School of Acts

The Gifts and Operations of God

By Eric Casto

MMXXII

School of Acts: The Gifts and Operations of God
Trilogy Christian Publishers A Wholly Owned Subsidiary of Trinity Broadcasting Network
2442 Michelle Drive Tustin, CA 92780
Copyright © 2022 by Eric Casto
All Scripture quotations are taken from the King James Version. Public domain.
References to other works:
Questions and Answers on Spiritual Gifts, Howard Carter. Harrison House Inc. Tulsa, OK.
The Ministries of the Holy Spirit, Study Guide, Dr. Lester Sumrall. Sumrall Publishing South Bend, Indiana. 2002
The Gifts of the Holy Spirit, Study Guide, Dr. Lester Sumrall. Sumrall Publishing, South Bend, Indiana reprint August 2000
Bereishis Genesis, ArtScroll Tanach Series, Volume I(a) Published by Mesorah Publications, Ltd. Brooklyn, NY.
Word Studies in the Greek New Testament, Volume 1. Kenneth S. Wuest. Eerdman Publishing. Grand Rapids, MI
Front Cover Photo Masang Kang Mountain Bhutan
Compliments Eric Casto and FourSmiles Productions
For More Information: www.foursmiles.com
FourSmiles Productions is a media production company of Eric Casto and is used solely on behalf of Global Reach Ministries, inc. P.O. Box 1050 Apopka, Florida, 32712 USA.
No part of this book may be reproduced, stored in a retrieval system, or transmitted by any means without written permission from the author. All rights reserved. Printed in the USA.
Rights Department, 2442 Michelle Drive, Tustin, CA 92780.
Trilogy Christian Publishing/TBN and colophon are trademarks of Trinity Broadcasting Network.
Cover design by: Eric Casto
For information about special discounts for bulk purchases, please contact Trilogy Christian Publishing.
Manufactured in the United States of America
10 9 8 7 6 5 4 3 2 1
Library of Congress Cataloging-in-Publication Data is available.
ISBN: 978-1-68556-805-4
E-ISBN: 978-1-68556-806-1s

School of Acts

The Gifts and Operations of God

Table of Contents

For Further Study

School of Acts Training Videos

https://www.foursmiles.com/school-of-acts

or

www.Youtube.com Eric Casto School of Acts
www.Rumble.com SchoolofActs

Keep posted with all new teaching content
Sign up for email updates

schoolofacts@foursmiles.com

FIRST WORDS: THE WHY OF THIS STUDY

Christianity is a torch that must be passed on. It was given to give light, a light for all men to see. This life-giving light was never intended to be concealed but rather placed high upon a lampstand. Over the past two thousand years of church history, regions of the earth have come alive through the preaching of the Christian message, demonstrated through the power of God. Then those same regions of light and glory dissipated, and the sands of time returned those same regions back to darkness. Christianity in a region can bloom and can also die. This study on Acts is designed for the student disciple to grasp truths from the early church and then be able to incorporate these truths into their own lives and local fellowships.

In admonishing the church in Sardis, the Lord commanded them to strengthen the things that remained which were ready to die. I believe this one verse encapsulates the purpose of this book–that being that the church must be continually strengthened.

"Be watchful, and strengthen the things which remain, that are ready to die: for I have not found thy works perfect before God."
Revelation 3:2

In closing, it is important to note that the book of Acts was never written solely for a historic account of the early church, but rather it was provided as a living blueprint for all churches until the Lord's return.

HOW TO USE THIS STUDY

This study is designed for the individual as well as church discipleship groups, home groups, and Bible schools. The study is broken into two parts. Part I of this study is the actual King James Version of the New Testament book of Acts while the second part (Part II) is divided into modules or commentaries written to help bring the various keys found in Part I to life.

In Part I, which is the book of Acts, keys are used to bring forth a visual conception of all that was happening in each chapter or event. This was done to assist the student in studying both the church as well as the moving of the Holy Spirit. The educational concept is to see it and then to study it.

In Part II, I have separated each topical key into modules that can be used for concise study. Simply meaning that each module of study corresponds with the various topical keys found in Part I of this book. For example, the key WOW, which stands for the word of wisdom, is one of the modules of study found in Part II. This key, because it is a gift of the Holy Spirit will be listed on the right side of the scripture in Part I.

I have chosen the King James Version of the Bible primarily because of the authority it carries in clearly defining the operations of the Holy Spirit. The student is encouraged to use other translations as well.

KEY

GIFTS OF THE HOLY SPIRIT
(Keys will be listed to the right side of scripture in Part I)

REVELATION GIFTS	
WORD OF WISDOM	WOW
WORD OF KNOWLEDGE	WOK
DISCERNING OF SPIRITS	DISC
POWER GIFTS	
GIFT OF FAITH	GOF
GIFTS OF HEALINGS	GOH
WORKING OF MIRACLES	WOM
GIFTS OF INSPIRATION	
PROPHECY	PRO
TONGUES	TONG
INTERPRETATION OF TONGUES	INT

DEFINITIVE STUDY
(Keys will be listed to the left side of scripture in Part I)

DOCUMENTED RESURRECTION	RES
DOCUMENTED PRAYER	PRAY
BAPTISM OF THE HOLY SPIRIT	BHS
DOCUMENTED HARVEST	HARV
DOCUMENTED PERSECUTION	PERS
DOCUMENTED ANGELS	ANG
DOCUMENTED JUDGMENTS	JUDG
*OLD TESTAMENT WORD of WISDOM	OT WOW

(OT WOW FOR REFERENCE ONLY)

Facts of Acts

- I have documented 138 manifestations of the Holy Spirit in Acts.
- There are 69 manifestations of the gifts of revelation (gifts that see).
  1. Word of Wisdom 40
  2. Word of Knowledge 11
  3. Discerning of Spirits 18
- There are 56 manifestations of the gifts of power (gifts that do).
  1. Gift of Faith 24
  2. Gifts of Healings 20
  3. Working of Miracles 12
- There are 13 manifestations of the gifts of inspiration (gifts that speak).
  1. Prophecy 10
  2. Tongues 2
  3. Interpretation of Tongues 1
- The book of Acts does not have a conclusion—it is still being written.
- The book of Acts covers approximately 30–33 years of church history. From Christ's ascension around AD 33 to Paul's imprisonment in Rome, roughly AD 63–65. Both the Gospels and the book of Acts cover approximately the same amount of time—approximately 30 years.
- The book of Acts begins in Jerusalem, where the church is born, and ends 28 chapters later in Rome.
- There are 36 examples of harvest in the book of Acts. These harvest examples range from multitudes, households, and single individuals.
- There are 23 references to the baptism of the Holy Spirit.
- There are 9 occurrences of angels and their ministry.
- There are 26 references to resurrection.
- There are 28 references to prayer.
- There are 31 references to persecution.
- There are 6 references to judgment.
- There are 21 Old Testament prophesies (OT WOW) fulfilled.
- The book of Acts is the reality of God's love for the entire world. This love was demonstrated through the preaching of the gospel, which is still preached today.
- The baptism of the Holy Spirit was administered supernaturally by the Lord Himself, by the Lord through His apostles, and by the Lord through laymen, such as Ananias.
- Every consequential breakthrough in church growth or direction came through the manifestation of the gifts and operations of the Holy Spirit.

- Only three chapters (17, 24, and 25) have no account of the gifts of the Holy Spirit in operation.
- The book of Acts is a historical record that deals primarily with the operations of the Holy Spirit to the Church and through the Church, rather than a record of the fruit of the Holy Spirit in the lives of believers (*Contrasted to the message in the Epistles*).
- The three principal players in the book of Acts are: Paul, Peter, and Barnabas—who was known as the son of encouragement. Following these men would be Philip the evangelist, who not only was listed as one of the first deacons with Stephen, but spearheaded a move of God into Samaria, then Ethiopia, and finally Caesarea, where Cornelius the Roman lived.
- The book of Acts is divided into two major divisions. The first division is the church in Jerusalem and the leadership of Peter and his ministry. The second division is the movement of the church Westward into Europe and Rome under the leadership of Paul. History shows us that both Peter and Paul, the two chief apostles, were martyred in Rome. Thus, showing the shift of the Christian power base from Asia to Europe, from Jerusalem—which would be destroyed in AD 70—to Rome. These two apostles were seeds planted into Europe. The other apostles of the Lord went in different directions with the gospel, but Peter and Paul's ministries were in line with Daniel's vision concerning the direction of four world empires that would affect human history until the coming of the Messiah, both as a baby in Bethlehem and His second coming as King of Kings. Therefore, the book of Acts, along with the book of Daniel, is a record of the strategic shift of power from Jerusalem to the nations, or more precisely with the book of Acts the shift is to Rome (Daniel 2:40–41, Daniel 7:19).
- The Bible lists five things that hinder the church from walking in the power of the Holy Spirit:

    - Lack of desire (1 Corinthians 14:1)
    - Ignorance (1 Corinthians 12:1)
    - Unbelief (Mark 16:14)
    - Hardness of heart (Mark 16:14)
    - Prayerlessness (Luke 11:13, Luke 18:1)

School of Acts

The Gifts and Operations of God

PART I

The Book of Acts
Chapters 1–28
with Keys

PART I (a):
Jerusalem, Judea, and Samaria (Acts 1–12)

PART I (b):
Paul to Rome–the Uttermost Parts of the Earth (Acts 13–28)

The Book of Acts (with keys)

PART I (a): Jerusalem, Judea, and Samaria (Acts 1–12)

Acts 1:1–26

1 The former treatise have I made, O Theophilus, of all that Jesus began both to do
and teach,
BHS 2 Until the day in which he was taken up, after that he through the Holy Ghost had
given commandments unto the apostles whom he had chosen:
RES 3 To whom also he showed himself alive after his passion by many infallible
proofs, being seen of them forty days, and speaking of the things pertaining to the
kingdom of God:
4 And, being assembled together with *them*, commanded them that they should not
BHS depart from Jerusalem, but wait for the promise of the Father, which, *saith he*, ye
have heard of me.
5 For John truly baptized with water; but ye shall be baptized with the Holy Ghost WOW
not many days hence.
6 When they therefore were come together, they asked of him, saying, Lord, wilt
thou at this time restore again the kingdom to Israel?
7 And he said unto them, It is not for you to know the times or the seasons, which
the Father hath put in his own power.
BHS 8 But ye shall receive power, after that the Holy Ghost is come upon you: and ye WOW
shall be witnesses unto me both in Jerusalem, and in all Judaea, and in Samaria,
and unto the uttermost part of the earth.
9 And when he had spoken these things, while they beheld, he was taken up; and a GOF
cloud received him out of their sight.
10 And while they looked steadfastly toward heaven as he went up, behold, two
ANG men stood by them in white apparel;
11 Which also said, Ye men of Galilee, why stand ye gazing up into heaven? this
same Jesus, which is taken up from you into heaven, shall so come in like manner WOW
as ye have seen him go into heaven.
12 Then returned they unto Jerusalem from the mount called Olivet, which is from
Jerusalem a sabbath day's journey.
13 And when they were come in, they went up into an upper room, where abode
both Peter, and James, and John, and Andrew, Philip, and Thomas, Bartholomew,
and Matthew, James *the son* of Alphaeus, and Simon Zelotes, and Judas *the
brother* of James.
PRAY 14 These all continued with one accord in prayer and supplication, with the women,
and Mary the mother of Jesus, and with his brethren.
15 And in those days Peter stood up in the midst of the disciples, and said, (the
number of names together were about a hundred and twenty,)

JUDG 16 Men *and* brethren, this scripture must needs have been fulfilled, which the Holy
Ghost by the mouth of David spake before concerning Judas, which was guide to
them that took Jesus.
17 For he was numbered with us and had obtained part of this ministry.
18 Now this man purchased a field with the reward of iniquity; and falling
headlong, he burst asunder in the midst, and all his bowels gushed out.
19 And it was known unto all the dwellers at Jerusalem; insomuch as that field is
called in their proper tongue, Aceldama, that is to say, The field of blood.
OTW 20 For it is written in the book of Psalms, *Let his habitation be desolate, and let no*
OTW *man dwell therein: and his bishopric let another take*. (Psalms 69:25, 109:8)
21 Wherefore of these men which have companied with us all the time that the
Lord Jesus went in and out among us,
BHS 22 Beginning from the baptism of John, unto that same day that he was taken up
RES from us, must one be ordained to be a witness with us of his resurrection.
23 And they appointed two, Joseph called Barsabas, who was surnamed Justus, and
Matthias.
PRAY 24 And they prayed, and said, Thou, Lord, which knowest the hearts of all *men*,
show whether of these two thou hast chosen,
25 That he may take part of this ministry and apostleship, from which Judas by
transgression fell, that he might go to his own place.
26 And they gave forth their lots; and the lot fell upon Matthias; and he was
numbered with the eleven apostles.

Acts 2:1–47

1 And when the day of Pentecost was fully come, they were all with one accord in
one place.
2 And suddenly there came a sound from heaven as of a rushing mighty wind, and
it filled all the house where they were sitting.
3 And there appeared unto them cloven tongues like as of fire, and it sat upon each
of them.
BHS 4 And they were all filled with the Holy Ghost, and began to speak with other GOF
tongues, as the Spirit gave them utterance. TONG
5 And there were dwelling at Jerusalem Jews, devout men, out of every nation
under heaven.
6 Now when this was noised abroad, the multitude came together, and were
confounded, because that every man heard them speak in his own language.
7 And they were all amazed and marveled, saying one to another, Behold, are not
all these which speak Galilaeans?
8 And how hear we every man in our own tongue, wherein we were born?
9 Parthians, and Medes, and Elamites, and the dwellers in Mesopotamia, and in
Judaea, and Cappadocia, in Pontus, and Asia,
10 Phrygia, and Pamphylia, in Egypt, and in the parts of Libya about Cyrene, and
strangers of Rome, Jews and proselytes,
11 Cretes and Arabians, we do hear them speak in our tongues the wonderful works
of God.
12 And they were all amazed, and were in doubt, saying one to another, What
meaneth this?
13 Others mocking said, These men are full of new wine.
14 But Peter, standing up with the eleven, lifted up his voice, and said unto them,
Ye men of Judaea, and all *ye* that dwell at Jerusalem, be this known unto you, and
hearken to my words:
15 For these are not drunken, as ye suppose, seeing it is *but* the third hour of the
day.
OTW 16 *But this is that which was spoken by the prophet Joel;*
17 *And it shall come to pass in the last days, saith God, I will pour out of my Spirit*
upon all flesh: and your sons and your daughters shall prophesy, and your young
men shall see visions, and your old men shall dream dreams:
18 *And on my servants and on my handmaidens I will pour out in those days of my*
Spirit; and they shall prophesy:
19 *And I will show wonders in heaven above, and signs in the earth beneath; blood,*
and fire, and vapor of smoke:
20 *The sun shall be turned into darkness, and the moon into blood, before that*
great and notable day of the Lord come:

21 *And it shall come to pass, that whosoever shall call on the name of the Lord*
shall be saved. (Joel 2:28–32)
22 Ye men of Israel, hear these words; Jesus of Nazareth, a man approved of God
among you by miracles and wonders and signs, which God did by him in the
midst of you, as ye yourselves also know:
23 Him, being delivered by the determinate counsel and foreknowledge of God, ye
have taken, and by wicked hands have crucified and slain:
RES 24 Whom God hath raised up, having loosed the pains of death: because it was not
possible that he should be holden of it.
OTW 25 For David speaketh concerning him, *I foresaw the Lord always before my face,*
for he is on my right hand, that I should not be moved:
26 *Therefore did my heart rejoice, and my tongue was glad; moreover also my*
flesh shall rest in hope:
27 *Because thou wilt not leave my soul in hell, neither wilt thou suffer thine Holy*
One to see corruption.
28 *Thou hast made known to me the ways of life; thou shalt make me full of joy*
with thy countenance. (Psalms 16:8–10)
29 Men *and* brethren, let me freely speak unto you of the patriarch David, that he is
both dead and buried, and his sepulchre is with us unto this day.
30 Therefore being a prophet, and knowing that God had sworn with an oath to
him, that of the fruit of his loins, according to the flesh, he would raise up Christ
to sit on his throne;
RES 31 He seeing this before spake of the resurrection of Christ, that his soul was not
left in hell, neither his flesh did see corruption.
32 This Jesus hath God raised up, whereof we all are witnesses.
33 Therefore being by the right hand of God exalted, and having received of the
BHS Father the promise of the Holy Ghost, he hath shed forth this, which ye now see
and hear.
OTW 34 For David is not ascended into the heavens: but he saith himself, *The LORD*
said unto my Lord, Sit thou on my right hand,
35 *Until I make thy foes thy footstool.* (Psalms 110:1)
36 Therefore let all the house of Israel know assuredly, that God hath made that
same Jesus, whom ye have crucified, both Lord and Christ.
37 Now when they heard *this*, they were pricked in their heart, and said unto Peter
and to the rest of the apostles, Men *and* brethren, what shall we do?
38 Then Peter said unto them, Repent, and be baptized every one of you in the
BHS name of Jesus Christ for the remission of sins, and ye shall receive the gift of the
Holy Ghost.
39 For the promise is unto you, and to your children, and to all that are afar WOW
off, *even* as many as the Lord our God shall call.

40 And with many other words did he testify and exhort, saying, Save yourselves
from this untoward generation.
HARV 41 Then they that gladly received his word were baptized: and the same day there
were added *unto them* about three thousand souls.
42 And they continued steadfastly in the apostles' doctrine and fellowship, and in
PRAY breaking of bread, and in prayers.
43 And fear came upon every soul: and many wonders and signs were done by the GOH
apostles. WOM
44 And all that believed were together, and had all things common;
45 And sold their possessions and goods, and parted them to all *men*, as every man
had need.
46 And they, continuing daily with one accord in the temple, and breaking bread
from house to house, did eat their meat with gladness and singleness of heart,
47 Praising God, and having favour with all the people. And the Lord added to the
HARV church daily such as should be saved.

Acts 3:1–26

PRAY 1 Now Peter and John went up together into the temple at the hour of prayer, *being*
the ninth *hour*.
2 And a certain man lame from his mother's womb was carried, whom they laid
daily at the gate of the temple which is called Beautiful, to ask alms of them that
entered into the temple;
3 Who seeing Peter and John about to go into the temple asked an alms.
4 And Peter, fastening his eyes upon him with John, said, Look on us.
5 And he gave heed unto them, expecting to receive something of them.
6 Then Peter said, Silver and gold have I none; but such as I have give I thee: In
the name of Jesus Christ of Nazareth rise up and walk. GOH
7 And he took him by the right hand, and lifted *him* up: and immediately his feet
and ankle bones received strength.
8 And he leaping up stood, and walked, and entered with them into the temple,
walking, and leaping, and praising God.
9 And all the people saw him walking and praising God:
10 And they knew that it was he which sat for alms at the Beautiful gate of the
temple: and they were filled with wonder and amazement at that which had
happened unto him.
11 And as the lame man which was healed held Peter and John, all the people ran
together unto them in the porch that is called Solomon's, greatly wondering.
12 And when Peter saw *it*, he answered unto the people, Ye men of Israel, why
marvel ye at this? or why look ye so earnestly on us, as though by our own power
or holiness we had made this man to walk?
13 The God of Abraham, and of Isaac, and of Jacob, the God of our fathers, hath
glorified his Son Jesus; whom ye delivered up, and denied him in the presence of
Pilate, when he was determined to let *him* go.
14 But ye denied the Holy One and the Just, and desired a murderer to be granted
unto you;
RES 15 And killed the Prince of life, whom God hath raised from the dead; whereof we
are witnesses.
16 And his name through faith in his name hath made this man strong, whom ye
see and know: yea, the faith which is by him hath given him this perfect
soundness in the presence of you all.
17 And now, brethren, I wot that through ignorance ye did *it*, as *did* also your
rulers.
OTW 18 But those things, which *God before had showed by the mouth of all his
prophets, that Christ should suffer, he hath so fulfilled*.
19 Repent ye therefore, and be converted, that your sins may be blotted out, when
the times of refreshing shall come from the presence of the Lord;

[20]And he shall send Jesus Christ, which before was preached unto you:
[21]Whom the heaven must receive until the times of restitution of all things, which WOW
God hath spoken by the mouth of all his holy prophets since the world began.
OTW [22]For Moses truly said unto the fathers, *A prophet shall the Lord your God raise up unto you of your brethren, like unto me; him shall ye hear in all things whatsoever he shall say unto you.*
[23]*And it shall come to pass, that every soul, which will not hear that prophet, shall be destroyed from among the people*. (Deut. 18:15,18, 19)
[24]Yea, and all the prophets from Samuel and those that follow after, as many as have spoken, have likewise foretold of these days.
[25]Ye are the children of the prophets, and of the covenant which God made with
OTW our fathers, saying unto Abraham, *And in thy seed shall all the kindreds of the earth be blessed*. (Genesis 12:3)
RES [26]Unto you first God, having raised up his Son Jesus, sent him to bless you, in WOW
turning away every one of you from his iniquities.

Acts 4:1–37

1 And as they spake unto the people, the priests, and the captain of the temple, and
PERS the Sadducees, came upon them,
2 Being grieved that they taught the people, and preached through Jesus the
RES resurrection from the dead.
3 And they laid hands on them and put *them* in hold unto the next day: for it was
now eventide.
HARV 4 Howbeit many of them which heard the word believed; and the number of the
men was about five thousand.
5 And it came to pass on the morrow, that their rulers, and elders, and scribes,
6 And Annas the high priest, and Caiaphas, and John, and Alexander, and as many
as were of the kindred of the high priest, were gathered together at Jerusalem.
7 And when they had set them in the midst, they asked, By what power, or by what
name, have ye done this?
BHS 8 Then Peter, filled with the Holy Ghost, said unto them, Ye rulers of the people,
and elders of Israel,
9 If we this day be examined of the good deed done to the impotent man, by what
means he is made whole;
10 Be it known unto you all, and to all the people of Israel, that by the name of
RES Jesus Christ of Nazareth, whom ye crucified, whom God raised from the
dead, *even* by him doth this man stand here before you whole.
11 This is the stone which was set at nought of you builders, which is become the
head of the corner.
12 Neither is there salvation in any other: for there is none other name under WOW
heaven given among men, whereby we must be saved.
13 Now when they saw the boldness of Peter and John, and perceived that they
were unlearned and ignorant men, they marveled; and they took knowledge of
them, that they had been with Jesus.
14 And beholding the man which was healed standing with them, they could say
nothing against it.
15 But when they had commanded them to go aside out of the council, they
conferred among themselves,
16 Saying, What shall we do to these men? for that indeed a notable miracle hath
been done by them *is* manifest to all them that dwell in Jerusalem; and we cannot
deny *it*.
17 But that it spread no further among the people, let us straightly threaten them,
that they speak henceforth to no man in this name.
PERS 18 And they called them, and commanded them not to speak at all nor teach in the
name of Jesus.
19 But Peter and John answered and said unto them, Whether it be right in the sight

of God to hearken unto you more than unto God, judge ye.
20 For we cannot but speak the things which we have seen and heard.
21 So when they had further threatened them, they let them go, finding nothing
how they might punish them, because of the people: for all *men* glorified God for
that which was done.
22 For the man was above forty years old, on whom this miracle of healing was
showed.
23 And being let go, they went to their own company, and reported all that the
chief priests and elders had said unto them.
PRAY 24 And when they heard that, they lifted up their voice to God with one accord, and
said, Lord, thou *art* God, which hast made heaven, and earth, and the sea, and all
that in them is:
OTW 25 Who by the mouth of thy servant David hast said, *Why did the heathen rage,
and the people imagine vain things?*
26 *The kings of the earth stood up, and the rulers were gathered together against
the Lord, and against his Christ*. (Psalms 2:1–2)
27 For of a truth against thy holy child Jesus, whom thou hast anointed, both
Herod, and Pontius Pilate, with the Gentiles, and the people of Israel, were
gathered together,
28 For to do whatsoever thy hand and thy counsel determined before to be done.
29 And now, Lord, behold their threatenings: and grant unto thy servants, that with
all boldness they may speak thy word,
30 By stretching forth thine hand to heal; and that signs and wonders may be done
by the name of thy holy child Jesus.
BHS 31 And when they had prayed, the place was shaken where they were assembled GOF
together; and they were all filled with the Holy Ghost, and they spake the word of
God with boldness.
32 And the multitude of them that believed were of one heart and of one soul:
neither said any *of them* that ought of the things which he possessed was his own;
ut they had all things common. GOH
RES 33 And with great power gave the apostles witness of the resurrection of the Lord
Jesus: and great grace was upon them all. WOM
34 Neither was there any among them that lacked: for as many as were possessors GOF
of lands or houses sold them, and brought the prices of the things that were sold,
35 And laid *them* down at the apostles' feet: and distribution was made unto every
man according as he had need.
36 And Joses, who by the apostles was surnamed Barnabas, (which is, being
interpreted, The son of consolation,) a Levite, *and* of the country of Cyprus,
37 Having land, sold *it*, and brought the money, and laid *it* at the apostles' feet.

Acts 5:1–42

1 But a certain man named Ananias, with Sapphira his wife, sold a possession,
2 And kept back *part* of the price, his wife also being privy *to it*, and brought a
certain part, and laid *it* at the apostles' feet.
3 But Peter said, Ananias, why hath Satan filled thine heart to lie to the Holy DISC
Ghost, and to keep back *part* of the price of the land? WOK
4 Whiles it remained, was it not thine own? and after it was sold, was it not in thine
own power? why hast thou conceived this thing in thine heart? thou hast not lied
unto men, but unto God.
JUDG 5 And Ananias hearing these words fell down, and gave up the ghost: and great
fear came on all them that heard these things.
6 And the young men arose, wound him up, and carried *him* out, and buried *him*.
7 And it was about the space of three hours after, when his wife, not knowing what
was done, came in.
8 And Peter answered unto her, Tell me whether ye sold the land for so much? And
she said, Yes, for so much.
9 Then Peter said unto her, How is it that ye have agreed together to tempt the
Spirit of the Lord? behold, the feet of them which have buried thy husband *are* at WOK
the door, and shall carry thee out. WOW
JUDG 10 Then fell she down straightway at his feet, and yielded up the ghost: and the
young men came in, and found her dead, and, carrying *her* forth, buried *her* by
her husband.
11 And great fear came upon all the church, and upon as many as heard these
things. GOH
12 And by the hands of the apostles were many signs and wonders wrought among
the people; (and they were all with one accord in Solomon's porch. WOM
13 And of the rest durst no man join himself to them: but the people magnified
them.
HARV 14 And believers were the more added to the Lord, multitudes both of men and
women.
15 Insomuch that they brought forth the sick into the streets, and laid *them* on beds
and couches, that at the least the shadow of Peter passing by might overshadow GOH
some of them.
16 There came also a multitude *out* of the cities round about unto Jerusalem,
bringing sick folks, and them which were vexed with unclean spirits: and they
were healed every one. GOH
17 Then the high priest rose up, and all they that were with him, (which is the sect
of the Sadducees,) and were filled with indignation,
PERS 18 And laid their hands on the apostles, and put them in the common prison.
ANG 19 But the angel of the Lord by night opened the prison doors, and brought them GOF

forth, and said,
20Go, stand and speak in the temple to the people all the words of this life. WOW
21And when they heard *that*, they entered into the temple early in the morning,
and taught. But the high priest came, and they that were with him, and called the
council together, and all the senate of the children of Israel, and sent to the prison
to have them brought.
22But when the officers came, and found them not in the prison, they returned, and
told,
23Saying, The prison truly found we shut with all safety, and the keepers standing
without before the doors: but when we had opened, we found no man within.
24Now when the high priest and the captain of the temple and the chief priests
heard these things, they doubted of them whereunto this would grow.
25Then came one and told them, saying, Behold, the men whom ye put in prison
are standing in the temple, and teaching the people.
26Then went the captain with the officers, and brought them without violence: for
they feared the people, lest they should have been stoned.
27And when they had brought them, they set *them* before the council: and the high
priest asked them,
28Saying, Did not we straightly command you that ye should not teach in this
name? and, behold, ye have filled Jerusalem with your doctrine, and intend to
bring this man's blood upon us.
29Then Peter and the *other* apostles answered and said, We ought to obey God
rather than men.
RES 30The God of our fathers raised up Jesus, whom ye slew and hanged on a tree.
31Him hath God exalted with his right hand *to be* a Prince and a Saviour, for to
give repentance to Israel, and forgiveness of sins.
BHS 32And we are his witnesses of these things; and *so is* also the Holy Ghost, whom
God hath given to them that obey him.
33When they heard *that*, they were cut *to the heart*, and took counsel to slay them.
34Then stood there up one in the council, a Pharisee, named Gamaliel, a doctor of
the law, had in reputation among all the people, and commanded to put the
apostles forth a little space;
35And said unto them, Ye men of Israel, take heed to yourselves what ye intend to
do as touching these men.
36For before these days rose up Theudas, boasting himself to be somebody; to
whom a number of men, about four hundred, joined themselves: who was slain;
and all, as many as obeyed him, were scattered, and brought to nought.
37After this man rose up Judas of Galilee in the days of the taxing, and drew away
much people after him: he also perished; and all, *even* as many as obeyed him,
were dispersed.

[38]And now I say unto you, Refrain from these men, and let them alone: for if this
counsel or this work be of men, it will come to nought:
[39]But if it be of God, ye cannot overthrow it; lest haply ye be found even to fight
against God.
PERS [40]And to him they agreed: and when they had called the apostles, and beaten *them*,
they commanded that they should not speak in the name of Jesus, and let them
go.
[41]And they departed from the presence of the council, rejoicing that they were
counted worthy to suffer shame for his name.
[42]And daily in the temple, and in every house, they ceased not to teach and preach
Jesus Christ.

Acts 6:1–15

1 And in those days, when the number of the disciples was multiplied, there arose a
murmuring of the Grecians against the Hebrews, because their widows were
neglected in the daily ministration.
2 Then the twelve called the multitude of the disciples *unto them*, and said, It is not
reason that we should leave the word of God, and serve tables.
BHS 3 Wherefore, brethren, look ye out among you seven men of honest report, full of
the Holy Ghost and wisdom, whom we may appoint over this business.
PRAY 4 But we will give ourselves continually to prayer, and to the ministry of the word.
5 And the saying pleased the whole multitude: and they chose Stephen, a man full
of faith and of the Holy Ghost, and Philip, and Prochorus, and Nicanor, and
Timon, and Parmenas, and Nicolas a proselyte of Antioch:
PRAY 6 Whom they set before the apostles: and when they had prayed, they laid *their*
hands on them.
HARV 7 And the word of God increased; and the number of the disciples multiplied in
HARV Jerusalem greatly; and a great company of the priests were obedient to the faith. GOH
8 And Stephen, full of faith and power, did great wonders and miracles among the
people. WOM
PERS 9 Then there arose certain of the synagogue, which is called *the synagogue* of the
Libertines, and Cyrenians, and Alexandrians, and of them of Cilicia and of Asia,
disputing with Stephen.
BHS 10 And they were not able to resist the wisdom and the spirit by which he spake.
11 Then they suborned men, which said, We have heard him speak blasphemous
words against Moses, and *against* God.
12 And they stirred up the people, and the elders, and the scribes, and came
upon *him*, and caught him, and brought *him* to the council,
13 And set up false witnesses, which said, This man ceaseth not to speak
blasphemous words against this holy place, and the law:
14 For we have heard him say, that this Jesus of Nazareth shall destroy this place,
and shall change the customs which Moses delivered us.
15 And all that sat in the council, looking steadfastly on him, saw his face as it had
been the face of an angel.

Acts 7:1–60

1 Then said the high priest, Are these things so?
2 And he said, Men, brethren, and fathers, hearken; The God of glory appeared
unto our father Abraham, when he was in Mesopotamia, before he dwelt in
Charran,
3 And said unto him, Get thee out of thy country, and from thy kindred, and come
into the land which I shall show thee.
4 Then came he out of the land of the Chaldaeans, and dwelt in Charran: and from
thence, when his father was dead, he removed him into this land, wherein ye now
dwell.
5 And he gave him none inheritance in it, no, not *so much as* to set his foot on: yet
he promised that he would give it to him for a possession, and to his seed after
him, when *as yet* he had no child.
6 And God spake on this wise, That his seed should sojourn in a strange land; and
that they should bring them into bondage, and entreat *them* evil four hundred
years.
7 And the nation to whom they shall be in bondage will I judge, said God: and
after that shall they come forth, and serve me in this place.
8 And he gave him the covenant of circumcision: and so *Abraham* begat Isaac, and
circumcised him the eighth day; and Isaac *begat* Jacob; and Jacob *begat* the
twelve patriarchs.
9 And the patriarchs, moved with envy, sold Joseph into Egypt: but God was with
him,
10 And delivered him out of all his afflictions, and gave him favour and wisdom in
the sight of Pharaoh king of Egypt; and he made him governor over Egypt and all
his house.
11 Now there came a dearth over all the land of Egypt and Chanaan, and great
affliction: and our fathers found no sustenance.
12 But when Jacob heard that there was corn in Egypt, he sent out our fathers first.
13 And at the second *time* Joseph was made known to his brethren; and Joseph's
kindred was made known unto Pharaoh.
14 Then sent Joseph, and called his father Jacob to *him*, and all his kindred,
threescore and fifteen souls.
15 So Jacob went down into Egypt, and died, he, and our fathers,
16 And were carried over into Sychem, and laid in the sepulchre that Abraham
bought for a sum of money of the sons of Emmor *the father* of Sychem.
17 But when the time of the promise drew nigh, which God had sworn to Abraham,
the people grew and multiplied in Egypt,
18 Till another king arose, which knew not Joseph.
19 The same dealt subtly with our kindred, and evil entreated our fathers, so that

they cast out their young children, to the end they might not live.
20 In which time Moses was born, and was exceeding fair, and nourished up in his
father's house three months:
21 And when he was cast out, Pharaoh's daughter took him up, and nourished him
for her own son.
22 And Moses was learned in all the wisdom of the Egyptians, and was mighty in
words and in deeds.
23 And when he was full forty years old, it came into his heart to visit his brethren
the children of Israel.
24 And seeing one *of them* suffer wrong, he defended *him*, and avenged him that
was oppressed, and smote the Egyptian:
25 For he supposed his brethren would have understood how that God by his hand
would deliver them: but they understood not.
26 And the next day he showed himself unto them as they strove, and would have
set them at one again, saying, Sirs, ye are brethren; why do ye wrong one to
another?
27 But he that did his neighbour wrong thrust him away, saying, Who made thee a
ruler and a judge over us?
28 Wilt thou kill me, as thou diddest the Egyptian yesterday?
29 Then fled Moses at this saying, and was a stranger in the land of Madian, where
he begat two sons.
30 And when forty years were expired, there appeared to him in the wilderness of
mount Sina an angel of the Lord in a flame of fire in a bush.
31 When Moses saw *it*, he wondered at the sight: and as he drew near to behold *it*,
the voice of the Lord came unto him,
32 *Saying*, I *am* the God of thy fathers, the God of Abraham, and the God of Isaac,
and the God of Jacob. Then Moses trembled, and durst not behold.
33 Then said the Lord to him, Put off thy shoes from thy feet: for the place where
thou standest is holy ground.
34 I have seen, I have seen the affliction of my people which is in Egypt, and I
have heard their groaning, and am come down to deliver them. And now come, I
will send thee into Egypt.
35 This Moses whom they refused, saying, Who made thee a ruler and a judge? the
same did God send *to be* a ruler and a deliverer by the hand of the angel which
appeared to him in the bush.
36 He brought them out, after that he had showed wonders and signs in the land of
Egypt, and in the Red sea, and in the wilderness forty years.
OTW 37 This is that Moses, which said unto the children of Israel, *A prophet shall the*
Lord your God raise up unto you of your brethren, like unto me; him shall ye hear
(Deuteronomy 18:15).

38 This is he, that was in the church in the wilderness with the angel which spake to him in the mount Sina, and *with* our fathers: who received the lively oracles to give unto us:
39 To whom our fathers would not obey, but thrust *him* from them, and in their hearts turned back again into Egypt,
40 Saying unto Aaron, Make us gods to go before us: for *as for* this Moses, which brought us out of the land of Egypt, we wot not what is become of him.
41 And they made a calf in those days, and offered sacrifice unto the idol, and rejoiced in the works of their own hands.
42 Then God turned, and gave them up to worship the host of heaven; as it is written in the book of the prophets, O ye house of Israel, have ye offered to me slain beasts and sacrifices *by the space of* forty years in the wilderness?
43 Yea, ye took up the tabernacle of Moloch, and the star of your god Remphan, figures which ye made to worship them: and I will carry you away beyond Babylon.
44 Our fathers had the tabernacle of witness in the wilderness, as he had appointed, speaking unto Moses, that he should make it according to the fashion that he had seen.
45 Which also our fathers that came after brought in with Jesus (Joshua) into the possession of the Gentiles, whom God drave out before the face of our fathers, unto the days of David;
46 Who found favour before God, and desired to find a tabernacle for the God of Jacob.
47 But Solomon built him an house.
48 Howbeit the most High dwelleth not in temples made with hands; as saith the prophet,
49 Heaven *is* my throne, and earth *is* my footstool: what house will ye build me? saith the Lord: or what *is* the place of my rest?
50 Hath not my hand made all these things?
51 Ye stiffnecked and uncircumcised in heart and ears, ye do always resist the Holy Ghost: as your fathers *did*, so *do* ye.
52 Which of the prophets have not your fathers persecuted? and they have slain them which showed before of the coming of the Just One; of whom ye have been now the betrayers and murderers:
53 Who have received the law by the disposition of angels, and have not kept *it*.
54 When they heard these things, they were cut to the heart, and they gnashed on him with *their* teeth.
BHS 55 But he, being full of the Holy Ghost, looked up stedfastly into heaven, and saw the glory of God, and Jesus standing on the right hand of God, DISC
56 And said, Behold, I see the heavens opened, and the Son of man standing on the

right hand of God.
[57]Then they cried out with a loud voice, and stopped their ears, and ran upon him
with one accord,
PERS [58]And cast *him* out of the city, and stoned *him*: and the witnesses laid down their
clothes at a young man's feet, whose name was Saul.
[59]And they stoned Stephen, calling upon *God*, and saying, Lord Jesus, receive my
spirit.
PRAY [60]And he kneeled down, and cried with a loud voice, Lord, lay not this sin to their
charge. And when he had said this, he fell asleep.

Acts 8:1–40

1 And Saul was consenting unto his death. And at that time there was a great
PERS persecution against the church which was at Jerusalem; and they were all
scattered abroad throughout the regions of Judaea and Samaria, except the
apostles.
2 And devout men carried Stephen *to his burial*, and made great lamentation over
him.
3 As for Saul, he made havock of the church, entering every house, and haling men
and women committed *them* to prison.
4 Therefore they that were scattered abroad went everywhere preaching the word.
5 Then Philip went down to the city of Samaria, and preached Christ unto them.
6 And the people with one accord gave heed unto those things which Philip spake, GOF
hearing and seeing the miracles which he did. WOM
7 For unclean spirits, crying with loud voice, came out of many that were
possessed *with them*: and many taken with palsies, and that were lame, were
healed. GOH
8 And there was great joy in that city.
9 But there was a certain man, called Simon, which before time in the same city
used sorcery, and bewitched the people of Samaria, giving out that himself was
some great one:
10 To whom they all gave heed, from the least to the greatest, saying, This man is
the great power of God.
11 And to him they had regard, because that of long time he had bewitched them
with sorceries.
HARV 12 But when they believed Philip preaching the things concerning the kingdom of
God, and the name of Jesus Christ, they were baptized, both men and women.
HARV 13 Then Simon himself believed also: and when he was baptized, he continued
with Philip, and wondered, beholding the miracles and signs which were done. WOM
14 Now when the apostles which were at Jerusalem heard that Samaria had
received the word of God, they sent unto them Peter and John:
PRAY 15 Who, when they were come down, prayed for them, that they might receive the
Holy Ghost:
16 (For as yet he was fallen upon none of them: only they were baptized in the
name of the Lord Jesus.)
BHS 17 Then laid they *their* hands on them, and they received the Holy Ghost. GOF
18 And when Simon saw that through laying on of the apostles' hands the Holy
Ghost was given, he offered them money,
19 Saying, Give me also this power, that on whomsoever I lay hands, he may
receive the Holy Ghost.
20 But Peter said unto him, Thy money perish with thee, because thou hast thought

that the gift of God may be purchased with money.
21Thou hast neither part nor lot in this matter: for thy heart is not right in the sight
of God.
22Repent therefore of this thy wickedness, and pray God, if perhaps the thought of
thine heart may be forgiven thee.
23For I perceive that thou art in the gall of bitterness, and *in* the bond of iniquity. DISC
24Then answered Simon, and said, Pray ye to the Lord for me, that none of these
things which ye have spoken come upon me.
25And they, when they had testified and preached the word of the Lord, returned
to Jerusalem, and preached the gospel in many villages of the Samaritans.
ANG 26And the angel of the Lord spake unto Philip, saying, Arise, and go toward the DISC
south unto the way that goeth down from Jerusalem unto Gaza, which is desert. WOW
27And he arose and went: and, behold, a man of Ethiopia, an eunuch of great
authority under Candace queen of the Ethiopians, who had the charge of all her
treasure, and had come to Jerusalem for to worship,
28Was returning, and sitting in his chariot read Esaias the prophet.
29Then the Spirit said unto Philip, Go near, and join thyself to this chariot. WOW
30And Philip ran thither to *him*, and heard him read the prophet Esaias, and said,
Understandest thou what thou readest?
31And he said, How can I, except some man should guide me? And he desired
Philip that he would come up and sit with him.
32The place of the scripture which he read was this, He was led as a sheep to the
slaughter; and like a lamb dumb before his shearer, so opened he not his mouth:
33In his humiliation his judgment was taken away: and who shall declare his
generation? for his life is taken from the earth.
34And the eunuch answered Philip, and said, I pray thee, of whom speaketh the
prophet this? of himself, or of some other man?
35Then Philip opened his mouth, and began at the same scripture, and preached
unto him Jesus.
36And as they went on *their* way, they came unto a certain water: and the eunuch
said, See, *here is* water; what doth hinder me to be baptized?
37And Philip said, If thou believest with all thine heart, thou mayest. And he
HARV answered and said, I believe that Jesus Christ is the Son of God.
38And he commanded the chariot to stand still: and they went down both into the
water, both Philip and the eunuch; and he baptized him.
39And when they were come up out of the water, the Spirit of the Lord caught GOF
away Philip, that the eunuch saw him no more: and he went on his way rejoicing.
40But Philip was found at Azotus: and passing through he preached in all the
cities, till he came to Caesarea.

Acts 9:1–43

PERS 1And Saul, yet breathing out threatenings and slaughter against the disciples of the
Lord, went unto the high priest,
2And desired of him letters to Damascus to the synagogues, that if he found any of
this way, whether they were men or women, he might bring them bound unto
Jerusalem.
3And as he journeyed, he came near Damascus: and suddenly there shined round DISC
about him a light from heaven:
ANG 4And he fell to the earth, and heard a voice saying unto him, Saul, Saul, why
persecutest thou me?
5And he said, Who art thou, Lord? And the Lord said, I am Jesus whom thou
persecutest: *it is* hard for thee to kick against the pricks.
PRAY 6And he trembling and astonished said, Lord, what wilt thou have me to do? And
the Lord *said* unto him, Arise, and go into the city, and it shall be told thee what WOW
thou must do.
7And the men which journeyed with him stood speechless, hearing a voice, but
seeing no man.
JUDG 8And Saul arose from the earth; and when his eyes were opened, he saw no man:
but they led him by the hand, and brought *him* into Damascus.
9And he was three days without sight, and neither did eat nor drink.
10And there was a certain disciple at Damascus, named Ananias; and to him said
the Lord in a vision, Ananias. And he said, Behold, I *am here*, Lord. DISC
11And the Lord *said* unto him, Arise, and go into the street which is called WOW
Straight, and inquire in the house of Judas for *one* called Saul, of Tarsus: for, WOK
PRAY behold, he prayeth,
12 And hath seen in a vision a man named Ananias coming in, and putting *his* hand DISC
on him, that he might receive his sight. WOK
13Then Ananias answered, Lord, I have heard by many of this man, how much WOW
evil he hath done to thy saints at Jerusalem:
14And here he hath authority from the chief priests to bind all that call on thy
name.
15But the Lord said unto him, Go thy way: for he is a chosen vessel unto me, to WOW
bear my name before the Gentiles, and kings, and the children of Israel:
16For I will show him how great things he must suffer for my name's sake.
17And Ananias went his way, and entered into the house; and putting his hands on
him said, Brother Saul, the Lord, *even* Jesus, that appeared unto thee in the way as
thou camest, hath sent me, that thou mightest receive thy sight, and be filled with GOF
BHS the Holy Ghost.
18And immediately there fell from his eyes as it had been scales: and he received
HARV sight forthwith, and arose, and was baptized.

19 And when he had received meat, he was strengthened. Then was Saul certain
days with the disciples which were at Damascus.
20 And straightway he preached Christ in the synagogues, that he is the Son of
God.
21 But all that heard *him* were amazed, and said; Is not this he that destroyed them
which called on this name in Jerusalem, and came hither for that intent, that he
might bring them bound unto the chief priests?
22 But Saul increased the more in strength, and confounded the Jews which dwelt
at Damascus, proving that this is very Christ.
PERS 23 And after that many days were fulfilled, the Jews took counsel to kill him:
24 But their laying await was known of Saul. And they watched the gates day and
night to kill him.
25 Then the disciples took him by night, and let *him* down by the wall in a basket.
26 And when Saul was come to Jerusalem, he assayed to join himself to the
disciples: but they were all afraid of him, and believed not that he was a disciple.
27 But Barnabas took him, and brought *him* to the apostles, and declared unto them
how he had seen the Lord in the way, and that he had spoken to him, and how he
had preached boldly at Damascus in the name of Jesus.
28 And he was with them coming in and going out at Jerusalem.
29 And he spake boldly in the name of the Lord Jesus, and disputed against the
PERS Grecians: but they went about to slay him.
30 *Which* when the brethren knew, they brought him down to Caesarea, and sent
him forth to Tarsus.
31 Then had the churches rest throughout all Judaea and Galilee and Samaria, and
were edified; and walking in the fear of the Lord, and in the comfort of the Holy PRO
HARV Ghost, were multiplied.
32 And it came to pass, as Peter passed throughout all *quarters*, he came down also
to the saints which dwelt at Lydda.
33 And there he found a certain man named Aeneas, which had kept his bed eight
years, and was sick of the palsy.
34 And Peter said unto him, Aeneas, Jesus Christ maketh thee whole: arise, and GOH
make thy bed. And he arose immediately.
HARV 35 And all that dwelt at Lydda and Saron saw him, and turned to the Lord.
36 Now there was at Joppa a certain disciple named Tabitha, which by
interpretation is called Dorcas: this woman was full of good works and almsdeeds
which she did.
37 And it came to pass in those days, that she was sick, and died: whom when they
had washed, they laid *her* in an upper chamber.
38 And forasmuch as Lydda was nigh to Joppa, and the disciples had heard that
Peter was there, they sent unto him two men, desiring *him* that he would not delay

to come to them.
39 Then Peter arose and went with them. When he was come, they brought him
into the upper chamber: and all the widows stood by him weeping, and showing
the coats and garments which Dorcas made, while she was with them.
PRAY 40 But Peter put them all forth, and kneeled down, and prayed; and turning *him* to GOF
RES the body said, Tabitha, arise. And she opened her eyes: and when she saw Peter, WOM
she sat up. GOH
41 And he gave her *his* hand, and lifted her up, and when he had called the saints
and widows, presented her alive.
HARV 42 And it was known throughout all Joppa; and many believed in the Lord.
43 And it came to pass, that he tarried many days in Joppa with one Simon a
tanner.

Acts 10:1–48

1 There was a certain man in Caesarea called Cornelius, a centurion of the band
called the Italian *band*,
2 *A* devout *man*, and one that feared God with all his house, which gave much alms
PRAY to the people, and prayed to God alway.
ANG 3 He saw in a vision evidently about the ninth hour of the day an angel of God DISC
coming in to him, and saying unto him, Cornelius.
4 And when he looked on him, he was afraid, and said, What is it, Lord? And he
said unto him, Thy prayers and thine alms are come up for a memorial before
God.
5 And now send men to Joppa, and call for *one* Simon, whose surname is Peter: WOK
6 He lodgeth with one Simon a tanner, whose house is by the sea side: he shall tell WOW
thee what thou oughtest to do.
7 And when the angel which spake unto Cornelius was departed, he called two of
his household servants, and a devout soldier of them that waited on him
continually;
8 And when he had declared all *these* things unto them, he sent them to Joppa.
9 On the morrow, as they went on their journey, and drew nigh unto the city, Peter
PRAY went up upon the housetop to pray about the sixth hour:
10 And he became very hungry, and would have eaten: but while they made ready,
he fell into a trance, DISC
11 And saw heaven opened, and a certain vessel descending unto him, as it had
been a great sheet knit at the four corners, and let down to the earth:
12 Wherein were all manner of fourfooted beasts of the earth, and wild beasts, and
creeping things, and fowls of the air.
13 And there came a voice to him, Rise, Peter; kill, and eat.
14 But Peter said, Not so, Lord; for I have never eaten any thing that is common or
unclean.
15 And the voice *spake* unto him again the second time, What God hath WOW
cleansed, *that* call not thou common.
16 This was done thrice: and the vessel was received up again into heaven.
17 Now while Peter doubted in himself what this vision which he had seen should
mean, behold, the men which were sent from Cornelius had made inquiry for
Simon's house, and stood before the gate,
18 And called, and asked whether Simon, which was surnamed Peter, were lodged
there.
19 While Peter thought on the vision, the Spirit said unto him, Behold, three men WOK
seek thee.
20 Arise therefore, and get thee down, and go with them, doubting nothing: for I WOW
have sent them. GOF

21Then Peter went down to the men which were sent unto him from Cornelius; and said, Behold, I am he whom ye seek: what *is* the cause wherefore ye are come?
22And they said, Cornelius the centurion, a just man, and one that feareth God, and of good report among all the nation of the Jews, was warned from God by an holy angel to send for thee into his house, and to hear words of thee.
23Then called he them in, and lodged *them*. And on the morrow Peter went away with them, and certain brethren from Joppa accompanied him.
24And the morrow after they entered into Caesarea. And Cornelius waited for them, and had called together his kinsmen and near friends.
25And as Peter was coming in, Cornelius met him, and fell down at his feet, and worshipped *him*.
26But Peter took him up, saying, Stand up; I myself also am a man.
27And as he talked with him, he went in, and found many that were come together.
28And he said unto them, Ye know how that it is an unlawful thing for a man that is a Jew to keep company, or come unto one of another nation; but God hath showed me that I should not call any man common or unclean.
29Therefore came I *unto you* without gainsaying, as soon as I was sent for: I ask therefore for what intent ye have sent for me?
30And Cornelius said, Four days ago I was fasting until this hour; and at the ninth hour I prayed in my house, and, behold, a man stood before me in bright clothing,
31And said, Cornelius, thy prayer is heard, and thine alms are had in remembrance in the sight of God.
32Send therefore to Joppa, and call hither Simon, whose surname is Peter; he is lodged in the house of *one* Simon a tanner by the sea side: who, when he cometh, shall speak unto thee.
33Immediately therefore I sent to thee; and thou hast well done that thou art come. Now therefore are we all here present before God, to hear all things that are commanded thee of God.
34Then Peter opened *his* mouth, and said, Of a truth I perceive that God is no respecter of persons:
35But in every nation he that feareth him, and worketh righteousness, is accepted with him.
36The word which *God* sent unto the children of Israel, preaching peace by Jesus Christ: (he is Lord of all:)
37That word, *I say*, ye know, which was published throughout all Judaea, and began from Galilee, after the baptism which John preached;
38How God anointed Jesus of Nazareth with the Holy Ghost and with power: who went about doing good, and healing all that were oppressed of the devil; for God

was with him.
39 And we are witnesses of all things which he did both in the land of the Jews, and
in Jerusalem; whom they slew and hanged on a tree:
RES 40 Him God raised up the third day, and showed him openly;
41 Not to all the people, but unto witnesses chosen before of God, *even* to us, who
did eat and drink with him after he rose from the dead.
42 And he commanded us to preach unto the people, and to testify that it is he
which was ordained of God *to be* the Judge of quick and dead.
43 To him give all the prophets witness, that through his name whosoever believeth
in him shall receive remission of sins.
BHS 44 While Peter yet spake these words, the Holy Ghost fell on all them which heard GOF
the word.
45 And they of the circumcision which believed were astonished, as many as came
with Peter, because that on the Gentiles also was poured out the gift of the Holy
Ghost.
46 For they heard them speak with tongues and magnify God. Then answered
Peter,
47 Can any man forbid water, that these should not be baptized, which have
received the Holy Ghost as well as we?
HARV 48 And he commanded them to be baptized in the name of the Lord. Then prayed
they him to tarry certain days.

Acts 11:1–30

1And the apostles and brethren that were in Judaea heard that the Gentiles had
also received the word of God.
2And when Peter was come up to Jerusalem, they that were of the circumcision
contended with him,
3Saying, Thou wentest in to men uncircumcised, and didst eat with them.
4But Peter rehearsed *the matter* from the beginning, and expounded *it* by order
unto them, saying,
5I was in the city of Joppa praying: and in a trance I saw a vision, A certain vessel
descend, as it had been a great sheet, let down from heaven by four corners; and it
came even to me:
6Upon the which when I had fastened mine eyes, I considered, and saw fourfooted
beasts of the earth, and wild beasts, and creeping things, and fowls of the air.
7And I heard a voice saying unto me, Arise, Peter; slay and eat.
8But I said, Not so, Lord: for nothing common or unclean hath at any time entered
into my mouth.
9But the voice answered me again from heaven, What God hath cleansed, *that* call
not thou common.
10And this was done three times: and all were drawn up again into heaven.
11And, behold, immediately there were three men already come unto the house
where I was, sent from Caesarea unto me.
12And the Spirit bade me go with them, nothing doubting. Moreover these six
brethren accompanied me, and we entered into the man's house:
13And he showed us how he had seen an angel in his house, which stood and said
unto him, Send men to Joppa, and call for Simon, whose surname is Peter;
14Who shall tell thee words, whereby thou and all thy house shall be saved.
BHS 15And as I began to speak, the Holy Ghost fell on them, as on us at the beginning.
16Then remembered I the word of the Lord, how that he said, John indeed
baptized with water; but ye shall be baptized with the Holy Ghost.
17Forasmuch then as God gave them the like gift as *he did* unto us, who believed
on the Lord Jesus Christ; what was I, that I could withstand God?
18When they heard these things, they held their peace, and glorified God, saying,
Then hath God also to the Gentiles granted repentance unto life.
19Now they which were scattered abroad upon the persecution that arose about
Stephen travelled as far as Phenice, and Cyprus, and Antioch, preaching the word
to none but unto the Jews only.
20And some of them were men of Cyprus and Cyrene, which, when they were
come to Antioch, spake unto the Grecians, preaching the Lord Jesus.
HARV 21And the hand of the Lord was with them: and a great number believed, and GOH
turned unto the Lord. WOM

22 Then tidings of these things came unto the ears of the church which was in
Jerusalem: and they sent forth Barnabas, that he should go as far as Antioch.
23 Who, when he came, and had seen the grace of God, was glad, and exhorted
them all, that with purpose of heart they would cleave unto the Lord.
BHS 24 For he was a good man, and full of the Holy Ghost and of faith: and much
HARV people was added unto the Lord.
25 Then departed Barnabas to Tarsus, for to seek Saul:
26 And when he had found him, he brought him unto Antioch. And it came to pass,
that a whole year they assembled themselves with the church, and taught much
people. And the disciples were called Christians first in Antioch. PRO
27 And in these days came prophets from Jerusalem unto Antioch.
28 And there stood up one of them named Agabus, and signified by the Spirit that WOW
there should be great dearth throughout all the world: which came to pass in the
days of Claudius Caesar.
29 Then the disciples, every man according to his ability, determined to send relief
unto the brethren which dwelt in Judaea:
30 Which also they did, and sent it to the elders by the hands of Barnabas and Saul.

Acts 12:1–25

PERS 1 Now about that time Herod the king stretched forth *his* hands to vex certain of
the church.
2 And he killed James the brother of John with the sword.
3 And because he saw it pleased the Jews, he proceeded further to take Peter also.
(Then were the days of unleavened bread.)
4 And when he had apprehended him, he put *him* in prison, and delivered *him* to
four quaternions of soldiers to keep him; intending after Easter to bring him forth
to the people.
PRAY 5 Peter therefore was kept in prison: but prayer was made without ceasing of the
church unto God for him.
6 And when Herod would have brought him forth, the same night Peter was
sleeping between two soldiers, bound with two chains: and the keepers before the
door kept the prison.
ANG 7 And, behold, the angel of the Lord came upon *him*, and a light shined in the
prison: and he smote Peter on the side, and raised him up, saying, Arise up
quickly. And his chains fell off from *his* hands. GOF
8 And the angel said unto him, Gird thyself, and bind on thy sandals. And so he
did. And he saith unto him, Cast thy garment about thee, and follow me.
9 And he went out, and followed him; and wist not that it was true which was done
by the angel; but thought he saw a vision.
10 When they were past the first and the second ward, they came unto the iron gate
that leadeth unto the city; which opened to them of his own accord: and they went
out, and passed on through one street; and forthwith the angel departed from him.
11 And when Peter was come to himself, he said, Now I know of a surety, that the
Lord hath sent his angel, and hath delivered me out of the hand of Herod,
and *from* all the expectation of the people of the Jews.
12 And when he had considered *the thing*, he came to the house of Mary the mother
PRAY of John, whose surname was Mark; where many were gathered together praying.
13 And as Peter knocked at the door of the gate, a damsel came to hearken, named
Rhoda.
14 And when she knew Peter's voice, she opened not the gate for gladness, but ran
in, and told how Peter stood before the gate.
15 And they said unto her, Thou art mad. But she constantly affirmed that it was
ANG even so. Then said they, It is his angel.
16 But Peter continued knocking: and when they had opened *the door*, and saw
him, they were astonished.
17 But he, beckoning unto them with the hand to hold their peace, declared unto
them how the Lord had brought him out of the prison. And he said, Go show these
things unto James, and to the brethren. And he departed, and went into another

place.
18Now as soon as it was day, there was no small stir among the soldiers, what was
become of Peter.
19And when Herod had sought for him, and found him not, he examined the
keepers, and commanded that *they* should be put to death. And he went down
from Judaea to Caesarea, and *there* abode.
20And Herod was highly displeased with them of Tyre and Sidon: but they came
with one accord to him, and, having made Blastus the king's chamberlain their
friend, desired peace; because their country was nourished by the king's *country*.
21And upon a set day Herod, arrayed in royal apparel, sat upon his throne, and
made an oration unto them.
22And the people gave a shout, *saying, It is* the voice of a god, and not of a man.
ANG 23And immediately the angel of the Lord smote him, because he gave not God the WOK
JUDG glory: and he was eaten of worms, and gave up the ghost.
HARV 24But the word of God grew and multiplied.
25And Barnabas and Saul returned from Jerusalem, when they had fulfilled *their*
ministry, and took with them John, whose surname was Mark.

PART I (b): Paul to Rome–the Uttermost Parts of the Earth (Acts 13–28)

Acts 13:1–52

1 Now there were in the church that was at Antioch certain prophets and teachers;
as Barnabas, and Simeon that was called Niger, and Lucius of Cyrene, and
Manaen, which had been brought up with Herod the tetrarch, and Saul.
PRAY 2 As they ministered to the Lord, and fasted, the Holy Ghost said, Separate me WOW
Barnabas and Saul for the work whereunto I have called them.
PRAY 3 And when they had fasted and prayed, and laid *their* hands on them, they
sent *them* away.
4 So they, being sent forth by the Holy Ghost, departed unto Seleucia; and from
thence they sailed to Cyprus.
5 And when they were at Salamis, they preached the word of God in the
synagogues of the Jews: and they had also John to *their* minister.
6 And when they had gone through the isle unto Paphos, they found a certain
sorcerer, a false prophet, a Jew, whose name *was* Barjesus:
7 Which was with the deputy of the country, Sergius Paulus, a prudent man; who
called for Barnabas and Saul, and desired to hear the word of God.
PERS 8 But Elymas the sorcerer (for so is his name by interpretation) withstood them,
seeking to turn away the deputy from the faith.
BHS 9 Then Saul, (who also *is called* Paul,) filled with the Holy Ghost, set his eyes on
him,
10 And said, O full of all subtlety and all mischief, *thou* child of the devil, *thou* DISC
enemy of all righteousness, wilt thou not cease to pervert the right ways of the
Lord?
11 And now, behold, the hand of the Lord *is* upon thee, and thou shalt be blind, not WOW
JUDG seeing the sun for a season. And immediately there fell on him a mist and a
darkness; and he went about seeking some to lead him by the hand.
HARV 12 Then the deputy, when he saw what was done, believed, being astonished at the
doctrine of the Lord.
13 Now when Paul and his company loosed from Paphos, they came to Perga in
Pamphylia: and John departing from them returned to Jerusalem.
14 But when they departed from Perga, they came to Antioch in Pisidia, and went
into the synagogue on the sabbath day, and sat down.
15 And after the reading of the law and the prophets the rulers of the synagogue
sent unto them, saying, *Ye* men *and* brethren, if ye have any word of exhortation
for the people, say on.
16 Then Paul stood up, and beckoning with *his* hand said, Men of Israel, and ye
that fear God, give audience.
17 The God of this people of Israel chose our fathers, and exalted the people when
they dwelt as strangers in the land of Egypt, and with an high arm brought he

them out of it.
18 And about the time of forty years suffered he their manners in the wilderness.
19 And when he had destroyed seven nations in the land of Chanaan, he divided
their land to them by lot.
20 And after that he gave *unto them* judges about the space of four hundred and
fifty years, until Samuel the prophet.
21 And afterward they desired a king: and God gave unto them Saul the son of Cis,
a man of the tribe of Benjamin, by the space of forty years.
22 And when he had removed him, he raised up unto them David to be their king;
to whom also he gave testimony, and said, I have found David the *son* of Jesse, a
man after mine own heart, which shall fulfil all my will.
23 Of this man's seed hath God according to *his* promise raised unto Israel a
Saviour, Jesus:
24 When John had first preached before his coming the baptism of repentance to all
the people of Israel.
25 And as John fulfilled his course, he said, Whom think ye that I am? I am not *he*.
But, behold, there cometh one after me, whose shoes of *his* feet I am not worthy
to loose.
26 Men *and* brethren, children of the stock of Abraham, and whosoever among you
feareth God, to you is the word of this salvation sent.
27 For they that dwell at Jerusalem, and their rulers, because they knew him not,
nor yet the voices of the prophets which are read every sabbath day, they have
fulfilled *them* in condemning *him*.
28 And though they found no cause of death *in him*, yet desired they Pilate that he
should be slain.
OTW 29 And when they had fulfilled all that was written of him, they took *him* down
from the tree, and laid *him* in a sepulcher.
RES 30 But God raised him from the dead:
31 And he was seen many days of them which came up with him from Galilee to
Jerusalem, who are his witnesses unto the people.
32 And we declare unto you glad tidings, how that the promise which was made
unto the fathers,
RES 33 God hath fulfilled the same unto us their children, in that he hath raised up Jesus
OTW again; as it is also written in the second psalm, Thou art my Son, this day have I
begotten thee (Psalms 2:7).
RES 34 And as concerning that he raised him up from the dead, *now* no more to return
OTW to corruption, he said on this wise, I will give you the sure mercies of David.
OTW 35 Wherefore he saith also in another *psalm*, Thou shalt not suffer thine Holy One
to see corruption (Isaiah 55:3 Psalms 16:10).
36 For David, after he had served his own generation by the will of God, fell on

sleep, and was laid unto his fathers, and saw corruption:
RES 37 But he, whom God raised again, saw no corruption.
38 Be it known unto you therefore, men *and* brethren, that through this man is
preached unto you the forgiveness of sins:
39 And by him all that believe are justified from all things, from which ye could
not be justified by the law of Moses.
40 Beware therefore, lest that come upon you, which is spoken of in the prophets;
OTW 41 Behold, ye despisers, and wonder, and perish: for I work a work in your days, a
work which ye shall in no wise believe, though a man declare it unto you
(Habakkuk 1:5).
42 And when the Jews were gone out of the synagogue, the Gentiles besought that
these words might be preached to them the next sabbath.
HARV 43 Now when the congregation was broken up, many of the Jews and religious
proselytes followed Paul and Barnabas: who, speaking to them, persuaded them to
continue in the grace of God.
44 And the next sabbath day came almost the whole city together to hear the word
of God.
PERS 45 But when the Jews saw the multitudes, they were filled with envy, and spake
against those things which were spoken by Paul, contradicting and blaspheming.
46 Then Paul and Barnabas waxed bold, and said, It was necessary that the word of GOF
God should first have been spoken to you: but seeing ye put it from you, and
judge yourselves unworthy of everlasting life, lo, we turn to the Gentiles.
OTW 47 For so hath the Lord commanded us, *saying*, I have set thee to be a light of the WOW
Gentiles, that thou shouldest be for salvation unto the ends of the earth (Isaiah 49:6).
48 And when the Gentiles heard this, they were glad, and glorified the word of the
HARV Lord: and as many as were ordained to eternal life believed.
49 And the word of the Lord was published throughout all the region.
PERS 50 But the Jews stirred up the devout and honourable women, and the chief men of
the city, and raised persecution against Paul and Barnabas, and expelled them out
of their coasts.
51 But they shook off the dust of their feet against them, and came unto Iconium.
BHS 52 And the disciples were filled with joy, and with the Holy Ghost.

Acts 14:1–28

1 And it came to pass in Iconium, that they went both together into the synagogue
HARV of the Jews, and so spake, that a great multitude both of the Jews and also of the
Greeks believed.
PERS 2 But the unbelieving Jews stirred up the Gentiles, and made their minds evil
affected against the brethren.
3 Long time therefore abode they speaking boldly in the Lord, which gave GOF
testimony unto the word of his grace, and granted signs and wonders to be done GOH
by their hands.
4 But the multitude of the city was divided: and part held with the Jews, and part WOM
with the apostles.
PERS 5 And when there was an assault made both of the Gentiles, and also of the Jews
with their rulers, to use *them* despitefully, and to stone them,
6 They were ware of *it*, and fled unto Lystra and Derbe, cities of Lycaonia, and
unto the region that lieth round about:
7 And there they preached the gospel.
8 And there sat a certain man at Lystra, impotent in his feet, being a cripple from
his mother's womb, who never had walked:
9 The same heard Paul speak: who stedfastly beholding him, and perceiving that he DISC
had faith to be healed, GOH
10 Said with a loud voice, Stand upright on thy feet. And he leaped and walked.
11 And when the people saw what Paul had done, they lifted up their voices, saying
in the speech of Lycaonia, The gods are come down to us in the likeness of men.
12 And they called Barnabas, Jupiter; and Paul, Mercurius, because he was the
chief speaker.
13 Then the priest of Jupiter, which was before their city, brought oxen and
garlands unto the gates, and would have done sacrifice with the people.
14 *Which* when the apostles, Barnabas and Paul, heard *of*, they rent their clothes,
and ran in among the people, crying out,
15 And saying, Sirs, why do ye these things? We also are men of like passions with
you, and preach unto you that ye should turn from these vanities unto the living
God, which made heaven, and earth, and the sea, and all things that are therein:
16 Who in times past suffered all nations to walk in their own ways.
17 Nevertheless he left not himself without witness, in that he did good, and gave
us rain from heaven, and fruitful seasons, filling our hearts with food and
gladness.
18 And with these sayings scarce restrained they the people, that they had not done
sacrifice unto them.
19 And there came thither *certain* Jews from Antioch and Iconium, who persuaded
PERS the people, and, having stoned Paul, drew *him* out of the city, supposing he had

been dead.
20 Howbeit, as the disciples stood round about him, he rose up, and came into the GOH
city: and the next day he departed with Barnabas to Derbe.
21 And when they had preached the gospel to that city, and had taught many, they
returned again to Lystra, and *to* Iconium, and Antioch,
22 Confirming the souls of the disciples, *and* exhorting them to continue in the
faith, and that we must through much tribulation enter into the kingdom of God.
PRAY 23 And when they had ordained them elders in every church, and had prayed with
fasting, they commended them to the Lord, on whom they believed.
24 And after they had passed throughout Pisidia, they came to Pamphylia.
25 And when they had preached the word in Perga, they went down into Attalia:
26 And thence sailed to Antioch, from whence they had been recommended to the
grace of God for the work which they fulfilled.
27 And when they were come, and had gathered the church together, they rehearsed
OTW all that God had done with them, and how he had opened the door of faith unto GOF
OTW the Gentiles (Isaiah 42:6, Isaiah 49:6).
28 And there they abode long time with the disciples.

Acts 15:1–41

1 And certain men which came down from Judaea taught the brethren, *and said,*
Except ye be circumcised after the manner of Moses, ye cannot be saved.
2 When therefore Paul and Barnabas had no small dissension and disputation with
them, they determined that Paul and Barnabas, and certain other of them, should
go up to Jerusalem unto the apostles and elders about this question.
3 And being brought on their way by the church, they passed through Phenice and
Samaria, declaring the conversion of the Gentiles: and they caused great joy unto
all the brethren.
4 And when they were come to Jerusalem, they were received of the church, and *of*
the apostles and elders, and they declared all things that God had done with them.
5 But there rose up certain of the sect of the Pharisees which believed, saying, That
it was needful to circumcise them, and to command *them* to keep the law of
Moses.
6 And the apostles and elders came together for to consider of this matter.
7 And when there had been much disputing, Peter rose up, and said unto them,
Men *and* brethren, ye know how that a good while ago God made choice among
us, that the Gentiles by my mouth should hear the word of the gospel, and
believe.
BHS 8 And God, which knoweth the hearts, bare them witness, giving them the Holy
Ghost, even as *he did* unto us;
9 And put no difference between us and them, purifying their hearts by faith.
10 Now therefore why tempt ye God, to put a yoke upon the neck of the disciples,
which neither our fathers nor we were able to bear?
11 But we believe that through the grace of the Lord Jesus Christ we shall be saved,
even as they.
12 Then all the multitude kept silence, and gave audience to Barnabas and Paul, GOH
declaring what miracles and wonders God had wrought among the Gentiles by WOM
them. GOF
13 And after they had held their peace, James answered, saying, Men *and* brethren,
hearken unto me:
14 Simeon hath declared how God at the first did visit the Gentiles, to take out of
them a people for his name.
15 And to this agree the words of the prophets; as it is written,
OTW 16 After this I will return, and will build again the tabernacle of David, which is
fallen down; and I will build again the ruins thereof and I will set it up (Isaiah 16:5).
OTW 17 That the residue of men might seek after the Lord, and all the Gentiles, upon
whom my name is called, saith the Lord, who doeth all these things (Amos 9:11).
18 Known unto God are all his works from the beginning of the world.
19 Wherefore my sentence is, that we trouble not them, which from among the

Gentiles are turned to God:
[20]But that we write unto them, that they abstain from pollutions of idols, and *from*
fornication, and *from* things strangled, and *from* blood.
[21]For Moses of old time hath in every city them that preach him, being read in the
synagogues every sabbath day.
[22]Then pleased it the apostles and elders, with the whole church, to send chosen
men of their own company to Antioch with Paul and Barnabas; *namely*, Judas
surnamed Barsabas, and Silas, chief men among the brethren:
[23]And they wrote *letters* by them after this manner; The apostles and elders and
brethren *send* greeting unto the brethren which are of the Gentiles in Antioch and
Syria and Cilicia:
[24]Forasmuch as we have heard, that certain which went out from us have troubled
you with words, subverting your souls, saying, *Ye must* be circumcised, and keep
the law: to whom we gave no *such* commandment:
[25]It seemed good unto us, being assembled with one accord, to send chosen men
unto you with our beloved Barnabas and Paul,
[26]Men that have hazarded their lives for the name of our Lord Jesus Christ.
[27]We have sent therefore Judas and Silas, who shall also tell *you* the same things
by mouth.
[28]For it seemed good to the Holy Ghost, and to us, to lay upon you no greater
burden than these necessary things;
[29]That ye abstain from meats offered to idols, and from blood, and from things
strangled, and from fornication: from which if ye keep yourselves, ye shall do
well. Fare ye well.
[30]So when they were dismissed, they came to Antioch: and when they had
gathered the multitude together, they delivered the epistle:
[31]*Which* when they had read, they rejoiced for the consolation.
[32]And Judas and Silas, being prophets also themselves, exhorted the brethren with PRO
many words, and confirmed *them*.
[33]And after they had tarried *there* a space, they were let go in peace from the
brethren unto the apostles.
[34]Notwithstanding it pleased Silas to abide there still.
[35]Paul also and Barnabas continued in Antioch, teaching and preaching the word
of the Lord, with many others also.
[36]And some days after Paul said unto Barnabas, Let us go again and visit our
brethren in every city where we have preached the word of the Lord, *and see* how
they do.
[37]And Barnabas determined to take with them John, whose surname was Mark.
[38]But Paul thought not good to take him with them, who departed from them from
Pamphylia, and went not with them to the work.

39 And the contention was so sharp between them, that they departed asunder one
from the other: and so Barnabas took Mark, and sailed unto Cyprus;
40 And Paul chose Silas, and departed, being recommended by the brethren unto
the grace of God.
41 And he went through Syria and Cilicia, confirming the churches.

Acts 16:1–40
[1]Then came he to Derbe and Lystra: and, behold, a certain disciple was there,
named Timotheus, the son of a certain woman, which was a Jewess, and believed;
but his father *was* a Greek:
[2]Which was well reported of by the brethren that were at Lystra and Iconium.
[3]Him would Paul have to go forth with him; and took and circumcised him
because of the Jews which were in those quarters: for they knew all that his father
was a Greek.
[4]And as they went through the cities, they delivered them the decrees for to keep,
that were ordained of the apostles and elders which were at Jerusalem.
HARV [5]And so were the churches established in the faith, and increased in number daily.
[6]Now when they had gone throughout Phrygia and the region of Galatia, and were WOW
forbidden of the Holy Ghost to preach the word in Asia,
[7]After they were come to Mysia, they assayed to go into Bithynia: but the Spirit
suffered them not. WOW
[8]And they passing by Mysia came down to Troas.
[9]And a vision appeared to Paul in the night; There stood a man of Macedonia, and DISC
prayed him, saying, Come over into Macedonia, and help us.
[10]And after he had seen the vision, immediately we endeavoured to go into
Macedonia, assuredly gathering that the Lord had called us for to preach the WOW
gospel unto them.
[11]Therefore loosing from Troas, we came with a straight course to Samothracia,
and the next *day* to Neapolis;
[12]And from thence to Philippi, which is the chief city of that part of
Macedonia, *and* a colony: and we were in that city abiding certain days.
PRAY [13]And on the sabbath we went out of the city by a river side, where prayer was
wont to be made; and we sat down, and spake unto the women which
resorted *thither*.
[14]And a certain woman named Lydia, a seller of purple, of the city of Thyatira,
which worshipped God, heard *us*: whose heart the Lord opened, that she attended PRO
unto the things which were spoken of Paul.
HARV [15]And when she was baptized, and her household, she besought *us*, saying, If ye
have judged me to be faithful to the Lord, come into my house, and abide *there*. DISC
And she constrained us.
PRAY [16]And it came to pass, as we went to prayer, a certain damsel possessed with a
spirit of divination met us, which brought her masters much gain by soothsaying:
[17]The same followed Paul and us, and cried, saying, These men are the servants of
the most high God, which show unto us the way of salvation.
[18]And this did she many days. But Paul, being grieved, turned and said to the DISC
spirit, I command thee in the name of Jesus Christ to come out of her. And he GOF
came out the same hour.
PERS [19]And when her masters saw that the hope of their gains was gone, they caught WOM
Paul and Silas, and drew *them* into the marketplace unto the rulers,
[20]And brought them to the magistrates, saying, These men, being Jews, do
exceedingly trouble our city,
[21]And teach customs, which are not lawful for us to receive, neither to observe,

being Romans.
22 And the multitude rose up together against them: and the magistrates rent off
their clothes, and commanded to beat *them.*
23 And when they had laid many stripes upon them, they cast *them* into prison,
charging the jailor to keep them safely:
24 Who, having received such a charge, thrust them into the inner prison, and made
their feet fast in the stocks.
PRAY 25 And at midnight Paul and Silas prayed, and sang praises unto God: and the
prisoners heard them.
26 And suddenly there was a great earthquake, so that the foundations of the prison GOF
were shaken: and immediately all the doors were opened, and every one's bands
were loosed.
27 And the keeper of the prison awaking out of his sleep, and seeing the prison
doors open, he drew out his sword, and would have killed himself, supposing that
the prisoners had been fled.
28 But Paul cried with a loud voice, saying, Do thyself no harm: for we are all WOK
here.
29 Then he called for a light, and sprang in, and came trembling, and fell down
before Paul and Silas,
HARV 30 And brought them out, and said, Sirs, what must I do to be saved?
31 And they said, Believe on the Lord Jesus Christ, and thou shalt be saved, and
thy house.
32 And they spake unto him the word of the Lord, and to all that were in his house.
33 And he took them the same hour of the night, and washed *their* stripes; and was
baptized, he and all his, straightway.
34 And when he had brought them into his house, he set meat before them, and
rejoiced, believing in God with all his house.
35 And when it was day, the magistrates sent the serjeants, saying, Let those men
go.
36 And the keeper of the prison told this saying to Paul, The magistrates have sent
to let you go: now therefore depart, and go in peace.
37 But Paul said unto them, They have beaten us openly uncondemned, being
Romans, and have cast *us* into prison; and now do they thrust us out privily? nay
verily; but let them come themselves and fetch us out.
38 And the serjeants told these words unto the magistrates: and they feared, when
they heard that they were Romans.
39 And they came and besought them, and brought *them* out, and desired *them* to
depart out of the city.
40 And they went out of the prison, and entered into *the house of* Lydia: and when
they had seen the brethren, they comforted them, and departed.

Acts 17:1–34

1 Now when they had passed through Amphipolis and Apollonia, they came to
Thessalonica, where was a synagogue of the Jews:
2 And Paul, as his manner was, went in unto them, and three sabbath days
reasoned with them out of the scriptures,
RES 3 Opening and alleging, that Christ must needs have suffered, and risen again from
the dead; and that this Jesus, whom I preach unto you, is Christ.
HARV 4 And some of them believed, and consorted with Paul and Silas; and of the devout
HARV Greeks a great multitude, and of the chief women not a few.
HARV 5 But the Jews which believed not, moved with envy, took unto them certain lewd
fellows of the baser sort, and gathered a company, and set all the city on an
PERS uproar, and assaulted the house of Jason, and sought to bring them out to the
people.
6 And when they found them not, they drew Jason and certain brethren unto the
rulers of the city, crying, These that have turned the world upside down are come
hither also;
7 Whom Jason hath received: and these all do contrary to the decrees of Caesar,
saying that there is another king, *one* Jesus.
8 And they troubled the people and the rulers of the city, when they heard these
things.
9 And when they had taken security of Jason, and of the other, they let them go.
10 And the brethren immediately sent away Paul and Silas by night unto Berea:
who coming *thither* went into the synagogue of the Jews.
11 These were more noble than those in Thessalonica, in that they received the
word with all readiness of mind, and searched the scriptures daily, whether those
things were so.
HARV 12 Therefore many of them believed; also of honourable women which were
HARV Greeks, and of men, not a few.
13 But when the Jews of Thessalonica had knowledge that the word of God was
PERS preached of Paul at Berea, they came thither also, and stirred up the people.
14 And then immediately the brethren sent away Paul to go as it were to the sea:
but Silas and Timotheus abode there still.
15 And they that conducted Paul brought him unto Athens: and receiving a
commandment unto Silas and Timotheus for to come to him with all speed, they
departed.
16 Now while Paul waited for them at Athens, his spirit was stirred in him, when
he saw the city wholly given to idolatry.
17 Therefore disputed he in the synagogue with the Jews, and with the devout
persons, and in the market daily with them that met with him.
18 Then certain philosophers of the Epicureans, and of the Stoicks, encountered

him. And some said, What will this babbler say? other some, He seemeth to be a
setter forth of strange gods: because he preached unto them Jesus, and the
RES resurrection.
19 And they took him, and brought him unto Areopagus, saying, May we know
what this new doctrine, whereof thou speakest, *is*?
20 For thou bringest certain strange things to our ears: we would know therefore
what these things mean.
21 (For all the Athenians and strangers which were there spent their time in nothing
else, but either to tell, or to hear some new thing.)
22 Then Paul stood in the midst of Mars' hill, and said, *Ye* men of Athens, I
perceive that in all things ye are too superstitious.
23 For as I passed by, and beheld your devotions, I found an altar with this
inscription, TO THE UNKNOWN GOD. Whom therefore ye ignorantly worship,
him declare I unto you.
24 God that made the world and all things therein, seeing that he is Lord of heaven
and earth, dwelleth not in temples made with hands;
25 Neither is worshipped with men's hands, as though he needed any thing, seeing
he giveth to all life, and breath, and all things;
26 And hath made of one blood all nations of men for to dwell on all the face of the
earth, and hath determined the times before appointed, and the bounds of their
habitation;
27 That they should seek the Lord, if haply they might feel after him, and find him,
though he be not far from every one of us:
28 For in him we live, and move, and have our being; as certain also of your own
poets have said, For we are also his offspring.
29 Forasmuch then as we are the offspring of God, we ought not to think that the
Godhead is like unto gold, or silver, or stone, graven by art and man's device.
30 And the times of this ignorance God winked at; but now commandeth all men
everywhere to repent:
31 Because he hath appointed a day, in the which he will judge the world in
righteousness by *that* man whom he hath ordained; *whereof* he hath given
RES assurance unto all *men*, in that he hath raised him from the dead.
RES 32 And when they heard of the resurrection of the dead, some mocked: and others
said, We will hear thee again of this *matter*.
33 So Paul departed from among them.
HARV 34 Howbeit certain men clave unto him, and believed: among the which *was*
Dionysius the Areopagite, and a woman named Damaris, and others with them.

Acts 18:1–28

1After these things Paul departed from Athens, and came to Corinth;
2And found a certain Jew named Aquila, born in Pontus, lately come from Italy,
with his wife Priscilla; (because that Claudius had commanded all Jews to depart
from Rome:) and came unto them.
3And because he was of the same craft, he abode with them, and wrought: for by
their occupation they were tentmakers.
4And he reasoned in the synagogue every sabbath, and persuaded the Jews and the
Greeks.
5And when Silas and Timotheus were come from Macedonia, Paul was pressed in
the spirit, and testified to the Jews *that* Jesus *was* Christ.
PERS 6And when they opposed themselves, and blasphemed, he shook *his* raiment, and
said unto them, Your blood *be* upon your own heads; I *am* clean: from henceforth
I will go unto the Gentiles.
7And he departed thence, and entered into a certain *man's* house, named
Justus, *one* that worshipped God, whose house joined hard to the synagogue.
HARV 8And Crispus, the chief ruler of the synagogue, believed on the Lord with all his
HARV house; and many of the Corinthians hearing believed, and were baptized.
9Then spake the Lord to Paul in the night by a vision, Be not afraid, but speak, DISC
and hold not thy peace: PRO
10For I am with thee, and no man shall set on thee to hurt thee: for I have much WOW
people in this city.
11And he continued *there* a year and six months, teaching the word of God among WOK
them.
PERS 12And when Gallio was the deputy of Achaia, the Jews made insurrection with
one accord against Paul, and brought him to the judgment seat,
13Saying, This *fellow* persuadeth men to worship God contrary to the law.
14And when Paul was now about to open *his* mouth, Gallio said unto the Jews, If
it were a matter of wrong or wicked lewdness, O *ye* Jews, reason would that I
should bear with you:
15But if it be a question of words and names, and *of* your law, look ye *to it*; for I
will be no judge of such *matters*.
16And he drave them from the judgment seat.
17Then all the Greeks took Sosthenes, the chief ruler of the synagogue, and
beat *him* before the judgment seat. And Gallio cared for none of those things.
18And Paul *after this* tarried *there* yet a good while, and then took his leave of the
brethren, and sailed thence into Syria, and with him Priscilla and Aquila; having
shorn *his* head in Cenchrea: for he had a vow.
19And he came to Ephesus, and left them there: but he himself entered into the
synagogue, and reasoned with the Jews.

20When they desired *him* to tarry longer time with them, he consented not;
21But bade them farewell, saying, I must by all means keep this feast that cometh
in Jerusalem: but I will return again unto you, if God will. And he sailed from
Ephesus.
22And when he had landed at Caesarea, and gone up, and saluted the church, he
went down to Antioch.
23And after he had spent some time *there*, he departed, and went over *all* the
country of Galatia and Phrygia in order, strengthening all the disciples.
24And a certain Jew named Apollos, born at Alexandria, an eloquent man, *and*
mighty in the scriptures, came to Ephesus.
25This man was instructed in the way of the Lord; and being fervent in the spirit,
he spake and taught diligently the things of the Lord, knowing only the baptism of
John.
26And he began to speak boldly in the synagogue: whom when Aquila and
BHS Priscilla had heard, they took him unto *them*, and expounded unto him the way of
God more perfectly.
27And when he was disposed to pass into Achaia, the brethren wrote, exhorting
the disciples to receive him: who, when he was come, helped them much which
had believed through grace:
28For he mightily convinced the Jews, *and that* publicly, showing by the scriptures
that Jesus was Christ.

Acts 19:1–41

1 And it came to pass, that, while Apollos was at Corinth, Paul having passed
through the upper coasts came to Ephesus: and finding certain disciples,
2 He said unto them, Have ye received the Holy Ghost since ye believed? And they
said unto him, We have not so much as heard whether there be any Holy Ghost.
3 And he said unto them, Unto what then were ye baptized? And they said, Unto
John's baptism.
4 Then said Paul, John verily baptized with the baptism of repentance, saying unto
the people, that they should believe on him which should come after him, that is,
on Christ Jesus.
HARV 5 When they heard *this*, they were baptized in the name of the Lord Jesus. GOF
BHS 6 And when Paul had laid *his* hands upon them, the Holy Ghost came on them; and TONG
they spake with tongues and prophesied. PRO
7 And all the men were about twelve.
8 And he went into the synagogue, and spake boldly for the space of three months, INT
disputing and persuading the things concerning the kingdom of God.
PERS 9 But when divers were hardened, and believed not, but spake evil of that way
before the multitude, he departed from them, and separated the disciples,
disputing daily in the school of one Tyrannus.
10 And this continued by the space of two years; so that all they which dwelt in
Asia heard the word of the Lord Jesus, both Jews and Greeks.
11 And God wrought special miracles by the hands of Paul:
12 So that from his body were brought unto the sick handkerchiefs or aprons, and GOH
the diseases departed from them, and the evil spirits went out of them.
13 Then certain of the vagabond Jews, exorcists, took upon them to call over them
which had evil spirits the name of the Lord Jesus, saying, We adjure you by Jesus
whom Paul preacheth.
14 And there were seven sons of *one* Sceva, a Jew, *and* chief of the priests, which
did so.
15 And the evil spirit answered and said, Jesus I know, and Paul I know; but who
are ye?
16 And the man in whom the evil spirit was leaped on them, and overcame them,
and prevailed against them, so that they fled out of that house naked and
wounded.
17 And this was known to all the Jews and Greeks also dwelling at Ephesus; and
fear fell on them all, and the name of the Lord Jesus was magnified.
HARV 18 And many that believed came, and confessed, and showed their deeds.
19 Many of them also which used curious arts brought their books together, and
burned them before all *men*: and they counted the price of them, and found *it* fifty
thousand *pieces* of silver.

GOF

GOH

WOM

WOW

20 So mightily grew the word of God and prevailed.
21 After these things were ended, Paul purposed in the spirit, when he had passed through Macedonia and Achaia, to go to Jerusalem, saying, After I have been there, I must also see Rome.
22 So he sent into Macedonia two of them that ministered unto him, Timotheus and Erastus; but he himself stayed in Asia for a season.

PERS

23 And the same time there arose no small stir about that way.
24 For a certain *man* named Demetrius, a silversmith, which made silver shrines for Diana, brought no small gain unto the craftsmen;
25 Whom he called together with the workmen of like occupation, and said, Sirs, ye know that by this craft we have our wealth.
26 Moreover ye see and hear, that not alone at Ephesus, but almost throughout all Asia, this Paul hath persuaded and turned away much people, saying that they be no gods, which are made with hands:
27 So that not only this our craft is in danger to be set at nought; but also that the temple of the great goddess Diana should be despised, and her magnificence should be destroyed, whom all Asia and the world worshippeth.
28 And when they heard *these sayings*, they were full of wrath, and cried out, saying, Great *is* Diana of the Ephesians.
29 And the whole city was filled with confusion: and having caught Gaius and Aristarchus, men of Macedonia, Paul's companions in travel, they rushed with one accord into the theatre.
30 And when Paul would have entered in unto the people, the disciples suffered him not.
31 And certain of the chief of Asia, which were his friends, sent unto him, desiring *him* that he would not adventure himself into the theatre.
32 Some therefore cried one thing, and some another: for the assembly was confused; and the more part knew not wherefore they were come together.
33 And they drew Alexander out of the multitude, the Jews putting him forward. And Alexander beckoned with the hand, and would have made his defense unto the people.
34 But when they knew that he was a Jew, all with one voice about the space of two hours cried out, Great *is* Diana of the Ephesians.
35 And when the town clerk had appeased the people, he said, *Ye* men of Ephesus, what man is there that knoweth not how that the city of the Ephesians is a worshipper of the great goddess Diana, and of the *image* which fell down from Jupiter?
36 Seeing then that these things cannot be spoken against, ye ought to be quiet, and to do nothing rashly.
37 For ye have brought hither these men, which are neither robbers of churches,

nor yet blasphemers of your goddess.
38Wherefore if Demetrius, and the craftsmen which are with him, have a matter
against any man, the law is open, and there are deputies: let them implead one
another.
39But if ye inquire anything concerning other matters, it shall be determined in a
lawful assembly.
40For we are in danger to be called in question for this day's uproar, there being
no cause whereby we may give an account of this concourse.
41And when he had thus spoken, he dismissed the assembly.

Acts 20:1–38

1And after the uproar was ceased, Paul called unto *him* the disciples, and
embraced *them*, and departed for to go into Macedonia.
2And when he had gone over those parts, and had given them much exhortation,
he came into Greece,
PERS 3And *there* abode three months. And when the Jews laid wait for him, as he was
about to sail into Syria, he purposed to return through Macedonia.
4And there accompanied him into Asia Sopater of Berea; and of the
Thessalonians, Aristarchus and Secundus; and Gaius of Derbe, and Timotheus;
and of Asia, Tychicus and Trophimus.
5These going before tarried for us at Troas.
6And we sailed away from Philippi after the days of unleavened bread, and came
unto them to Troas in five days; where we abode seven days.
7And upon the first *day* of the week, when the disciples came together to break
bread, Paul preached unto them, ready to depart on the morrow; and continued his
speech until midnight.
8And there were many lights in the upper chamber, where they were gathered
together.
9And there sat in a window a certain young man named Eutychus, being fallen
into a deep sleep: and as Paul was long preaching, he sunk down with sleep, and
fell down from the third loft, and was taken up dead. GOF
RES 10And Paul went down, and fell on him, and embracing *him* said, Trouble not WOM
yourselves; for his life is in him. GOH
11When he therefore was come up again, and had broken bread, and eaten, and
talked a long while, even till break of day, so he departed.
12And they brought the young man alive, and were not a little comforted.
13And we went before to ship, and sailed unto Assos, there intending to take in
Paul: for so had he appointed, minding himself to go afoot.
14And when he met with us at Assos, we took him in, and came to Mitylene.
15And we sailed thence, and came the next *day* over against Chios; and the
next *day* we arrived at Samos, and tarried at Trogyllium; and the next *day* we
came to Miletus.
16For Paul had determined to sail by Ephesus, because he would not spend the
time in Asia: for he hasted, if it were possible for him, to be at Jerusalem the day
of Pentecost.
17And from Miletus he sent to Ephesus, and called the elders of the church.
18And when they were come to him, he said unto them, Ye know, from the first
day that I came into Asia, after what manner I have been with you at all seasons,

19Serving the Lord with all humility of mind, and with many tears, and
temptations, which befell me by the lying in wait of the Jews:
20*And* how I kept back nothing that was profitable *unto you*, but have showed you,
and have taught you publicly, and from house to house,
21Testifying both to the Jews, and also to the Greeks, repentance toward God, and
faith toward our Lord Jesus Christ.
22And now, behold, I go bound in the spirit unto Jerusalem, not knowing the
things that shall befall me there:
23Save that the Holy Ghost witnesseth in every city, saying that bonds and WOW
afflictions abide me.
24But none of these things move me, neither count I my life dear unto myself, so
that I might finish my course with joy, and the ministry, which I have received of
the Lord Jesus, to testify the gospel of the grace of God.
25And now, behold, I know that ye all, among whom I have gone preaching the
kingdom of God, shall see my face no more. WOW
26Wherefore I take you to record this day, that I *am* pure from the blood of
all *men*.
27For I have not shunned to declare unto you all the counsel of God.
28Take heed therefore unto yourselves, and to all the flock, over the which the
Holy Ghost hath made you overseers, to feed the church of God, which he hath
purchased with his own blood.
29For I know this, that after my departing shall grievous wolves enter in among WOW
you, not sparing the flock.
30Also of your own selves shall men arise, speaking perverse things, to draw away
disciples after them.
31Therefore watch, and remember, that by the space of three years I ceased not to
warn every one night and day with tears.
32And now, brethren, I commend you to God, and to the word of his grace, which
is able to build you up, and to give you an inheritance among all them which are
sanctified.
33I have coveted no man's silver, or gold, or apparel.
34Yea, ye yourselves know, that these hands have ministered unto my necessities,
and to them that were with me.
35I have showed you all things, how that so labouring ye ought to support the
weak, and to remember the words of the Lord Jesus, how he said, It is more
blessed to give than to receive.
PRAY 36And when he had thus spoken, he kneeled down, and prayed with them all.
37And they all wept sore, and fell on Paul's neck, and kissed him,
38Sorrowing most of all for the words which he spake, that they should see his
face no more. And they accompanied him unto the ship.

Acts 21:1–40

[1]And it came to pass, that after we were gotten from them, and had launched, we
came with a straight course unto Coos, and the *day* following unto Rhodes, and
from thence unto Patara:
[2]And finding a ship sailing over unto Phenicia, we went aboard, and set forth.
[3]Now when we had discovered Cyprus, we left it on the left hand, and sailed into
Syria, and landed at Tyre: for there the ship was to unlade her burden.
[4]And finding disciples, we tarried there seven days: who said to Paul through the WOW
Spirit, that he should not go up to Jerusalem.
[5]And when we had accomplished those days, we departed and went our way; and
they all brought us on our way, with wives and children, till *we were* out of the
PRAY city: and we kneeled down on the shore, and prayed.
[6]And when we had taken our leave one of another, we took ship; and they
returned home again.
[7]And when we had finished *our* course from Tyre, we came to Ptolemais, and
saluted the brethren, and abode with them one day.
[8]And the next *day* we that were of Paul's company departed, and came unto
Caesarea: and we entered into the house of Philip the evangelist, which was *one*
of the seven; and abode with him.
[9]And the same man had four daughters, virgins, which did prophesy. PRO
[10]And as we tarried *there* many days, there came down from Judaea a certain
prophet, named Agabus.
[11]And when he was come unto us, he took Paul's girdle, and bound his own hands
and feet, and said, Thus saith the Holy Ghost, So shall the Jews at Jerusalem bind WOW
the man that owneth this girdle, and shall deliver *him* into the hands of the
Gentiles.
[12]And when we heard these things, both we, and they of that place, besought him
not to go up to Jerusalem.
[13]Then Paul answered, What mean ye to weep and to break mine heart? for I am
ready not to be bound only, but also to die at Jerusalem for the name of the Lord
Jesus.
[14]And when he would not be persuaded, we ceased, saying, The will of the Lord
be done.
[15]And after those days we took up our carriages, and went up to Jerusalem.
[16]There went with us also *certain* of the disciples of Caesarea, and brought with
them one Mnason of Cyprus, an old disciple, with whom we should lodge.
[17]And when we were come to Jerusalem, the brethren received us gladly.
[18]And the *day* following Paul went in with us unto James; and all the elders were
present.
[19]And when he had saluted them, he declared particularly what things God had

wrought among the Gentiles by his ministry.
20And when they heard *it*, they glorified the Lord, and said unto him, Thou seest, brother, how many thousands of Jews there are which believe; and they are all zealous of the law:
21And they are informed of thee, that thou teachest all the Jews which are among the Gentiles to forsake Moses, saying that they ought not to circumcise *their* children, neither to walk after the customs.
22What is it therefore? the multitude must needs come together: for they will hear that thou art come.
23Do therefore this that we say to thee: We have four men which have a vow on them;
24Them take, and purify thyself with them, and be at charges with them, that they may shave *their* heads: and all may know that those things, whereof they were informed concerning thee, are nothing; but *that* thou thyself also walkest orderly, and keepest the law.
25As touching the Gentiles which believe, we have written *and* concluded that they observe no such thing, save only that they keep themselves from *things* offered to idols, and from blood, and from strangled, and from fornication.
26Then Paul took the men, and the next day purifying himself with them entered into the temple, to signify the accomplishment of the days of purification, until that an offering should be offered for every one of them.
27And when the seven days were almost ended, the Jews which were of Asia,
PERS when they saw him in the temple, stirred up all the people, and laid hands on him,
28Crying out, Men of Israel, help: This is the man, that teacheth all *men* every where against the people, and the law, and this place: and further brought Greeks also into the temple, and hath polluted this holy place.
29(For they had seen before with him in the city Trophimus an Ephesian, whom they supposed that Paul had brought into the temple.)
30And all the city was moved, and the people ran together: and they took Paul, and drew him out of the temple: and forthwith the doors were shut.
31And as they went about to kill him, tidings came unto the chief captain of the band, that all Jerusalem was in an uproar.
32Who immediately took soldiers and centurions, and ran down unto them: and
PERS when they saw the chief captain and the soldiers, they left beating of Paul.
33Then the chief captain came near, and took him, and commanded *him* to be bound with two chains; and demanded who he was, and what he had done.
34And some cried one thing, some another, among the multitude: and when he could not know the certainty for the tumult, he commanded him to be carried into the castle.
35And when he came upon the stairs, so it was, that he was borne of the soldiers

for the violence of the people.
36For the multitude of the people followed after, crying, Away with him.
37And as Paul was to be led into the castle, he said unto the chief captain, May I
speak unto thee? Who said, Canst thou speak Greek?
38Art not thou that Egyptian, which before these days madest an uproar, and
leddest out into the wilderness four thousand men that were murderers?
39But Paul said, I am a man *which am* a Jew of Tarsus, *a city* in Cilicia, a citizen
of no mean city: and, I beseech thee, suffer me to speak unto the people.
40And when he had given him licence, Paul stood on the stairs, and beckoned with
the hand unto the people. And when there was made a great silence, he spake
unto *them* in the Hebrew tongue, saying,

Acts 22:1–30

1 Men, brethren, and fathers, hear ye my defense *which I make* now unto you.
2 (And when they heard that he spake in the Hebrew tongue to them, they kept the
more silence: and he saith,)
3 I am verily a man *which am* a Jew, born in Tarsus, *a city* in Cilicia, yet brought
up in this city at the feet of Gamaliel, *and* taught according to the perfect manner
of the law of the fathers, and was zealous toward God, as ye all are this day.
4 And I persecuted this way unto the death, binding and delivering into prisons
both men and women.
5 As also the high priest doth bear me witness, and all the estate of the elders: from
whom also I received letters unto the brethren, and went to Damascus, to bring
them which were there bound unto Jerusalem, for to be punished.
6 And it came to pass, that, as I made my journey, and was come nigh unto
Damascus about noon, suddenly there shone from heaven a great light round
about me.
7 And I fell unto the ground, and heard a voice saying unto me, Saul, Saul, why
persecutest thou me?
8 And I answered, Who art thou, Lord? And he said unto me, I am Jesus of
Nazareth, whom thou persecutest.
9 And they that were with me saw indeed the light, and were afraid; but they heard
not the voice of him that spake to me.
10 And I said, What shall I do, Lord? And the Lord said unto me, Arise, and go
into Damascus; and there it shall be told thee of all things which are appointed for
thee to do.
11 And when I could not see for the glory of that light, being led by the hand of
them that were with me, I came into Damascus.
12 And one Ananias, a devout man according to the law, having a good report of
all the Jews which dwelt *there*,
13 Came unto me, and stood, and said unto me, Brother Saul, receive thy sight.
And the same hour I looked up upon him.
14 And he said, The God of our fathers hath chosen thee, that thou shouldest know
his will, and see that Just One, and shouldest hear the voice of his mouth.
15 For thou shalt be his witness unto all men of what thou hast seen and heard.
16 And now why tarriest thou? arise, and be baptized, and wash away thy sins,
calling on the name of the Lord.
17 And it came to pass, that, when I was come again to Jerusalem, even while I DISC
PRAY prayed in the temple, I was in a trance;
18 And saw him saying unto me, Make haste, and get thee quickly out of WOW
Jerusalem: for they will not receive thy testimony concerning me. WOK
19 And I said, Lord, they know that I imprisoned and beat in every synagogue them

that believed on thee:
20 And when the blood of thy martyr Stephen was shed, I also was standing by,
and consenting unto his death, and kept the raiment of them that slew him.
21 And he said unto me, Depart: for I will send thee far hence unto the Gentiles. WOW
22 And they gave him audience unto this word, and *then* lifted up their voices, and
said, Away with such a *fellow* from the earth: for it is not fit that he should live.
23 And as they cried out, and cast off *their* clothes, and threw dust into the air,
24 The chief captain commanded him to be brought into the castle, and bade that he
should be examined by scourging; that he might know wherefore they cried so
against him.
25 And as they bound him with thongs, Paul said unto the centurion that stood by,
Is it lawful for you to scourge a man that is a Roman, and uncondemned?
26 When the centurion heard *that*, he went and told the chief captain, saying, Take
heed what thou doest: for this man is a Roman.
27 Then the chief captain came, and said unto him, Tell me, art thou a Roman? He
said, Yea.
28 And the chief captain answered, With a great sum obtained I this freedom. And
Paul said, But I was *free* born.
29 Then straightway they departed from him which should have examined him: and
the chief captain also was afraid, after he knew that he was a Roman, and because
he had bound him.
30 On the morrow, because he would have known the certainty wherefore he was
accused of the Jews, he loosed him from *his* bands, and commanded the chief
priests and all their council to appear, and brought Paul down, and set him before
them.

Acts 23:1–35

1 And Paul, earnestly beholding the council, said, Men *and* brethren, I have lived
in all good conscience before God until this day.
PERS 2 And the high priest Ananias commanded them that stood by him to smite him on
the mouth.
3 Then said Paul unto him, God shall smite thee, *thou* whited wall: for sittest thou
to judge me after the law, and commandest me to be smitten contrary to the law?
4 And they that stood by said, Revilest thou God's high priest?
5 Then said Paul, I wist not, brethren, that he was the high priest: for it is written,
Thou shalt not speak evil of the ruler of thy people.
6 But when Paul perceived that the one part were Sadducees, and the other
Pharisees, he cried out in the council, Men *and* brethren, I am a Pharisee, the son
RES of a Pharisee: of the hope and resurrection of the dead I am called in question.
7 And when he had so said, there arose a dissension between the Pharisees and the
Sadducees: and the multitude was divided.
8 For the Sadducees say that there is no resurrection, neither angel, nor spirit: but
the Pharisees confess both.
9 And there arose a great cry: and the scribes *that were* of the Pharisees' part arose,
and strove, saying, We find no evil in this man: but if a spirit or an angel hath
spoken to him, let us not fight against God.
PERS 10 And when there arose a great dissension, the chief captain, fearing lest Paul
should have been pulled in pieces of them, commanded the soldiers to go down,
and to take him by force from among them, and to bring *him* into the castle. DISC
11 And the night following the Lord stood by him, and said, Be of good cheer, PRO
Paul: for as thou hast testified of me in Jerusalem, so must thou bear witness also WOW
at Rome.
PERS 12 And when it was day, certain of the Jews banded together, and bound
themselves under a curse, saying that they would neither eat nor drink till they
had killed Paul.
13 And they were more than forty which had made this conspiracy.
14 And they came to the chief priests and elders, and said, We have bound
ourselves under a great curse, that we will eat nothing until we have slain Paul.
15 Now therefore ye with the council signify to the chief captain that he bring him
down unto you to morrow, as though ye would inquire something more perfectly
concerning him: and we, or ever he come near, are ready to kill him.
16 And when Paul's sister's son heard of their lying in wait, he went and entered
into the castle, and told Paul.
17 Then Paul called one of the centurions unto *him*, and said, Bring this young man
unto the chief captain: for he hath a certain thing to tell him.
18 So he took him, and brought *him* to the chief captain, and said, Paul the prisoner

called me unto *him*, and prayed me to bring this young man unto thee, who hath
something to say unto thee.
19Then the chief captain took him by the hand, and went *with him* aside privately,
and asked *him*, What is that thou hast to tell me?
20And he said, The Jews have agreed to desire thee that thou wouldest bring down
Paul to morrow into the council, as though they would inquire somewhat of him
more perfectly.
21But do not thou yield unto them: for there lie in wait for him of them more than
forty men, which have bound themselves with an oath, that they will neither eat
nor drink till they have killed him: and now are they ready, looking for a promise
from thee.
22So the chief captain *then* let the young man depart, and charged *him, See thou*
tell no man that thou hast showed these things to me.
23And he called unto *him* two centurions, saying, Make ready two hundred
soldiers to go to Caesarea, and horsemen threescore and ten, and spearmen two
hundred, at the third hour of the night;
24And provide *them* beasts, that they may set Paul on, and bring *him* safe unto
Felix the governor.
25And he wrote a letter after this manner:
26Claudius Lysias unto the most excellent governor Felix *sendeth* greeting.
27This man was taken of the Jews, and should have been killed of them: then came
I with an army, and rescued him, having understood that he was a Roman.
28And when I would have known the cause wherefore they accused him, I brought
him forth into their council:
29Whom I perceived to be accused of questions of their law, but to have nothing
laid to his charge worthy of death or of bonds.
30And when it was told me how that the Jews laid wait for the man, I sent
straightway to thee, and gave commandment to his accusers also to say before
thee what *they had* against him. Farewell.
31Then the soldiers, as it was commanded them, took Paul, and brought *him* by
night to Antipatris.
32On the morrow they left the horsemen to go with him, and returned to the
castle:
33Who, when they came to Caesarea, and delivered the epistle to the governor,
presented Paul also before him.
34And when the governor had read *the letter*, he asked of what province he was.
And when he understood that *he was* of Cilicia;
35I will hear thee, said he, when thine accusers are also come. And he commanded
him to be kept in Herod's judgment hall.

Acts 24:1–27

1And after five days Ananias the high priest descended with the elders, and *with* a certain orator *named* Tertullus, who informed the governor against Paul.
2And when he was called forth, Tertullus began to accuse *him*, saying, Seeing that by thee we enjoy great quietness, and that very worthy deeds are done unto this nation by thy providence,
3We accept *it* always, and in all places, most noble Felix, with all thankfulness.
4Notwithstanding, that I be not further tedious unto thee, I pray thee that thou wouldest hear us of thy clemency a few words.
5For we have found this man *a* pestilent *fellow*, and a mover of sedition among all the Jews throughout the world, and a ringleader of the sect of the Nazarenes:
6Who also hath gone about to profane the temple: whom we took, and would have judged according to our law.
7But the chief captain Lysias came *upon us*, and with great violence took *him* away out of our hands,
8Commanding his accusers to come unto thee: by examining of whom thyself mayest take knowledge of all these things, whereof we accuse him.
9And the Jews also assented, saying that these things were so.
10Then Paul, after that the governor had beckoned unto him to speak, answered, Forasmuch as I know that thou hast been of many years a judge unto this nation, I do the more cheerfully answer for myself:
11Because that thou mayest understand, that there are yet but twelve days since I went up to Jerusalem for to worship.
12And they neither found me in the temple disputing with any man, neither raising up the people, neither in the synagogues, nor in the city:
13Neither can they prove the things whereof they now accuse me.
14But this I confess unto thee, that after the way which they call heresy, so worship I the God of my fathers, believing all things which are written in the law and in the prophets:
15And have hope toward God, which they themselves also allow, that there shall be a resurrection of the dead, both of the just and unjust.
16And herein do I exercise myself, to have always a conscience void of offence toward God, and *toward* men.
17Now after many years I came to bring alms to my nation, and offerings.
18Whereupon certain Jews from Asia found me purified in the temple, neither with multitude, nor with tumult.
19Who ought to have been here before thee, and object, if they had ought against me.
20Or else let these same *here* say, if they have found any evil doing in me, while I stood before the council,

[21]Except it be for this one voice, that I cried standing among them, Touching the
RES resurrection of the dead I am called in question by you this day.
[22]And when Felix heard these things, having more perfect knowledge of *that* way,
he deferred them, and said, When Lysias the chief captain shall come down, I will
know the uttermost of your matter.
[23]And he commanded a centurion to keep Paul, and to let *him* have liberty, and
that he should forbid none of his acquaintance to minister or come unto him.
[24]And after certain days, when Felix came with his wife Drusilla, which was a
Jewess, he sent for Paul, and heard him concerning the faith in Christ.
[25]And as he reasoned of righteousness, temperance, and judgment to come, Felix
trembled, and answered, Go thy way for this time; when I have a convenient
season, I will call for thee.
[26]He hoped also that money should have been given him of Paul, that he might
loose him: wherefore he sent for him the oftener, and communed with him.
[27]But after two years Porcius Festus came into Felix' room: and Felix, willing to
show the Jews a pleasure, left Paul bound.

Acts 25:1–27

1Now when Festus was come into the province, after three days he ascended from
Caesarea to Jerusalem.
2Then the high priest and the chief of the Jews informed him against Paul, and
besought him,
3And desired favour against him, that he would send for him to Jerusalem, laying
wait in the way to kill him.
4But Festus answered, that Paul should be kept at Caesarea, and that he himself
would depart shortly *thither*.
5Let them therefore, said he, which among you are able, go down with *me*, and
accuse this man, if there be any wickedness in him.
6And when he had tarried among them more than ten days, he went down unto
Caesarea; and the next day sitting on the judgment seat commanded Paul to be
brought.
7And when he was come, the Jews which came down from Jerusalem stood round
about, and laid many and grievous complaints against Paul, which they could not
prove.
8While he answered for himself, Neither against the law of the Jews, neither
against the temple, nor yet against Caesar, have I offended any thing at all.
9But Festus, willing to do the Jews a pleasure, answered Paul, and said, Wilt thou
go up to Jerusalem, and there be judged of these things before me?
10Then said Paul, I stand at Caesar's judgment seat, where I ought to be judged: to
the Jews have I done no wrong, as thou very well knowest.
11For if I be an offender, or have committed any thing worthy of death, I refuse
not to die: but if there be none of these things whereof these accuse me, no man
may deliver me unto them. I appeal unto Caesar.
12Then Festus, when he had conferred with the council, answered, Hast thou
appealed unto Caesar? unto Caesar shalt thou go.
13And after certain days king Agrippa and Bernice came unto Caesarea to salute
Festus.
14And when they had been there many days, Festus declared Paul's cause unto the
king, saying, There is a certain man left in bonds by Felix:
15About whom, when I was at Jerusalem, the chief priests and the elders of the
Jews informed *me*, desiring *to have* judgment against him.
16To whom I answered, It is not the manner of the Romans to deliver any man to
die, before that he which is accused have the accusers face to face, and have
licence to answer for himself concerning the crime laid against him.
17Therefore, when they were come hither, without any delay on the morrow I sat
on the judgment seat, and commanded the man to be brought forth.
18Against whom when the accusers stood up, they brought none accusation of

such things as I supposed:
19But had certain questions against him of their own superstition, and of one
RES Jesus, which was dead, whom Paul affirmed to be alive.
20And because I doubted of such manner of questions, I asked *him* whether he would go to Jerusalem, and there be judged of these matters.
21But when Paul had appealed to be reserved unto the hearing of Augustus, I commanded him to be kept till I might send him to Caesar.
22Then Agrippa said unto Festus, I would also hear the man myself. To morrow, said he, thou shalt hear him.
23And on the morrow, when Agrippa was come, and Bernice, with great pomp, and was entered into the place of hearing, with the chief captains, and principal men of the city, at Festus' commandment Paul was brought forth.
24And Festus said, King Agrippa, and all men which are here present with us, ye see this man, about whom all the multitude of the Jews have dealt with me, both at Jerusalem, and *also* here, crying that he ought not to live any longer.
25But when I found that he had committed nothing worthy of death, and that he himself hath appealed to Augustus, I have determined to send him.
26Of whom I have no certain thing to write unto my lord. Wherefore I have brought him forth before you, and specially before thee, O king Agrippa, that, after examination had, I might have somewhat to write.
27For it seemeth to me unreasonable to send a prisoner, and not withal to signify the crimes *laid* against him.

Acts 26:1–32

1 Then Agrippa said unto Paul, Thou art permitted to speak for thyself. Then Paul
stretched forth the hand, and answered for himself:
2 I think myself happy, king Agrippa, because I shall answer for myself this day
before thee touching all the things whereof I am accused of the Jews:
3 Especially *because I know* thee to be expert in all customs and questions which
are among the Jews: wherefore I beseech thee to hear me patiently.
4 My manner of life from my youth, which was at the first among mine own nation
at Jerusalem, know all the Jews;
5 Which knew me from the beginning, if they would testify, that after the most
straitest sect of our religion I lived a Pharisee.
6 And now I stand and am judged for the hope of the promise made of God unto
our fathers:
7 Unto which *promise* our twelve tribes, instantly serving *God* day and night, hope
to come. For which hope's sake, king Agrippa, I am accused of the Jews.
RES 8 Why should it be thought a thing incredible with you, that God should raise the
dead?
9 I verily thought with myself, that I ought to do many things contrary to the name
of Jesus of Nazareth.
10 Which thing I also did in Jerusalem: and many of the saints did I shut up in
prison, having received authority from the chief priests; and when they were put
to death, I gave my voice against *them*.
11 And I punished them oft in every synagogue, and compelled *them* to blaspheme;
and being exceedingly mad against them, I persecuted *them* even unto strange
cities.
12 Whereupon as I went to Damascus with authority and commission from the
chief priests,
13 At midday, O king, I saw in the way a light from heaven, above the brightness
of the sun, shining round about me and them which journeyed with me.
14 And when we were all fallen to the earth, I heard a voice speaking unto me, and
saying in the Hebrew tongue, Saul, Saul, why persecutest thou me? *it is* hard for
thee to kick against the pricks.
15 And I said, Who art thou, Lord? And he said, I am Jesus whom thou
persecutest.
16 But rise, and stand upon thy feet: for I have appeared unto thee for this purpose, WOW
to make thee a minister and a witness both of these things which thou hast seen,
and of those things in the which I will appear unto thee;
17 Delivering thee from the people, and *from* the Gentiles, unto whom now I send
thee,
18 To open their eyes, *and* to turn *them* from darkness to light, and *from* the power

of Satan unto God, that they may receive forgiveness of sins, and inheritance
among them which are sanctified by faith that is in me.
19Whereupon, O king Agrippa, I was not disobedient unto the heavenly vision:
20But showed first unto them of Damascus, and at Jerusalem, and throughout all
the coasts of Judaea, and *then* to the Gentiles, that they should repent and turn to
God, and do works meet for repentance.
21For these causes the Jews caught me in the temple, and went about to kill *me*.
22Having therefore obtained help of God, I continue unto this day, witnessing both
to small and great, saying none other things than those which the prophets and
Moses did say should come:
RES 23That Christ should suffer, *and* that he should be the first that should rise from
the dead, and should show light unto the people, and to the Gentiles.
24And as he thus spake for himself, Festus said with a loud voice, Paul, thou art
beside thyself; much learning doth make thee mad.
25But he said, I am not mad, most noble Festus; but speak forth the words of truth
and soberness.
26For the king knoweth of these things, before whom also I speak freely: for I am
persuaded that none of these things are hidden from him; for this thing was not
done in a corner.
27King Agrippa, believest thou the prophets? I know that thou believest.
28Then Agrippa said unto Paul, Almost thou persuadest me to be a Christian.
29And Paul said, I would to God, that not only thou, but also all that hear me this
day, were both almost, and altogether such as I am, except these bonds.
30And when he had thus spoken, the king rose up, and the governor, and Bernice,
and they that sat with them:
31And when they were gone aside, they talked between themselves, saying, This
man doeth nothing worthy of death or of bonds.
32Then said Agrippa unto Festus, This man might have been set at liberty, if he
had not appealed unto Caesar.

Acts 27:1–44

1 And when it was determined that we should sail into Italy, they delivered Paul
and certain other prisoners unto *one* named Julius, a centurion of Augustus' band.
2 And entering into a ship of Adramyttium, we launched, meaning to sail by the
coasts of Asia; *one* Aristarchus, a Macedonian of Thessalonica, being with us.
3 And the next *day* we touched at Sidon. And Julius courteously entreated Paul,
and gave *him* liberty to go unto his friends to refresh himself.
4 And when we had launched from thence, we sailed under Cyprus, because the
winds were contrary.
5 And when we had sailed over the sea of Cilicia and Pamphylia, we came to
Myra, *a city* of Lycia.
6 And there the centurion found a ship of Alexandria sailing into Italy; and he put
us therein.
7 And when we had sailed slowly many days, and scarce were come over against
Cnidus, the wind not suffering us, we sailed under Crete, over against Salmone;
8 And, hardly passing it, came unto a place which is called The fair havens; nigh
whereunto was the city *of* Lasea.
9 Now when much time was spent, and when sailing was now dangerous, because
the fast was now already past, Paul admonished *them*,
10 And said unto them, Sirs, I perceive that this voyage will be with hurt and much WOW
damage, not only of the lading and ship, but also of our lives.
11 Nevertheless the centurion believed the master and the owner of the ship, more
than those things which were spoken by Paul.
12 And because the haven was not commodious to winter in, the more part advised
to depart thence also, if by any means they might attain to Phenice, *and there* to
winter; *which is* an haven of Crete, and lieth toward the south west and north
west.
13 And when the south wind blew softly, supposing that they had obtained *their*
purpose, loosing *thence*, they sailed close by Crete.
14 But not long after there arose against it a tempestuous wind, called Euroclydon.
15 And when the ship was caught, and could not bear up into the wind, we let *her*
drive.
16 And running under a certain island which is called Clauda, we had much work
to come by the boat:
17 Which when they had taken up, they used helps, undergirding the ship; and,
fearing lest they should fall into the quicksands, struck sail, and so were driven.
18 And we being exceedingly tossed with a tempest, the next *day* they lightened the
ship;
19 And the third *day* we cast out with our own hands the tackling of the ship.
20 And when neither sun nor stars in many days appeared, and no small tempest

lay on *us*, all hope that we should be saved was then taken away.
21 But after long abstinence Paul stood forth in the midst of them, and said, Sirs, ye
should have hearkened unto me, and not have loosed from Crete, and to have
gained this harm and loss.
22 And now I exhort you to be of good cheer: for there shall be no loss of *any* WOW
man's life among you, but of the ship.
ANG 23 For there stood by me this night the angel of God, whose I am, and whom I DISC
serve,
24 Saying, Fear not, Paul; thou must be brought before Caesar: and, lo, God hath PRO
given thee all them that sail with thee.
25 Wherefore, sirs, be of good cheer: for I believe God, that it shall be even as it GOF
was told me.
26 Howbeit we must be cast upon a certain island.
27 But when the fourteenth night was come, as we were driven up and down in
Adria, about midnight the shipmen deemed that they drew near to some country;
28 And sounded, and found *it* twenty fathoms: and when they had gone a little
further, they sounded again, and found *it* fifteen fathoms.
29 Then fearing lest we should have fallen upon rocks, they cast four anchors out
of the stern, and wished for the day.
30 And as the shipmen were about to flee out of the ship, when they had let down
the boat into the sea, under colour as though they would have cast anchors out of
the foreship,
31 Paul said to the centurion and to the soldiers, Except these abide in the ship, ye WOK
cannot be saved. WOW
32 Then the soldiers cut off the ropes of the boat, and let her fall off.
33 And while the day was coming on, Paul besought *them* all to take meat, saying,
This day is the fourteenth day that ye have tarried and continued fasting, having
taken nothing.
34 Wherefore I pray you to take *some* meat: for this is for your health: for there PRO
shall not a hair fall from the head of any of you.
PRAY 35 And when he had thus spoken, he took bread, and gave thanks to God in
presence of them all: and when he had broken *it*, he began to eat.
36 Then were they all of good cheer, and they also took *some* meat.
37 And we were in all in the ship two hundred threescore and sixteen souls.
38 And when they had eaten enough, they lightened the ship, and cast out the wheat
into the sea.
39 And when it was day, they knew not the land: but they discovered a certain
creek with a shore, into the which they were minded, if it were possible, to thrust
in the ship.
40 And when they had taken up the anchors, they committed *themselves* unto the

sea, and loosed the rudder bands, and hoisted up the mainsail to the wind, and
made toward shore.
41 And falling into a place where two seas met, they ran the ship aground; and the
forepart stuck fast, and remained unmoveable, but the hinder part was broken with
the violence of the waves.
42 And the soldiers' counsel was to kill the prisoners, lest any of them should swim
out, and escape.
43 But the centurion, willing to save Paul, kept them from *their* purpose; and
commanded that they which could swim should cast *themselves* first *into the sea,*
and get to land:
44 And the rest, some on boards, and some on *broken pieces* of the ship. And so it
came to pass, that they escaped all safe to land.

Acts 28:1–31

1 And when they were escaped, then they knew that the island was called Melita.
2 And the barbarous people showed us no little kindness: for they kindled a fire,
and received us every one, because of the present rain, and because of the cold.
3 And when Paul had gathered a bundle of sticks, and laid *them* on the fire, there
came a viper out of the heat, and fastened on his hand.
4 And when the barbarians saw the *venomous* beast hang on his hand, they said
among themselves, No doubt this man is a murderer, whom, though he hath
escaped the sea, yet vengeance suffereth not to live.
5 And he shook off the beast into the fire, and felt no harm. GOF
6 Howbeit they looked when he should have swollen, or fallen down dead
suddenly: but after they had looked a great while, and saw no harm come to him,
they changed their minds, and said that he was a god.
7 In the same quarters were possessions of the chief man of the island, whose name
was Publius; who received us, and lodged us three days courteously.
8 And it came to pass, that the father of Publius lay sick of a fever and of a bloody
PRAY flux: to whom Paul entered in, and prayed, and laid his hands on him, and healed GOH
him.
9 So when this was done, others also, which had diseases in the island, came, and
were healed: GOH
10 Who also honoured us with many honours; and when we departed, they laded *us*
with such things as were necessary.
11 And after three months we departed in a ship of Alexandria, which had wintered
in the isle, whose sign was Castor and Pollux.
12 And landing at Syracuse, we tarried *there* three days.
13 And from thence we fetched a compass, and came to Rhegium: and after one
day the south wind blew, and we came the next day to Puteoli:
14 Where we found brethren, and were desired to tarry with them seven days: and
so we went toward Rome.
15 And from thence, when the brethren heard of us, they came to meet us as far as
PRAY Appiiforum, and The three taverns: whom when Paul saw, he thanked God, and
took courage.
16 And when we came to Rome, the centurion delivered the prisoners to the captain
of the guard: but Paul was suffered to dwell by himself with a soldier that kept
him.
17 And it came to pass, that after three days Paul called the chief of the Jews
together: and when they were come together, he said unto them, Men *and*
brethren, though I have committed nothing against the people, or customs of our
fathers, yet was I delivered prisoner from Jerusalem into the hands of the
Romans.
18 Who, when they had examined me, would have let *me* go, because there was no
cause of death in me.
19 But when the Jews spake against *it*, I was constrained to appeal unto Caesar; not
that I had ought to accuse my nation of.
20 For this cause therefore have I called for you, to see *you*, and to speak with *you*:
because that for the hope of Israel I am bound with this chain.

21 And they said unto him, We neither received letters out of Judaea concerning
thee, neither any of the brethren that came showed or spake any harm of thee.
22 But we desire to hear of thee what thou thinkest: for as concerning this sect, we
PERS know that every where it is spoken against.
23 And when they had appointed him a day, there came many to him into *his*
lodging; to whom he expounded and testified the kingdom of God, persuading
them concerning Jesus, both out of the law of Moses, and *out of* the prophets,
from morning till evening.
HARV 24 And some believed the things which were spoken, and some believed not.
25 And when they agreed not among themselves, they departed, after that Paul had
spoken one word, Well spake the Holy Ghost by Esaias the prophet unto our
fathers,
26 Saying, Go unto this people, and say, Hearing ye shall hear, and shall not
understand; and seeing ye shall see, and not perceive:
OTW 27 For the heart of this people is waxed gross, and their ears are dull of hearing,
and their eyes have they closed; lest they should see with *their* eyes, and hear
with *their* ears, and understand with *their* heart, and should be converted, and I
should heal them (Isaiah 6:9).
28 Be it known therefore unto you, that the salvation of God is sent unto the
HARV Gentiles, and *that* they will hear it. WOW
29 And when he had said these words, the Jews departed, and had great reasoning
among themselves.
30 And Paul dwelt two whole years in his own hired house, and received all that
came in unto him,
31 Preaching the kingdom of God, and teaching those things which concern the
Lord Jesus Christ, with all confidence, no man forbidding him.

Acts 29:1—
Your Chapter–how you live your life for the Lord is in this chapter. Make it a chapter worth reading!

School of Acts

The Gifts and Operations of God

PART II

A DEFINITIVE STUDY

DOCUMENTED RESURRECTION

THE MESSAGE AND THE MANIFESTATION

"WITH GREAT POWER GAVE THE APOSTLES WITNESS OF THE RESURRECTION OF THE LORD JESUS: AND GREAT GRACE WAS UPON THEM ALL."

ACTS 4:33

DOCUMENTED RESURRECTION

THE MESSAGE AND THE MANIFESTATION IN THE BOOK OF ACTS

"By faith Abraham, when he was tried, offered up Isaac: and he that had received the promises offered up his only begotten son, Of whom it was said, That in Isaac shall thy seed be called: Accounting that God was able to raise him up, even from the dead; from whence also he received him in a figure."
Hebrews 11:17–19

PREFACE

When Abraham raised his knife to sacrifice his only son, the son of his love, God spoke and stopped him. Abraham's faith had been approved. God, with His man Abraham, had set an eternal mark of resurrection faith upon the Jewish nation. The story of Abraham and Isaac is more than a story of sacrifice; it reaches into the eternal realities of a man in covenant with God and the power of faith. This mark of resurrection faith is what opened the door for God to send His own Son, the Son of His love, to die and be raised to life so that all men might live. It is the power of Christ's resurrection that has carried the church through the centuries, sometimes facing impossible odds. It is this act of His defeating death that inspired Paul to know the Lord and the power of His resurrection (Philippians 3:10).

I have included every reference to resurrection mentioned, preached, or demonstrated in the book of Acts so that through consolidation of references it would be clear and undeniable that the message of resurrection was at the core of the life, message, and hope of the first-century Christian church.

As we take time to meditate upon these truths, we will see the importance of this doctrine as well as the power that is released through preaching it. As you study the following passages you will realize that a strong church has at the root of its message the revelation of resurrection. It is not enough to mentally agree with resurrection; the local church must adhere to it and declare it boldly in order to excel in its ministry of salt and light to her neighbors.

RESURRECTION
QUICK REFERENCE

Reference	Description of Resurrection
(Jerusalem, Judea, Samaria)	
1. Acts 1:3	Jesus showed Himself alive
2. Acts 1:21–22	Witnesses of His resurrection
3. Acts 2:24	Peter preaching resurrection
4. Acts 2:31–32	Peter preaching from the Psalms
5. Acts 3:15	Peter declares resurrection
6. Acts 3:26	Peter preaches resurrection
7. Acts 4:2	Jewish religious leaders grieved
8. Acts 4:10	Jesus' name empowered by resurrection
9. Acts 4:33	With great power they declared resurrection
10. Acts 5:30–32	Peter preaches resurrection and repentance
11. Acts 9:40	Tabitha (Dorcas) raised from the dead
12. Acts 10:40	Peter's last recorded message of resurrection
(To the Uttermost Parts of the Earth)	
13. Acts 13:30	Paul preaches resurrection
14. Acts 13:33	Paul preaches from the Psalms
15. Acts 13:34	Paul continues to preach from the Psalms
16. Acts 13:35–37	Paul continues to preach from the Psalms
17. Acts 17:3	Resurrection preaching births a church
18. Acts 17:18	Athens hears the message of resurrection
19. Acts 17:31	Christ's resurrection gives assurance to all men
20. Acts 17:32	Athens responds to the message of resurrection
21. Acts 20:9,10	Resurrection power demonstrated
22. Acts 23:6	Paul divides his accusers
23. Acts 24:21	The message of resurrection was the root of Paul's persecution by the religious Jews
24. Acts 25:19	Festus declares to Agrippa that it is Paul's message of resurrection that brought his troubles upon him
25. Acts 26:8	Paul preaching to Agrippa
26. Acts 26:23	Paul preaching to Agrippa and Festus

RESURRECTION
A DEFINITIVE LOOK

(Jerusalem, Judea, and Samaria)

1. **JESUS SHOWED HIMSELF ALIVE**
Acts 1:3
"To whom also he showed himself alive after his passion by many infallible proofs, being seen of them forty days, and speaking of the things pertaining to the kingdom of God."

Note: Being with Jesus after His resurrection must have been sheer joy. Hebrews 12:2 declares that it was for the joy set before Him that Jesus endured the cross. There, standing in resurrection life, the joy flowing from Jesus must have been pure ecstasy. Before His death on the cross, Jesus prayed and asked the Father to glorify Him with the glory He had before the world began (John 17:5). Now, a man, the Word made flesh, is seated and exalted at the right hand of the Father in glory. These disciples were standing in the presence of life Himself, and they were filled with joy—a joy no man could ever take (John 16:22). Also, though the disciples were extremely overjoyed to see Jesus, Jesus was extremely overjoyed to be with them.

The following passages give each appearance of the Lord. Remember, God the Father was not hiding Jesus but rather showing Him openly (Acts 10:40).

1. Mary Magdalene	Mark 16:9
2. Mary and other women	Matthew 28:9
3. Peter	Luke 24:34
4. Two disciples on the road	Mark 16:12–13, Luke 24:13–31
5. To apostles minus Thomas	John 20:19–20
6. To all disciples with Thomas	John 20:26
7. To the 11 disciples in Galilee	Matthew 28:16–17
8. Disciples and others	Luke 24:36
9. To seven disciples fishing	John 21:1–2
10. James	1 Corinthians 15:7
11. 500 disciples	1 Corinthians 15:6
12. Paul (Later)	1 Corinthians 15:8

2. **WITNESSES OF HIS RESURRECTION**
Acts 1:21–22
"Wherefore of these men which have companied with us–all the time that the Lord Jesus went in and out among us, beginning from the baptism of John, unto that same day that he was taken up from us, must one be ordained to be a witness with us of his resurrection."

Note: This passage shows the importance the apostles placed on being a witness of Jesus' resurrection. This verse also reveals that there were many others that followed Jesus during the three years of His ministry on earth. We usually focus our theological attention on the lives of the twelve apostles, but many other people loved Jesus and followed Him closely. Remember, Lazarus was a close friend of Jesus but was never called an apostle. Close friendship with Jesus does not come from a position of ministry but rather flows from a heart that spends time with Him.

3. PETER PREACHED RESURRECTION

Acts 2:24

"Whom God hath raised up, having loosed the pains of death: because it was not possible that he should be held of it."

Note: Jesus is not only alive—He is life! Death had no possibility of holding Jesus. John 1:4 declares that *"in Him was life."* Jesus also declared in John 14:6, *"I am the way, the truth, and the life."* We often think that life is the opposite of death but in this case, His life has no opposite. He is life, and death could not hold Him. This is what the Father knew pertaining to Jesus becoming a man and dying for our sins. This wisdom was found in the life of God that could not stay dead. Jesus' life not only conquered death, but it also conquered sin, Satan, hell, and the grave. This truth is clearly seen in 1 Corinthians 15:54, *"Death is swallowed up in victory!"*

4. PETER PREACHES FROM THE PSALMS

Acts 2:31–32

"He seeing this before spake of the resurrection of Christ, that his soul was not left in hell, neither his flesh did see corruption. This Jesus hath God raised up, whereof we all are witnesses."

Note: It must have been an amazing experience for Peter to know that what God revealed to King David a thousand years before concerning Israel's Messiah had come to pass in his life. He not only witnessed the fulfillment of what the prophets of the Old Testament had spoken but he touched it as well.

"That which was from the beginning, which we have heard, which we have seen with our eyes, which we have looked upon, and our hands have handled, of the Word of life."
1 John 1:1

Peter preaching from the Psalms is empowered by the Holy Spirit through Christ's resurrection. When reading the book of Acts, it seems that the apostles gave greater importance to being witnesses of Christ's resurrection than to be the organizers of church growth.

5. **PETER DECLARES RESURRECTION**
   Acts 3:15
   "And killed the Prince of life, whom God hath raised from the dead; whereof we are witnesses."

   Note: Peter declared two truths; we are witnesses that you killed Him, and we are witnesses that He is alive. These religious leaders had not only demanded Jesus' death but were present at His crucifixion and watched Him die. These same leaders, agitated that this miracle worker might be raised back to life, sealed His tomb, and set a guard over it. Now, these religious leaders were forced to behold an undeniable miracle of the Jesus kind, facing the reality that Jesus was alive, just as He said.

6. **PETER PREACHES RESURRECTION**
   Acts 3:26
   "Unto you first, God, having raised up his Son Jesus, sent Him to bless you, in turning away every one of you from his iniquities."

   Note: Peter, through a word of wisdom (revelation gift), was speaking forth the plan of God, though at that time he did not have complete understanding of it. It is important to note that Peter declared that it was God who raised Jesus, bringing great conviction upon all who listened. Also, we should note that it wasn't until the conversion of Cornelius in Acts chapter 10 that Peter completely understood the doctrine of *"unto you first."* The resurrection of Jesus was for the Jews first and then to be preached to the Gentiles. Paul, in his epistles, brings further revelation of this New Testament doctrine (Romans 1:16, Romans 2:9–10). The message of resurrection is the hope of all men.

7. **JEWISH RELIGIOUS LEADERS GRIEVED**
   Acts 4:2
   "Being grieved that they taught the people and preached through Jesus the resurrection from the dead."

   Note: There were many reasons why Jerusalem's religious leaders were grieved at the message of resurrection. First, the devil, who had worked through the religious hierarchy was still feeling the bruising he had received at the resurrection. Second, those same leaders who killed Jesus were now witnessing the power that is released through the preaching of His name backed by the message of His resurrection. They feared it greatly and sought to stop it. Third, they were under condemnation for what they had done to the Messiah, just as Joseph's brothers bore the guilt of selling their brother to Egypt as a type of killing him.

8. JESUS' NAME EMPOWERED BY RESURRECTION

Acts 4:10

"Be it known unto you all, and to all the people of Israel, that by the name of Jesus Christ of Nazareth, whom ye crucified, whom God raised from the dead, even by him doth this man stand here before you whole."

Note: The authority of Jesus' name is backed by the power of His resurrection. His name being used with faith in His name by His disciples was the same as Jesus being present and doing the miracle Himself.

"And whatsoever ye shall ask in my name, that will I do, that the Father may be glorified in the Son."
John 14:13

9. WITH GREAT POWER THEY DECLARED RESURRECTION

Acts 4:33

"And with great power gave the apostles witness of the resurrection of the Lord Jesus: and great grace was upon them all."

Note: The baptism of the Holy Spirit, which Christ commanded His followers to receive, was to empower their witness of the resurrection (Acts 1:4,5,8). In this passage we see that both *"great power"* flowed out of the believers and *"great grace"* was upon them all. It seems that God's plan for the church was to be defined by the word, *"great."*

10. PETER PREACHES RESURRECTION AND REPENTANCE

Acts 5:30–32

"The God of our fathers raised up Jesus, whom ye slew and hanged on a tree. Him hath God exalted with his right hand to be a Prince and a Saviour, for to give repentance to Israel, and forgiveness of sins. And we are his witnesses of these things; and so is also the Holy Ghost, whom God hath given to them that obey Him."

Note: The message of resurrection was at the core of New Testament preaching. It is the resurrection of Jesus and His exaltation to the right hand of the Father that gives repentance and forgiveness, not only to the Jews but to all men. Once again, Peter declares that *"we"* are witnesses of His resurrection and so is the Holy Ghost. With this sermon he brings to revelatory light that every believer, throughout all ages, would have this testimony in them through the Holy Spirit.

11. TABITHA (DORCAS) RAISED FROM THE DEAD

Acts 9:40

"But Peter put them all forth, and kneeled down, and prayed; and turning him to the body said, Tabitha, arise. And she opened her eyes: and when she saw Peter, she sat up."

Note: The declaration of the resurrection of Jesus was the core message of the church. All that was done was based upon one central truth; Jesus is alive, He has risen. The Jewish nation had been marked with resurrection faith by Abraham, and this mark of resurrection was firmly embedded into this early church. This birthmark of resurrection faith was efficacious, and they declared it everywhere they went. Coupled with the preaching of resurrection were also testimonies of people being raised from the dead.

These Jews knew their history. They knew about Elijah and Elisha, who both raised people from the dead (1 Kings 17:22, 2 Kings 4:35). They knew about the bones of Elisha that raised a dead man back to life (2 Kings 13:21). They also knew about Jesus, how He raised many from the dead—no matter how long they had been dead. They also knew that after His resurrection, graves had opened and saints of old had been seen walking around the city. The early church believed in God's ability to raise the dead.

Adding to this story is that the believers in Joppa had heard how the towns of Lydda and Sharon turned to the Lord through the healing of Aeneas. They also knew that Peter was staying in Lydda, so they sent messengers to bring him quickly to Joppa.

It is important to note that when Dorcas died, the faith of the local believers in Joppa had not accepted her death. They were believing for her to be raised back to life. She had been such a blessing and an encouragement; they did not want to be void of her presence. They washed her and put her in an upper room, just like the widow did with her dead son in Elisha's day (2 Kings 4:21).

When Peter arrived, I am sure he began to remember following Jesus to Jairus' house. What did Peter do? He did exactly what Jesus did in Mark 5:39–41. He put everybody out of the room and prayed to God. After he finished praying, with such confidence coming from his communion with the Lord, Peter turned to the dead body and simply said, *"Dorcas, get up!"* It must have been amazing to watch her eyes open, beaming with life. The Bible says that many turned to the Lord in Joppa because of this miracle. I imagine that many also believed because of the stories she told about heaven—though she had only been there for a short time.

12. PETER'S LAST RECORDED MESSAGE OF RESURRECTION

Acts 10:40

"Him (JESUS) God raised up the third day and showed him openly."

Note: Peter spoke plainly about Jesus being raised from the dead and concerning God showing Him openly. God never hid the resurrection. He not only showed Jesus alive, but He also poured out His Spirit upon the church to empower their witness of His resurrection. Though this is the last recorded reference to Peter declaring the resurrection of Jesus, we know that he carried the power of that message throughout the nations, and like a seed that falls into the ground and dies, he planted it into Rome (Europe).

(To the Uttermost Parts of the Earth)

13. PAUL PREACHES RESURRECTION

Acts 13:30

"But God raised him from the dead."

Note: In this passage we have the first sermon of Paul declaring resurrection. Up until now, the book of Acts has focused on Peter and the church in Jerusalem. Now, the message of resurrection, in the hands of Paul, is being declared to the Gentiles—on a westward push towards Rome.

14. PAUL PREACHES FROM THE PSALMS

Acts 13:33

"God hath fulfilled the same unto us their children, in that he hath raised up Jesus again; as it is also written in the second psalm, Thou art my Son, this day have I begotten thee."

Note: Remember, the early church did not have New Testament Bibles. They used the Old Testament to give light concerning the resurrection of Christ. They preached the New Testament realities from Old Testament scripture, thus underscoring that the Old Testament is not old. In fact, the Old Testament is still the Word of God, full of power and still speaking.

15. PAUL CONTINUES TO PREACH FROM THE PSALMS

Acts 13:34

"And as concerning that he raised him up from the dead, now no more to return to corruption, he said on this wise, I will give you the sure mercies of David."

Note: Once again, Paul is using the Psalms as His sermon text. I am sure that King David never knew that what he had declared in his writings, a thousand years before, would be used to turn the world upside down.

16. PAUL CONTINUES TO PREACH FROM THE PSALMS

Acts 13:35–37

"Wherefore he saith also in another psalm, Thou shalt not suffer thine Holy One to see corruption. For David, after he had served his own generation by the will of God, fell asleep, and was laid unto his fathers, and saw corruption: But he, whom God raised again, saw no corruption."

Note: Paul, using Old Testament scriptures, proves that the prophetic words *(which are a manifestation of the word of wisdom)* in the Psalms were not about David but were concerning Christ. When Jesus asked His disciples who men said He was, they answered Him with the names of prophets that had died—men whose bodies saw corruption. This passage in the Psalms and in Acts reveals that God's plan had no corruption in it. Therefore, only Christ's death and resurrection could have fulfilled this word.

17. RESURRECTION PREACHING BIRTHED A CHURCH

Acts 17:3

"Opening and alleging, that Christ must needs have suffered, and risen again from the dead; and that this Jesus, whom I preach unto you, is Christ."

Note: Paul preached Jesus' suffering and His resurrection. His preaching resulted in a church being planted in Thessalonica. Remember, Abraham's faith not only marked the Jewish nation with resurrection, but that eternal mark of faith ensures the blessing of God for all nations. Paul's preaching demonstrated the power of the Abrahamic blessing and its ability to touch all nations, tribes, and tongues. That which God scattered at Babel was now being gathered through the message of resurrection.

18. ATHENS HEARS THE MESSAGE OF RESURRECTION

Acts 17:18

"Then certain philosophers of the Epicureans, and of the Stoics, encountered him. And some said, What will this babbler say? other some, He seemeth to be a setter forth of strange gods: because he preached unto them Jesus, and the resurrection."

Note: When Paul encountered the Athenian intelligentsia, he wasted no time in confronting their wisdom. How did he do that? He began to declare Christ resurrected. This message of resurrection so grabbed their attention that they wanted to hear more, so they brought him into their most holy place, the Areopagus. In many ways, Paul's preaching in that place was part of the fulfillment of Nebuchadnezzar's dream which saw a stone roll into the image of the four world empires–completely demolishing them. The kingdoms of this world have no power to resist what Jesus did through the cross and resurrection, no more than the idol Dagan had when the Philistines housed the Ark of God inside its temple (1 Samuel 5:4). The Bible declares that when the Philistines opened the doors to the temple the following morning, they found Dagan prostrate before the Ark of God, with its hands and head cut off. In like manner, God directed Paul's steps into the Areopagus, a type of the center of global humanism—where man's wisdom is exalted above the knowledge of God. Paul, clothed in the power of the Holy Spirit, declared a resurrected

Christ—the Savior of the world. Paul's preaching gave testimony both against the wisdom of this world, which is coming to nothing, and against those who trust in that which God has called foolish.

"For the preaching of the cross is to them that perish–foolishness; but unto us which are saved it is the power of God. For it is written, I will destroy the wisdom of the wise, and will bring to nothing the understanding of the prudent. Where is the wise? where is the scribe? where is the disputer of this world? hath not God made foolish the wisdom of this world? For after that in the wisdom of God the world by wisdom knew not God, it pleased God by the foolishness of preaching to save them that believe. For the Jews require a sign, and the Greeks seek after wisdom."

1 Corinthians 1:18–22

19. CHRIST'S RESURRECTION GIVES ASSURANCE TO ALL MEN

Acts 17:31

"Because he hath appointed a day, in the which he will judge the world in righteousness by that man whom he hath ordained; whereof he hath given assurance unto all men, in that he hath raised him from the dead."

Note: Paul was a witness to the great and the small. In this passage, we see the Lord in His compassion reaching out to the elite of Greek culture. Paul later writes under the inspiration of the Holy Spirit that the carnal mind cannot receive the things of the Spirit of God. This is clearly understood through the sermon he gave in Athens (1 Corinthians 2:14).

20. ATHENS RESPONDS TO THE MESSAGE OF RESURRECTION

Acts 17:32

"And when they heard of the resurrection of the dead, some mocked: and others said, "We will hear thee again of this matter."

Note: Paul preached and those who were listening had to decide how to respond. This message has no middle ground. Jesus declared that when the Holy Spirit comes, He will convict the world of sin. As Paul preached, the Holy Spirit was convicting. Some of those listening went further into darkness while others came into light.

21. RESURRECTION POWER DEMONSTRATED

Acts 20:9–10

"And there sat in a window a certain young man named Eutychus, being fallen into a deep sleep: and as Paul was long preaching, he sunk down with sleep, and fell down from the third loft, and was taken up dead. And Paul went down, and fell on him, and embracing him said, Trouble not yourselves; for his life is in him."

Note: The day had been long and hot, and there in the cool of the evening, the church had gathered to hear Paul. As usual, Paul was full of the Holy Spirit and had much to share with them. They loved to hear the stories of Jesus working with Paul and His apostolic team. Unfortunately, a young man, upon dozing off, fell out of the window. As women screamed, Paul went outside and fell upon him just as Elisha did to the rich woman's son.

The Bible says that Paul fell on him, grabbing him forcefully. That energetic embrace is where the power of God shot through the lad and brought him back to the earth side of eternity. Once again, resurrection was at the core of the Christian message, and that night it was reinforced before the eyes of the congregation. I would imagine that this story spread like wildfire throughout that region.

22. PAUL DIVIDES HIS ACCUSERS

Acts 23:6

"But when Paul perceived that the one part were Sadducees, and the other Pharisees, he cried out in the council, Men and brethren, I am a Pharisee, the son of a Pharisee: of the hope and resurrection of the dead I am called in question."

Note: Paul, on trial, decides to use his knowledge as a former Pharisee to cause division within the ranks of those accusing him. Paul knew all too well the theological arguments Pharisees and Sadducees had with each other, and the theology of resurrection was right at the top.

23. THE MESSAGE OF RESURRECTION WAS THE ROOT OF PAUL'S PERSECUTION BY THE RELIGIOUS JEWS

Acts 24:21

"Except it be for this one voice, that I cried standing among them, Touching the resurrection of the dead I am called in question by you this day."

Note: It was Paul's message of resurrection that caused problems everywhere he went. This message carries the power of God that overthrows the idols in the hearts of men and ultimately lays waste the kingdoms of this world. The devil still feels the bruising he received when Jesus was raised from the dead; and this message of resurrection continues to remind him of the crushing defeat he received on that first Easter morning.

24. FESTUS DECLARES TO AGRIPPA THAT IT IS PAUL'S MESSAGE OF RESURRECTION THAT BROUGHT HIS TROUBLES UPON HIM

Acts 25:19

"But had certain questions against him of their own superstition, and of one Jesus, which was dead, whom Paul affirmed to be alive."

Note: Festus knew the details of Jesus' crucifixion under Pontus Pilot. The message of Jesus' death was not the issue concerning Paul's confinement but Jesus' resurrection. This intrigued King Agrippa to desire to hear Paul personally.

25. PAUL PREACHING TO AGRIPPA

Acts 26:8

"Why should it be thought a thing incredible with you, that God should raise the dead?"

Note: Paul knew that Agrippa had been educated in the Jewish religion. Therefore, Paul begins to build the case of resurrection before the king using the Jewish law and the prophets, for which Agrippa had respect. Paul was a master builder.

26. PAUL PREACHING TO AGRIPPA AND FESTUS

Acts 26:23

"That Christ should suffer, and that he should be the first that should rise from the dead, and should show light unto the people, and to the Gentiles."

Note: This is the last declaration of resurrection in the book of Acts. Paul, as a prisoner of Rome, declares to Governor Festus and King Agrippa that Christ's resurrection gives light unto all men, even to the Gentiles. Once again, we see Paul, who is a witness to both small and great, standing in the strength of God preaching resurrection. As he preached his sermon, the message of resurrection divided the crowd. Festus rejects but Agrippa is moved.

DOCUMENTED PRAYER

"PRAY YE THEREFORE THE LORD OF THE HARVEST, THAT HE WILL SEND FORTH LABORERS INTO HIS HARVEST."

MATTHEW 9:38

DOCUMENTED PRAYER

A DEFINITIVE LOOK AT PRAYER AND PRAYING IN THE BOOK OF ACTS

"And it came to pass, that, as he was praying in a certain place, when he ceased, one of his disciples said unto him, Lord, teach us to pray, as John also taught his disciples."
Luke 11:1

PREFACE

When Jesus finished praying, the disciples became very aware of a saturating peace that permeated the atmosphere around Jesus. That emanating flow of life touched the disciples so deeply that they requested, *"teach us to pray."* The spirit of prayer is a tangible presence of God upon those who spend time worshipping and communing with the Father. In the book of Acts, prayer was at the center of the life of the church. After spending time meditating on the following twenty-eight accounts of prayer in the book of Acts, one will have little difficulty understanding why the gifts of the Holy Spirit were so prevalent in the life of the early church.

Prayer created the fertile bed of expectancy that birthed the Christian church. Even more so now, prayer must be the priority of the church so that she will continue being a light on a hill and the salt of the earth until the great day of the Lord's return.

As you study prayer in the book of Acts earnestly desire a spirit of prayer. In thoughtful study, you will see that the purpose of the earth is for prayer to ascend to our heavenly Father and in return for heaven and all its blessings to descend upon man.

"And the smoke of the incense, which came with the prayers of the saints, ascended up before God out of the angel's hand. And the angel took the censer, and filled it with fire of the altar, and cast it into the earth: and there were voices, and thunderings, and lightnings, and an earthquake."
Revelation 8:4–5

PRAYER

PRAYER
QUICK REFERENCE

Reference	Description of Prayer
(Jerusalem, Judea, Samaria)	
1. Acts 1:14	Waiting for the promise of the Father
2. Acts 1:24–26	Eleven apostles choose Matthias
3. Acts 2:42	The church continued steadfast in prayer
4. Acts 3:1	Peter and John went to the temple to pray
5. Acts 4:24	After being persecuted by religious leaders
6. Acts 6:4	Apostles give themselves to prayer
7. Acts 6:6	Apostles ordain laborers through prayer
8. Acts 7:60	Stephen prays for his murderers
9. Acts 8:15	Peter and John pray for the Samaritans
10. Acts 9:6	Saul humbles himself and prays
11. Acts 9:11	Paul, a man of prayer
12. Acts 9:40	Peter, prayer, and resurrection power
13. Acts 10:2	Roman centurion who prayed
14. Acts 10:9	Peter praying, falls into a trance
15. Acts 12:5	The church prays without ceasing
16. Acts 12:12	A house church fervent in prayer
(To the Uttermost Parts of the Earth)	
17. Acts 13:2	Direction for ministry (Paul and Barnabas)
18. Acts 13:3	Prayer that releases missionaries
19. Acts 14:23	Paul ordains elders
20. Acts 16:13	Paul and Silas meet Lydia
21. Acts 16:16	Paul and Silas in Philippi, cast out a devil
22. Acts 16:25	Paul and Silas in jail
23. Acts 20:36–37	Paul saying goodbye to the Ephesians
24. Acts 21:5	Paul praying with believers on the shore
25. Acts 22:17	Paul recounts praying in the temple
26. Acts 27:35	Paul praying and giving thanks for food
27. Acts 28:8	Paul praying before ministering healing
28. Acts 28:15	Paul gives thanks and takes courage

PRAYER
A DEFINITIVE LOOK

(Jerusalem, Judea, Samaria)

1. **WAITING FOR THE PROMISE OF THE FATHER**
   Acts 1:14
   "These all continued with one accord in prayer and supplication, with the women, and Mary the mother of Jesus, and with his brethren."

   Note: Jesus had been their example of a life given to prayer. He had also been their teacher concerning prayer and praying. Jesus was always reaffirming their relationship with a heavenly Father who desires to hear them and to answer them. Now, with Jesus' ascension to the Father, the disciples are left with a command to receive the promise of the Holy Spirit. I am sure at some point, as they waited in prayer, the words of Jesus continued to echo in their spirits, *"wait for the promise of the Father."* In this passage, 120 believers were assembled and praying with great expectation for what was about to come. It must have been the continual praying that kept the atmosphere of expectation alive for what was about to change the world. Remember, the disciples had no New Testament Bibles to read in order to understand the baptism of the Holy Spirit. It was their dependency on fellowship and prayer that kept the purposes of God moving forward.

   A final thought on this passage deals with Mary, the mother of Jesus. I often wonder what it must have been like to experience the Holy Spirit the way Mary did at Christ's inception. The angel told her that the Holy Spirit would come upon her and the power of the Most High would overshadow her—placing Jesus into her womb (Luke 1:35). Mary walked in such heavenly glory with Jesus as a baby in her, so that when she greeted pregnant Elizabeth, both Elizabeth and baby John were filled with the Holy Spirit. Thirty-three years later Mary is positioned in prayer, ready to receive the Holy Spirit coming back upon her with the power of the Highest overshadowing her—as a new creation, born again through Jesus Christ, the baby she had carried.

2. **ELEVEN APOSTLES CHOOSE MATTHIAS**
   Acts 1:24, 26
   "And they prayed, and said, Thou, Lord, which knowest the hearts of all men, shew whether of these two thou hast chosen, And they gave forth their lots; and the lot fell upon Matthias; and he was numbered with the eleven apostles."

   Note: This prayer meeting involved the disciples' sense of need to fill Judas Iscariot's empty office. As the Lord established twelve founding tribes of Israel, so He also established twelve governing offices over the

PRAYER

church. These eleven apostles knew that this vacant office (Judas' bishopric) needed to be filled. Therefore, they took it upon themselves to seek a person to fill this sacred position. As we study this passage of scripture it gives us insight into the many other people that were close to Jesus, people that had followed Him from the very beginning of His ministry. Remember, there were seventy other evangelists that helped the Lord alongside the twelve apostles.

In this passage, this prayer meeting shows the human side of ministry. They earnestly believed that they needed to choose Judas' replacement. As you read further into Acts, you realize that the apostle Paul was the Lord's choice in filling that sacred seat of the twelfth apostle of the Lamb.

The apostles prayed, heard no clear answer from the Lord, and then chose a very archaic tradition of picking lots to discern the will of the Lord. It is important to note that Jesus never taught His disciples to pick lots, and that this is the only occasion where they did so. After this failed attempt at prayer, they changed and put these cultural traditions behind them.

The lot fell upon Matthias. The Bible says that Matthias was *"numbered"* with the eleven, not being mentioned as the one filling Judas' office. He was ordained to be with the eleven! It is also important to note that the Lord did not answer their prayer pertaining to filling Judas' office. It is probable to assume that the Lord had no problem with Matthias assisting the eleven. In fact, He personally knew Matthias and approved of him assisting them. (*It is important to note that Matthias was present at Jesus' baptism and began following him from that point.*) In closing, as church history marched forward, there was going to be a great need for many more laborers and helpers as the church grew, both locally and globally.

3. THE CHURCH CONTINUED STEADFAST IN PRAYER

Acts 2:42

"And they continued stedfastly in the apostles doctrine and fellowship, and in breaking of bread, <u>and in prayers</u>."

Note: The church is born! It is important to note that these people did not have Bibles. They had to rely on being together to be strong. Therefore, fellowship was crucial. They were diligent to gather together and hear the Word of God, observing the instructions of the apostles. They maintained a constant communion with the Lord and with each other. This dependency on prayer created a fertile bed of expectancy, which was the catalyst for church growth.

4. PETER AND JOHN WENT TO THE TEMPLE TO PRAY

Acts 3:1

"Now Peter and John went up together into the temple at the hour of prayer, being the ninth hour."

Note: The temple was God's idea. It was Holy and carried a calling to be a place of prayer for all nations. The temple mentioned during this period was known as the second temple. Solomon's temple, though dedicated with such glory and fire, had been destroyed by Nebuchadnezzar due to Israel's sin. After seventy years of captivity, the Jews, according to prophecy, returned to Jerusalem and built a second temple.

This second temple differed from the first temple in that it never was dedicated with such glory and fire. The second temple, though seemingly lacking in visible glory, had a very important role in that it received Jesus—the Lamb of God. Solomon's temple carried a visible shekinah glory; the second temple hosted the Son of God, who not only had been dedicated as a baby within its walls but taught and did many miracles there as well.

Once again, the temple was God's idea, and the Jewish church loved it! In this passage we see that the apostles still were very much involved with temple worship, just like Jesus had been. And just like Jesus they manifested the power of the Holy Spirit on its steps. God's plan is perfect!

5. AFTER BEING PERSECUTED BY RELIGIOUS LEADERS

Acts 4:24

"And when they heard that, they lifted up their voice to God with one accord, and said, Lord, thou art God, which hast made heaven, and earth, and the sea, and all that in them is."

Note: The apostles had never seen or witnessed Jesus back down from the will of God due to persecution. The resurrection of Jesus and the baptism of the Holy Spirit had so empowered and emboldened the apostles that nothing was going to make them afraid. Jesus had commanded them to preach the gospel to the ends of the earth. This commission of preaching the gospel was the life of the church's mission and these Jerusalem believers were not going to drop the baton. In this passage, the response to the first persecution was prayer. The prayer was not generic in form but with desire and fervency. It was bathed in the revelation of Christ's commission to preach the gospel to the ends of the earth. The church prayed with heated fervency, and the Lord responded to their desire with Holy Spirit fire. The kingdom of God suffers violence (Matthew 11:12), and in this passage we see a violent church taking it by force through prayer. We also see demonstrated in this passage the power of corporate intercession— *"where two or more are gathered together in my name"* (Matthew 18:20). Jesus truly walked into the midst of these praying saints and manifested His glory. It was this type of praying in the face of opposition that established the church and turned the world upside down.

6. **APOSTLES GIVE THEMSELVES TO PRAYER**
   Acts 6:4
   "But, we will give ourselves continually to prayer, and to the ministry of the word."

   Note: In the prior example of prayer, we witness the church, both apostles and disciples, fervently praying that the Lord would stretch out His hand. Evangelism, which included evangelistic prayer, was the priority of this newborn church. In this passage, we see another aspect of the apostles' dependency on prayer. The apostles did not just say prayers but rather gave themselves continually to prayer. There is a difference. Peter, James, John, and the others must have missed Jesus tremendously. They had known Him in the flesh for three years. They lived with Him, touched Him, and watched Him do miracles. Now with Jesus seated in heaven, prayer was how they could commune with Him through the Holy Spirit's presence in them. The apostles also were charting new ground and therefore had another reason to be dependent upon prayer.

   In this passage, because of the growth of the newborn church, the need for helpers arose. Waiting and serving tables was extremely important but not more important than staying in communion with the Lord through prayer. Thus, this passage sees the entrance of a new type of servant called *"deacons."* The ministry role of a deacon (one who serves in a position closest to the people, under the authority of a superior) came because of the dependency key leadership had in fulfilling the ministry of prayer. In other words, the apostles kept themselves set apart in prayer, and the deacons became their hands extended—serving the practical needs of the congregation on behalf of the apostles. These deacons, such as Stephen and Philip, were powerful in that their ministry to the people flowed out from the prayer life of these apostles. In short, the ministry of a deacon can only reach its fullest potential through a leadership structure given to prayer.

7. **APOSTLES ORDAIN LABORERS THROUGH PRAYER**
   Acts 6:6
   "Whom they set before the apostles: and when they had prayed, they laid their hands on them."

   Note: Before ordaining His twelve disciples, Jesus spent the night in prayer. The apostles learned from Jesus' example to pray before laying hands on any man suddenly (1 Timothy 5:22). The work of the Lord was Holy, every aspect of it, even the serving of tables. Therefore, ordination required prayer. We also see how much the Lord loved widows. Men full of the Holy Spirit and faith were chosen and ordained to minister to the needs of the seemingly weakest amongst them.

8. **STEPHEN PRAYS FOR HIS MURDERERS**
Acts 7:60
"And he kneeled down, and cried with a loud voice, Lord, lay not this sin to their charge. And when he had said this, he fell asleep."

Note: The Bible declares that Jesus is seated at the right hand of the Father, but in this passage, we see Jesus standing up on behalf of Stephen. Such a powerful encouragement to all who live righteously on the earth and are persecuted for it. To think that Jesus stands for His servants is overwhelming. The final thought is that Stephen prays for those taking his life. As Stephen's final prayer left his mouth, there standing as a witness to these things was a man that would later be eternally impacted by this event—his name was Saul. There is no scale that can measure the impact of a righteous man who lives holy before God and dies holy before God. Truly creation groans waiting for the manifestation of these sons of God (Romans 8:19). The world is not worthy of such (Hebrews 11:38).

9. **PETER AND JOHN PRAY FOR THE SAMARITANS**
Acts 8:15–17
"Who, when they were come down, prayed for them, that they might receive the Holy Ghost: (For as yet he was fallen upon none of them: only they were baptized in the name of the Lord Jesus.)
Then laid they their hands on them, and they received the Holy Ghost."

Note: Salvation from sin and the baptism in the Holy Spirit were both a priority to the early church. In the Jewish mind, if God is going to build a temple, then He also plans to glorify it—all of it. These Jewish apostles were heading back into Samaria to finish a work that Jesus had begun at a well several years before (John 4:4–30).

It is important to note that they took time to pray for the Samaritans before ministering to them. When the Lord spoke to Jeremiah to go down to the potter's house, he obeyed, not knowing the why of his visit. Once there, the prophet had to sit and watch, and then after some time, the Lord spoke. Even so here, these apostles went to Samaria, and upon arriving, they had to quiet themselves and pray. When they finished praying, they understood the will of the Lord.

Upon laying their hands upon these outcast people who were now born again by the Blood of Jesus, they watched the power of God come down upon them and then heard new languages flow forth from their mouths. They also realized that God was healing their own racial divisions as they reached out and touched the Samaritans.

10. SAUL HUMBLES HIMSELF AND PRAYS

Acts 9:6

"And he trembling and astonished said, Lord, what wilt thou have me to do? And the Lord said unto him, Arise, and go into the city, and it shall be told thee what thou must do."

Note: Every knee shall bow, and every tongue shall confess that Jesus Christ is Lord to the glory of God (Philippians 2:9–10). Paul had encountered Jesus, and through that experience, he became a man of prayer. Though Jesus was the same as He was during His earthly ministry, there was one little (maybe huge) difference. After His resurrection and seating at the right hand of the Father, Jesus was now clothed with the glory He had before creation (John 17:5). Paul was encountered by this Jesus, who held the title *"King of kings and Lord of lords"* (Revelation 19:6). Paul experienced just a touch of the living light of Jesus' face—burning his eyes shut. Though Paul could not see in the natural, the imprint of the Lord's face (*shining like the sun*) left such a mark on his heart and mind that he became a man of prayer.

11. PAUL, A MAN OF PRAYER

Acts 9:11

"And the Lord said unto him, Arise, and go into the street which is called Straight, and inquire in the house of Judas for one called Saul of Tarsus: for, behold, he prayeth,"

Note: Ananias was hesitant to find Saul. Saul was known as a religious zealot out to kill Christians. Therefore, the Lord had to assure Ananias that Saul had changed. In this passage, the Holy Spirit revealed through a word of knowledge that Paul had become a man of prayer. Because of the assurance of the Lord and the knowledge of Paul praying, Ananias went, and the Lord poured out His Spirit upon this soon-to-be chief apostle. The Lord was finally filling the twelfth seat of the foundation called the apostles (Acts 1:20).

"And are built upon the foundation of the apostles and prophets, Jesus Christ himself being the chief corner stone."
Ephesians 2:20

12. PETER, PRAYER, AND RESURRECTION POWER

Acts 9:40

"But Peter put them all forth, and kneeled down, and prayed; and turning to the body said, Tabitha, arise. And she opened her eyes: and when she saw Peter, she sat up."

Note: In this passage, we see Peter humbling himself in prayer. The strongest man is a humble man. For it is the humble man, through his praying, that finds the mighty hand of God resting upon him. Peter kneels and stirs up the gift of God (2 Timothy 1:5–7), thus giving the leadership of that situation to the Lord. As Peter prayed, the boldness of the power gifts of the Holy Spirit came upon him. Peter then simply turned and spoke to Tabitha, *"arise."* Prayerful communion set the course for Peter to follow the leadership of the Holy Spirit in this miracle of resurrection.

13. ROMAN CENTURION WHO PRAYED

Acts 10:2

"A devout man, and one that feared God with all his house, which gave much alms to the people, and prayed to God always."

Note: The story of Job is a historical record of a man, though not Jewish, who loved God and served Him with all his heart. God knew Job by name. So, it is in this passage with Roman Cornelius—a Gentile who loved God.

Here we see the power of a man, regardless of being a Jew or Gentile, who sought the Lord, and in this, the Lord chose him to be the catalyst to awaken the Jewish apostles to the scope of God's plan of salvation. Cornelius was a man who fervently prayed, and his prayers along with his offerings have been memorialized in heaven.

14. PETER PRAYING, FALLS INTO A TRANCE

Acts 10:9

"On the morrow, as they went on their journey, and drew nigh unto the city, Peter went up upon the housetop to pray about the sixth hour."

Note: Peter was a man of prayer! As Peter waited for lunch, a spirit of prayer fell upon him. As he prayed, the Lord used his natural hunger mixed with his fervency in prayer to speak to him about the Gentiles being cleansed.

15. THE CHURCH PRAYS WITHOUT CEASING

Acts 12:5

"Peter therefore was kept in prison: but prayer was made without ceasing of the church unto God for him."

Note: From chapter 7 to chapter 12, we see the murder of Christians as a new form of persecution. From the martyrdom of Stephen to Christians imprisoned and put to death at the hands of Saul, to now King Herod, we see a new chapter in church history open. There are different levels of persecution; obviously, murder is the highest form of this hatred. It is important to note that the church did not back down or give in. Jesus had warned them that He was sending them out as lambs amongst wolves, and they had now come to terms with that. They had given their lives in the service of the Lord, and now in this passage, we see the church turning to fervent prayer without ceasing.

It is in this passage that we see the authority of a praying church. First, a church that takes its place at the right hand of God (*in Christ*) has the authority to influence earthly government. The church that forsakes her place in this sacred position of authority will suffer at the hands of satanically inspired government. Isaiah had prophesied that the government would be upon His (Christ's) shoulders. The church is the body of Christ, seated in Him, with access to this authority.

We also see that there are angelic ministries released by a praying church. It is important to note that Jesus equipped the church with *"grace"* weapons. In Matthew 18:18, the Lord declared that His disciples had authority to bind and authority to loose, which affects change in the realm of the spirit. A church that does not corporately pray with authority has ceded this holy place to the devil within its society and has forsaken the grace that could be theirs. The result of a church that forsakes her holy position of prayer will be a weakened church—which in turn affects people being saved.

16. A HOUSE CHURCH FERVENT IN PRAYER

Acts 12:12

"And when he had considered the thing, he came to <u>the house</u> of Mary the mother of John, whose surname was Mark; <u>where many were gathered together praying</u>."

Note: Fervent praying coming from a house church is probably the most dangerous weapon on the planet. A home is a natural place of love and fellowship, and in these prayer meetings, there was no time restraint. They prayed until heaven answered. House church prayer meetings have been known to stop wars and bring down tyrannical governments. How we need prayer meetings flowing out of homes!

(To the Uttermost Parts of the Earth)

17. DIRECTION FOR MINISTRY (PAUL AND BARNABAS)

Acts 13:2

"As <u>they ministered to the Lord, and fasted</u>, the Holy Ghost said, Separate me Barnabas and Saul for the work whereunto I have called them."

Note: In this passage, we glean an understanding of the power of ministering to the Lord mixed with fasting. This type of praying and communion also opens the door for the gifts of the Holy Spirit to operate. Jesus had commanded His disciples to pray to the Lord of the harvest to send (Greek *ekballo*—to thrust out) laborers into His harvest. Most likely, they were obeying this call to prayer. There are callings and assignments that the Lord gives at certain seasons. A praying church will keep in step with the Lord and His call for laborers.

18. PRAYER THAT RELEASES MISSIONARIES
Acts 13:3
"And when they had fasted and prayed, and laid their hands on them, they sent them away."

Note: In the preceding example, the church leaders were praying and singing to the Lord mixed with fasting. After the Holy Spirit spoke, their praying changed towards the purpose and direction of the calling. In both examples, prayer was mixed with fasting. It is also important to note that this is the first reference in the New Testament (church age) to fasting. In closing, the word *"sent"* is the same word used concerning divorce between a man and a woman. In this usage, we see that through prayer, the church leaders were able to fully divorce themselves from attempting to interfere with the direction God was giving to Paul and Barnabas. When they prayed and released them, Paul and Barnabas were fully in the hands of the Holy Spirit.

19. PAUL ORDAINS ELDERS
Acts 14:23
"And when they had ordained them elders in every church, and had prayed with fasting, they commended them to the Lord, on whom they believed."

Note: In this passage, we see the importance of prayer in ordination. We also see the role of fasting mixed with prayer pertaining to the sending forth of laborers. When the prophet Samuel came to Jesse's house, the Lord spoke very clearly to the old seer to not judge with the eyes. God is a judge who knows the hearts of all men. Therefore, it is important for men to take time to pray and ask God for guidance in ordaining laborers to serve in the local assemblies.

20. PAUL AND SILAS MEET LYDIA
Acts 16:13
"And on the sabbath we went out of the city by a river side, where prayer was wont to be made; and we sat down, and spake unto the women which resorted thither."

Note: After receiving a vision to come to Macedonia, Paul and his team set out in the direction of God and arrived at Philippi. Upon arriving, there was no further supernatural vision to direct their steps. Therefore, Paul and the team went outside the city to pray and seek the Lord. It was during this time of prayer that God opened the door into the city, and ultimately, the region. Therefore, visions and dreams are very important tools from the Holy Spirit to help the gospel laborer understand direction. Though these are powerful tools, they should never take the place of continued communion with the Lord through prayer.

21. PAUL AND SILAS IN PHILIPPI, CAST OUT A DEVIL

Acts 16:16

"And it came to pass, as we went to prayer, a certain damsel possessed with a spirit of divination met us, which brought her masters much gain by soothsaying."

Note: Paul and his team followed the leading of the Holy Spirit through the vision of the man from Macedonia, and now in Philippi, they were waiting for the next step from the Lord. Until they meet Lydia, the Bible does not give any details on where they stayed. We do know that they had a habit of daily prayer down by the river just outside the city. It was while they prayed that a group of ladies began to listen, whose hearts the Lord was touching. The prayer meetings down by the river must have been extremely powerful and effective to cause demons to manifest as the apostles walked through the city. It is also important to note the authority in Jesus name. His name not only worked in Jerusalem, but it produced gospel results within the boundaries of every nation where Christ was preached. The name of Jesus has no geographical limits to its use!

22. PAUL AND SILAS IN JAIL

Acts 16:25

"And at midnight Paul and Silas prayed and sang praises unto God: and the prisoners heard them."

Note: Once again, we see that persecution has no bearing or effect on the disciple's dedication to prayer. God had delivered Daniel because of his dedication to prayer, and Paul must have believed the same. Chained, bleeding, and hurting, they defied the shame and the pain and lifted their voices with joy to the Lord. We have no accounts in the book of Acts of a church barely given to prayer. On the contrary, we see a church completely given to praying with fervency. They knew the realities of persecution and death. They also desired to be in constant communion with the Lord who could deliver them. Prayer was life to these missionaries, and life always conquers the grave.

23. PAUL SAYING GOODBYE TO THE EPHESIANS

Acts 20:36–37

"And when he had thus spoken, he kneeled down, and prayed with them all. And they all wept sore (deeply), and fell (hugging) on Paul's neck, and kissed him,"

Note: The battle for Ephesus had been intense. The power of God had fallen upon that city, and God, through His battle axe Paul, had established a strong church in that city. Paul and his team had invested much time in Ephesus. Now, probably one of the most emotional moments in the book of Acts is their final goodbye. Paul, through revelation (word of God's wisdom), let the church know they would never see his face again. They loved Paul, and Paul loved them. As they bowed down and prayed, there was a very special presence of God upon them.

24. PAUL PRAYING WITH BELIEVERS ON THE SHORE

Acts 21:5

"And when we had accomplished those days, we departed and went our way; and they all brought us on our way, with wives and children, till we were out of the city: and we kneeled down on the shore and prayed."

Note: *(Another final goodbye)* In this farewell, we see the first picture of families with children in a prayer meeting. Paul must have remembered the beautiful picture of those families (husbands, wives, and children) waving goodbye as he departed from them. I would imagine that during the trying times before him, Paul would often think back to the mighty victories the Spirit of God gave in establishing those churches, as well as the love he felt as they prayed together on the shoreline that day.

25. PAUL RECOUNTS PRAYING IN THE TEMPLE

Acts 22:17

"And it came to pass, that, when I was (had) come again to Jerusalem, even while I prayed in the temple, I was in a trance."

Note: Paul, in giving his testimony, reveals information that was not given earlier in Acts chapter nine. Paul declares that while he was *"in"* the temple praying, he was caught up in a trance. I would imagine the religious leaders struggled at hearing this.

26. PAUL PRAYING AND GIVING THANKS FOR FOOD

Acts 27:35

"And when he had thus spoken, he took bread, and gave thanks to God in (the) presence of them all: and when he had broken it, he began to eat."

Note: In the midst of a storm, Paul, before eating, prayed and gave thanks to God for the food. It is easy in good times to give thanks to God or even for an unbeliever to thank his idol, but in the midst of a dangerous storm, only a man with faith in the Almighty would pause to say, *"thank you."* As Paul began praying, the presence of the Lord brought further comfort to those gathered. I am sure this left a mark upon the hearts of every man on that boat, both slave and free.

27. PAUL PRAYING BEFORE MINISTERING HEALING

Acts 28:8

"And it came to pass, that the father of Publius lay sick of a fever and of a bloody flux: to whom Paul entered in, and prayed, and laid his hands on him, and healed him."

Note: Jesus commanded His disciples to go into all the world and preach the gospel. In Christ's great commission, He also commanded them to pray for the sick. Even though Paul did not know Jesus in the flesh or ever see Him minister to the sick, he was full of the Spirit of Jesus, doing the same works of the Lord. The same flow of Christ that poured forth from Peter was equally as strong in Paul through the power of the Holy Spirit (Galatians 2:8). In this passage, before Paul administers healing, he humbles himself and prays. I believe that during this time of prayer, Paul received a fresh filling of the Holy Spirit, which ultimately prepared him to minister to the islanders who would come to be healed after hearing of the healing of Publius' father.

28. PAUL GIVES THANKS AND TAKES COURAGE

Acts 28:15

"And from thence, when the brethren heard of us, they came to meet us as far as Appii Forum, and The Three Taverns: whom when Paul saw, he thanked God, and took courage."

Note: Courage comes in different ways. Sometimes courage drops down upon us from heaven under an operation of the gift of God's special faith. In this passage, after Paul spends time thanking God, he then takes courage—stirring up the courage already in his heart. It would seem that giving thanks purifies the heart so that what is residing in the heart, such as courage, can rise up. In similar manner, David, after the burning of Ziklag, losing all that he had, stirred up courage in his own heart (1Samuel 30:6). In either example, courage is still courage and serves as a necessary tool in our faith walk with the Lord. Though this is the last reference to prayer in the book of Acts, it is not the last prayer prayed. Talking to God is the very reason man was created, and the book of Acts is a historical record of men that walked and talked with God on the earth, thus turning the world upside down.

THE BAPTISM OF THE HOLY SPIRIT

“THAT THE BLESSING OF
ABRAHAM MIGHT COME ON
THE GENTILES THROUGH
JESUS CHRIST; THAT WE
MIGHT RECEIVE THE PROMISE
OF THE SPIRIT THROUGH
FAITH.”
GALATIANS 3:14

THE BAPTISM OF THE HOLY SPIRIT

A DEFINITIVE LOOK AT THE BAPTISM OF THE HOLY SPIRIT IN THE BOOK OF ACTS

Part A

TYPES, SHADOWS, AND PROPHECY

JACOB

"And Jacob rose up early in the morning and took the stone that he had put for his pillows, and set it up for a pillar, and poured oil upon the top of it."
Genesis 28:18

When Jacob laid down to sleep, his thoughts troubled him. He was alone, he was on the run, and he was heading to a country that was not his own. As he drifted off to sleep, the God of Abraham visited him with a dream which was designed to encourage him as well as to paint a prophetic picture that would show forth the church age—an age where the body of the Messiah, comprised of all nations, would be saturated in the oil of the Holy Spirit. When Jacob awakened from this holy visitation, trembling under the supernatural awe of God's presence, he took the rock he had used for his pillow and poured oil upon it as a place of remembrance.

DANIEL

"Thou sawest till that a stone was cut out without hands, which smote the image upon his feet that were of iron and clay, and brake them to pieces."
Daniel 2:34

As Daniel proceeded to explain the dream to King Nebuchadnezzar, the court of Babylon stood silent as the king and his wise men listened to the young Hebrew captive explain a dream that had never been told. Daniel declared, *"you saw a stone cut from a mountain without hands and that stone began to move in the earth and it struck the image at its feet causing the image to fall."* As Daniel finished explaining the dream, the power of the Holy Spirit fell in the room, causing the great king to fall off his throne and onto the floor. Nebuchadnezzar was getting a taste of the day of Pentecost that would one day empower the stone that would demolish the four earthly kingdoms explained in his dream. Once again, a stone is used to describe a spiritual truth.

JESUS

"And I say also unto thee, That thou art Peter, and upon this rock I will build my church; and the gates of hell shall not prevail against it."
Matthew 16:18

Jesus brings the fullness of these two prophetic visitations together one day when He asked His disciples who they personally said He was. When Peter answered, *"you are the Christ, the son of the living God,"* Jesus declared, *"On this rock of revelation of who I am, I will build my church and the gates of hell shall not prevail against it."* Jesus likened the revelation of who He is to a stone or giant boulder that would crush Satan's kingdom, just as Daniel's stone destroyed Nebuchadnezzar's giant statue.

Before the day of Pentecost occurred, Jesus had ascended into heaven. Having sat down upon His throne at the right hand of the Father, Jesus was fully clothed with the glory He had shared with the Father before creation. The difference now was that this Jesus, the Word made flesh, had become a man. This man Jesus, now seated at the right hand of God, prayed to His Father and our Father for the promise of the Holy Spirit to be granted. The word of God's wisdom had already been spoken prophetically by Joel, and now it was time for those words to birth a move of the Holy Spirit unlike any other time in history. It was time to gather the nations into one body, into one new man, into Christ.

There in Jerusalem, one hundred twenty disciples had gathered into an upper room; though not fully understanding what was about to happen, they were determined to receive what Jesus called *"the promise of the Father."* As the Father poured forth His Spirit upon those gathered, there came a sound likened to a mighty moving wind that literally shook the city. Those expectant disciples were now sitting under a glory spout, a river of fire from which tributaries streamed forth and sat fully upon each of the Lord's servants and handmaids. As the glory filled both the house and each disciple, Isaiah's prophetic word began to manifest, *"With stammering lips and another tongue will he speak to this people"* (Isaiah 28:11).

Though Jacob had no understanding of the prophetic depth of what he was doing when he poured oil over the stone he had used for his pillows, there was one thing for sure—God's plan had been established before creation; and through Jacob, the Eternal One was painting a prophetic picture or signpost of His plans and purposes for both the Jewish people and all nations.

Part B

THE GATHERING

"That the blessing of Abraham might come on the Gentiles through Jesus Christ. that we might receive the promise of the Spirit through faith."
Galatians 3:14

"Let us go down, and there confound their language, that they may not understand one another's speech. So, the Lord scattered them abroad from thence upon the face of all the earth: and they left off building the city. Therefore, is the

name of it called Babel; because the Lord did there confound the language of all the earth: and from thence did the Lord scatter them abroad upon the face of all the earth."
Genesis 11:7–9

"And when the day of Pentecost was fully come, they were all with one accord in one place. And suddenly there came a sound from heaven as of a rushing mighty wind, and it filled all the house where they were sitting. And there appeared unto them cloven tongues like as of fire, and it sat upon each of them. And they were all filled with the Holy Ghost, and began to speak with other tongues, as the Spirit gave them utterance. And there were dwelling at Jerusalem Jews, devout men, out of every nation under heaven. Now when this was noised abroad, the multitude came together, and were confounded, because that every man heard them speak in his own language. And they were all amazed and marveled, saying one to another, Behold, are not all these which speak Galilaeans? And how hear we every man in our own tongue, wherein we were born? Parthians, and Medes, and Elamites, and the dwellers in Mesopotamia, and in Judaea, and Cappadocia, in Pontus, and Asia, Phrygia, and Pamphylia, in Egypt, and in the parts of Libya about Cyrene, and strangers of Rome, Jews and proselytes, Cretes and Arabians, we do hear them speak in our tongues the wonderful works of God."
Acts 2:1–11

PREFACE

Once again, we find that the book of Genesis, the first book of the Bible, has much to say about the baptism of the Holy Spirit. The Tower of Babel is where God poured out His mercy as a judgment, dividing and scattering earth's rebellious nations and tribes by changing their languages. At Babel's lofty tower, humanity once again had embarked on a sinful career. This time humanity had lusted after an image and a name, turning away from the gospel of Noah, thus cementing into stone their idolatry. This act of rebellion sealed their sinful purpose before the throne of God. Though they were knowledgeable of the sin, of Noah's pre-flood generation, they still chose to continue down the same wicked path. God had every right to destroy man, but once again, mercy triumphed. At the core of their rebellion was the fear of being scattered—therefore, God judged humanity by what they feared.

As the wind of the Holy Spirit thrust (expelling) outward earth's families and tribes, they carried in their hearts the seeds of rebellion and idolatry. These divided nations, now relocated, sat in spiritual darkness by their own choosing, waiting for the appointed season when light would come. Jesus declared to Nicodemus, *"For God so loved the world"* (John 3:16). God loves man, and His plan of redemption is for the whole world. In His righteousness, the Almighty could not disregard man's rebellion, but in His mercy, He embarked on a plan to gather what had been scattered.

As God had done with Noah, so He started a new work with Abraham. According to Rabbinical tradition backed by biblical timelines, both Noah and Abraham were living at this time, and both witnessed the scattering of the nations. Both men were fathers of two different dispensations[1]. Noah had witnessed a judgment of a great flood destroy every living creature on the face of the earth, except for his own sons and their wives—who had been kept safe in an ark of gopher wood. The other man, Abraham, would give birth to a spiritual seed being Christ (Galatians 3:16). The seed of Christ, through a nation of people (being the Jewish nation), would bless all of Noah's seed—every scattered nation, tribe, and tongue. It must have been an amazing thing for Abraham to hear the Lord declare, *"In you, I will bless all nations"* (Genesis 22:18). Abraham had no idea as to the scope of what God was planning to do, but his faith accepted the steps God placed before him. Abraham went forward, and so did the plan of God.

CENTRIPETAL

acceleration inward—center seeking

"Now when Solomon had made an end of praying, the fire came down from heaven, and consumed the burnt offering and the sacrifices; and the glory of the Lord filled the house. And the priests could not enter into the house of the Lord, because the glory of the Lord had filled the Lord's house."
2 Chronicles 7:1–3

When Abraham met the priest Melchizedek, a spiritual blessing was imparted to him through the gift of God's special faith. This operation of God's power was then imparted into Isaac and Isaac into Jacob and from Jacob into every generation that proceeded. This blessing was more than mere words. It was an operation of the Holy Spirit, full of power and full of glory.

The blessing of Abraham upon the Jewish nation was readily perceived by the visible glory of God upon the first temple. The nations, because of the tangible blessing of Abraham upon the Jewish people, were to be drawn inward (centripetal) to Jerusalem to hear the Word of God. Jerusalem, the city that God had chosen as His own (a city whose foundations had been laid by Abraham's resurrection faith), was the hub of all nations. Everything that pertained to God's plan of redemption was Jerusalem-focused. The Queen of Sheba was drawn to Jerusalem to hear Solomon's wisdom and to see the manifest glory of God upon the temple. She was overwhelmed by what she saw (2 Chronicles 9:1–4). It is important to note that what the Queen of Sheba experienced was a manifestation of the blessing of Abraham—which was saturated in the holy presence of the God of Israel.

Once again, this blessing was more than words, but rather an operation of God's grace and ability that has kept the natural seed of Abraham as a nation of people, even throughout centuries of incredible struggles. God's purpose for the

[1] Page 359 Bereishis Genesis, ArtScroll Tanach Series, Volume I(a) Published by Mesorah Publications, Ltd. Brooklyn, NY.

Jewish nation will be accomplished precisely because of the promise of His word to Abraham and the impartation of God's special faith upon the Jewish people that energizes the plan of God on the earth.

CENTRIFUGAL

acceleration outward from the center

On the day of Pentecost, the blessing of Abraham was visible again in Jerusalem by the manifested (*shekinah*) glory of God upon the body of Christ—the church, God's new temple. With this sanctification, coupled with the Lord's great commission to go and tell all men, came a new concept to the Jewish mind, *"Jerusalem, Judea, Samaria, and to the ends of the earth"* (Acts 1:8). God's plan was now outward (centrifugal) to the nations. Jeremiah 31:10 reveals the promise of God to Israel concerning their own judgment, *"He that scattered Israel, will gather them."* This same mercy of God holds true for all nations through the power of the gospel. The God who divided and scattered earth's families at Babel had a plan to gather all men into one family where He would be restored as man's rightful Father.

The outpouring of the Holy Spirit on the day of Pentecost, grace filling grace, the double blessing, or simply put—the blessing of Abraham poured forth upon all flesh, is the power that propels the plan of God outward from Jerusalem to the ends of the earth. Now, by His passion and through the preaching of the gospel, the Lord, who is now our high priest after the order of Melchizedek, administrates this impartation of power and blessing—thus, unifying earth's families in the power of the Holy Spirit through one new man—Christ Jesus.

THE BAPTISM OF THE HOLY SPIRIT
QUICK REFERENCE

Reference	Descriptions
(Jerusalem, Judea, Samaria)	
1. Acts 1:2	He through the Holy Spirit
2. Acts 1:4–5	The Promise of the Father
3. Acts 1:8	Power to witness
4. Acts 1:22	Beginning from the baptism of John
5. Acts 2:1–4	The Holy Spirit is poured out—the church is born.
6. Acts 2:33	Both seen and heard
7. Acts 2:38	Repent, be baptized, and you shall receive
8. Acts 4:8	Power to witness and confront
9. Acts 4:31	Boldness to speak
10. Acts 5:32	The greatest witness of resurrection
11. Acts 6: 3,5	A prerequisite to serve
12. Acts 6:10	The Holy Spirit enhances speech
13. Acts 7:55	Stephen, a man full of the Holy Spirit
14. Acts 8:17	Samaritans are baptized in the Holy Spirit
15. Acts 9:17	Paul receives the baptism of the Holy Spirit
16. Acts 10:44	Gentiles receive the baptism of the Holy Spirit
17. Acts 11:15–16	John the Baptist and Jesus
18. Acts 11:24	Barnabas, a man full of the Holy Spirit
(To the Uttermost Parts of the Earth)	
19. Acts 13:9	Paul confronts a sorcerer
20. Acts 13:52	Filled with joy and the Holy Spirit
21. Acts 15:8	Speaking in tongues is the foremost sign
22. Acts 18:26	Apollos baptized in the Holy Spirit
23. Acts 19:6	Twelve are baptized in the Holy Spirit

THE BAPTISM OF THE HOLY SPIRIT
A DEFINITIVE LOOK

(Jerusalem, Judea, Samaria)

1. **HE THROUGH THE HOLY SPIRIT**
   Acts 1:2
   "Until the day in which he was taken up, after that he through the Holy Ghost had given commandments unto the apostles whom he had chosen."

   Note: In the second verse in the book of Genesis, the book of beginnings, we are introduced to the Holy Spirit. The earth was in a state of chaos, and darkness was upon the face of the deep. In the midst of this darkness, the Holy Spirit (who is God) was moving in immense strength. Then the words *"let there be light"* came forth from the throne of God. It is important to note that these words were spoken before the sun was created. As the word went forth from the Father, the Holy Spirit manifested such glorious light—a light that was shining not upon the earth but rather saturating the earth. The earth was literally submerged into the power of the Holy Spirit. God the Father and the Word of God were creating, and the Holy Spirit was manifested, bringing forth the creation of God.

   How important is the Holy Spirit? As it was in Genesis with the creation of the world, so it is in Acts with the preaching of the gospel. Meditate on the power of this simple phrase, *"He through the Holy Spirit."* How important is the Holy Spirit? He is everything, just as Jesus is everything. Therefore, how important is the baptism of the Holy Spirit, which is an immersion into the power of God? It is everything! As we enter this study, keep the words *"He through the Holy Spirit"* in your hearts. As you do, you will cherish even more the presence and the power of the Holy Spirit in your life.

2. **THE PROMISE OF THE FATHER**
   Acts 1:4–5
   "And, being assembled together with them, commanded them that they should not depart from Jerusalem, but wait for the promise of the Father, which, saith he, ye have heard of me. For John truly baptized with water; but ye shall be baptized with the Holy Ghost not many days hence."

   Note: The baptism of the Holy Spirit was never considered an option to the Lord Jesus. In Acts 1:4, the Lord reminds His disciples that the command to receive the baptism of the Holy Spirit came from Him. This one phrase carries such sobering weight pertaining to the Lord's command to receive this baptism of fire and power, and then to live in the grace of it.

HOLY SPIRIT

This blessing from heaven was not an option—it was a command! This passage also reveals that much had already been said concerning this holy submersion. It is also important to note that John the Baptist had spoken of this blessing. John, through revelation, declared that Jesus Himself was the one who would officiate this blessing.

Another powerful truth is that John the Baptist made it clear that he, as well as with all men, was not worthy to bend low and touch the latches of Jesus' shoes, but Jesus, on the other hand, would touch us and submerge us into the sacred power of the Holy Spirit.

"And Jesus, when he was baptized, went up straightway out of the water: and, lo, the heavens were opened unto him, and he saw the Spirit of God descending like a dove, and lighting upon him."
Matthew 3:16

3. POWER TO WITNESS

Acts 1:8

"But, ye shall receive power, after that the Holy Ghost is come upon you: and ye shall be witnesses unto me both in Jerusalem, and in all Judaea, and in Samaria, and unto the uttermost parts of the earth."

Note: In Matthew 24:1, the disciples showed Jesus the buildings of Jerusalem's beautiful temple. Jesus, being a prophet, operating under a word of wisdom, began teaching His disciples concerning things to come. It must have been shocking to hear Jesus declare that Jerusalem's majestic temple would be destroyed. These words obviously were never forgotten.

In Acts 1:6, before Jesus ascends to the Father, the disciples asked another end-time question. Perhaps they were hoping to hear more about the destruction of Jerusalem and of things to come. It is important to note that Jerusalem and its beautiful temple gave the Jewish nation hope and resilience in facing adversity. The stories of how Solomon built the first temple and how God dedicated it with fire and glory were more than history to the Jewish mind—it was a part of who they were as a people.

So here, in Acts chapter 1 verses 7 and 8, the disciples ask a question and receive a completely different answer than they did in Matthew chapter 24. Jesus wanted them ready, not with a focus on a new physical temple and a restored Davidic kingdom, but rather for them to become a new temple, prepared for the service of God. They did not know it at the time, but just as the glory fell with holy fire upon Solomon's temple, it was about to fall upon them. Jesus, through revelation concerning the will of God, revealed that they would receive miracle-working power when the Holy Spirit came upon them. The very power that flowed from Jesus as He walked on water, walked through angry crowds, multiplied loaves and fish, raised dead people, and healed the multitudes, was going to rest upon them. Jesus was about to dedicate a new temple, a masterpiece created through His passion. With the extreme price He paid with His own flesh and blood, He commands His disciples to receive the fullness of what He provided. The last thing He reveals in this verse is that this power would flow from Jerusalem outward to the ends of the earth as a witness to all nations of His resurrection.

4. **BEGINNING FROM THE BAPTISM OF JOHN**
Acts 1:22
"Beginning from the baptism of John, unto that same day that he was taken up from us, must one be ordained to be a witness with us of his resurrection."

Note: Jesus' baptism by John was a memorable event. Not only was Jesus, who had become a man, baptized in water, but those present saw the power of the Holy Spirit rest upon Him and heard the voice of the Father speak, *"This is my Son!"* The apostles, in choosing Judas' replacement, felt deeply that the person who would take Judas' ministry position had to not only be someone who carried a depth of devotion but who also had an experiential understanding of Jesus' ministry. Therefore, this event of Jesus' baptism in water and in the Holy Spirit became the threshold of the criteria needed for choosing one to be ordained into this holy service. Therefore, how important to the apostles was Jesus' baptism in the Holy Spirit? Everything!

5. **THE HOLY SPIRIT IS POURED OUT—THE CHURCH IS BORN**
Acts 2:1–4
"And when the day of Pentecost was fully come, they were all with one accord in one place. And suddenly there came a sound from heaven as of a rushing mighty wind, and it filled all the house where they were sitting. And there appeared unto them cloven tongues like as of fire, and it sat upon each of them. And they were all filled with the Holy Ghost, and began to speak with other tongues, as the Spirit gave them utterance."

Note: The feast of Pentecost was a harvest feast. This new temple, dedicated with glory, was a temple created for the harvest of the nations.

"Now when Solomon had made an end of praying, the fire came down from heaven, and consumed the burnt offering and the sacrifices; and the glory of the Lord filled the house. And the priests could not enter into the house of the Lord, because the glory of the Lord had filled the Lord's house. And when all the children of Israel saw how the fire came down, and the glory of the Lord upon the house, they bowed themselves with their faces to the ground upon the pavement, worshipped."
2 Chronicles 7:1–3

God's desire was for His glory to reside upon man. Unlike the baptism of Jesus, when the Holy Spirit baptized our Lord in a gentleness likened to a dove, these disciples were submerged into a mighty rushing wind—coming straight out of heaven. It would seem that on the day of Pentecost, earth was getting a taste of heaven's extreme joy. As the 120 disciples sat praying in the upper room, fire came down from heaven—literally sitting upon them. It was not a gentle flame on their heads. The fire sat on them—saturating them. The revelation John the Baptist preached, *"with fire,"* had come to pass!

"Marvel not that I said unto thee, Ye must be born again. The wind blows where it desires, and thou hearest the sound thereof, but canst not tell whence it cometh, and whither it goeth: so is every one that is born of the Spirit."
John 3:7–8

Jesus likened the Holy Spirit's work in salvation to the *"wind"* blowing. On the day of Pentecost, with Jesus seated in heaven, this mighty wind of salvation was released upon the earth. Now, with God's masterpiece of a new creation, we see the complete reversal of the judgment upon the nations at the Tower of Babel. The difference at Pentecost was that the disciples were speaking in the languages of many nations, and yet there was complete unity. This holy gift was not a divider but a unifier.

One often overlooked miracle was how the men from various nations heard (clearly) their own languages being spoken by the 120 disciples in the upper room. When a large group of people shout and give glory, the individual is typically drowned out by the corporate. But with this vocal miracle on the day of Pentecost, God gave the nations that were present ears to hear!

6. BOTH SEEN AND HEARD

Acts 2:33

"Therefore, being by the right hand of God exalted, and having received of the Father the promise of the Holy Ghost, he hath shed forth this, which ye now see and hear."

Note: In short, this powerful operation of the Holy Spirit is both seen and heard. As it was on the day of Pentecost and in the account of Cornelius and the Gentiles, it was the speaking in tongues that gave confirmation to this holy baptism of fire. As mentioned earlier, the carnal mind does not receive these truths (1 Corinthians 2:14).

7. **REPENT, BE BAPTIZED, AND YOU SHALL RECEIVE**
Acts 2:38
"Then Peter said unto them, Repent, and be baptized every one of you in the name of Jesus Christ for the remission of sins, and ye shall receive the gift of the Holy Ghost."

Note: Peter, speaking by revelation, included *"every one of you"* in the scope of this baptism. At that time, Peter still had much to learn about the Holy Spirit working in the lives of all believers—especially the Gentiles.

8. **POWER TO WITNESS AND CONFRONT**
Acts 4:8
"Then Peter, filled with the Holy Ghost, said unto them, Ye rulers of the people, and elders of Israel,"

Note: The baptism of the Holy Spirit was not limited to a simple glorification of this new temple but was also intended to fortify the believer in dealing with the devil and evil people. God has never failed to provide what was needed for His children and servants to effectively serve. If the world is filled with wickedness and demonic power, then God, through His triumphant Christ, provided for His temple to be filled with His own victorious power. Peter, filled fresh with miracle-working strength, responds to the religious leaders and confronts their hypocrisy.

9. **BOLDNESS TO SPEAK**
Acts 4:31
"And when they had prayed, the place was shaken where they were assembled together; and they were all filled with the Holy Ghost, and they spake the word of God with boldness."

Note: In this passage, we see none left out; all were filled with the Holy Spirit. Also, Paul, in the letter to the Ephesians, asked the church to pray that God would grant him boldness to speak as the gospel required. These believers understood that the gospel was supernatural and could not be preached effectively through mere human intellect. In this verse, we see the blueprint of evangelistic prayer and the necessity of boldness received through fresh refilling(s) of the Holy Spirit.

10. **THE GREATEST WITNESS OF RESURRECTION.**
Acts 5:32
"And we are his witnesses of these things; and so is also the Holy Ghost, whom God hath given to them that obey him."

Note: The utmost calling of the Holy Spirit is to bring conviction of sin to the hearts of people through the witness of Christ's resurrection. Romans 8:11 declares that it was the Holy Spirit who raised Jesus from the dead—

thus making the Spirit of God the greatest witness of resurrection. As we wait upon Him for His fullness, He fine-tunes our witness with His witness, making us likened to a sharp threshing sickle thrusting outward to bring in a harvest of souls.

11. A PREREQUISITE TO SERVE

Acts 6:3

"Wherefore, brethren, look ye out among you seven men of honest report, full of the Holy Ghost and wisdom, whom we may appoint over this business.

Acts 6:5

"And the saying pleased the whole multitude: and they chose Stephen, a man full of faith and of the Holy Ghost."

Note: During the six days of creation God created the galactic heavens, the firmament above our heads, the dry land beneath our feet, and the oceans that surround us. God never created a sphere without a plan to fill it. He created the atmosphere and filled it with oxygen, which would sustain the physical life of all things. He proceeded to fill the heavens with stars and planets. He filled the earth with animals. He filled the seas with fish as well as with so many other creatures. The living God who created us is a God of fullness. On the day of Pentecost, the Lord created the church and filled it with the Holy Spirit. Now, in this chapter, we see that every member of the body of Christ can live filled with faith and with the Holy Spirit. Also, in this chapter, we see that one of the key requirements of serving as a deacon is being filled with the Holy Spirit and living a spirit-filled life—which is both holy as well as supernatural. Stephen was a man who had received this holy baptism of fire and power and was known by the congregation as a man that lived full of God's presence.

12. THE HOLY SPIRIT ENHANCES SPEECH

Acts 6:10

"And they were not able to resist the wisdom and the spirit by which he spake."

Note: Not only does God give man language—He also, with that language, has the ability to enhance man's speech. In this passage, as it was with Daniel in Babylon, Stephen had received a speaking upgrade, and with this ability came great conviction upon the people—even those that hated him.

"The Lord GOD hath given me the tongue of the learned, that I should know how to speak a word in season to him that is weary."
Isaiah 50:4

13. STEPHEN, A MAN FULL OF THE HOLY SPIRIT

Acts 7:55

"But he, being full of the Holy Ghost, looked up steadfastly into heaven, and saw the glory of God, and Jesus standing on the right hand of God,"

Note: The Bible declares that Stephen's face was shining like the face of an angel. It reminds us of Moses' face when he came down from the mountain of God (Exodus 34:29). We see in the New Testament that the ministry of righteousness excels in glory (2 Corinthians 3:6–13) and that ministry was shining through Stephen's face as a witness of the finished work of God at Calvary. The religious leaders, having a form of godliness that denied the power God, were filled with envy as they stared at the glory upon Stephen's face—a glory they could have had but refused to humble themselves to receive.

14. SAMARITANS ARE BAPTIZED IN THE HOLY SPIRIT

Acts 8:17

"Then laid they their hands on them, and they received the Holy Ghost."

Note: Jesus declared, *"Jerusalem, Judea, Samaria..."* Now, because of the persecution of Saul (Paul), Samaritans hear and receive the Word of God and are baptized in the Holy Spirit. Unlike on the day of Pentecost, the Samaritan believers were baptized in the Holy Spirit by the apostles laying their hands upon them. Because of the division between Jews and Samaritans, I believe that the apostles were led to touch, with the hand of love, people who had been viewed earlier as low-class half breeds. Just as Jesus reached out and touched the leper, even so the Jewish apostles reached out, doing the unthinkable, touching the Samaritans. The Holy Spirit is wise in how He leads us. God was healing the racial prejudice between the two peoples through the preaching of the gospel and the baptism of the Holy Spirit. The Lord was teaching His Jewish apostles that one new man was and is *"one new man!"*

15. PAUL RECEIVES THE BAPTISM OF THE HOLY SPIRIT

Acts 9:17

"And Ananias went his way, and entered into the house; and putting his hands on him said, Brother Saul, the Lord, even Jesus, that appeared unto thee in the way as thou camest, hath sent me, that thou mightest receive thy sight, and be filled with the Holy Ghost."

Note: Paul, the former chief persecutor, was also a candidate for the baptism of the Holy Spirit. Even though it does not reveal that he prayed in tongues in this passage, his first epistle to the Corinthians clearly describes his personal prayer life and his constant dependency on praying in the Holy Spirit—otherwise known as praying in tongues. We also see that the Lord did not use a chief apostle such as Peter, James, or John to lay their hands on Paul. The Lord used a simple layman named Ananias. The Lord was instituting an eternal truth concerning the administration of this holy baptism being that every member of His body was an able minister of the gospel. The Lord also removed any future competition or condescension that could have risen by one of the original eleven apostles (or their followers), reminding Paul that Peter or John had prayed for him to receive the baptism of the Holy Spirit. Paul, as a chief apostle, received the baptism of the Holy Spirit by the hands of a simple layman. What a powerful truth as to the humility and gentleness of Jesus and how He chooses to use any and every member of His body.

It is also important to note that this operation of the baptism of the Holy Spirit occurred outside the boundaries of the land of Israel, thus revealing that there would be no limitations to the gospel. The power of the Holy Spirit administered within the borders of Israel, the Holy Land, would be the same power outside those borders as the gospel moved outward to the ends of the earth.

16. GENTILES RECEIVE THE BAPTISM OF THE HOLY SPIRIT

Acts 10:44
"While Peter yet spake these words, the Holy Ghost fell on all them which heard the word."

Acts 10:46
"For they heard them speak with tongues, and magnify God."

Note: The Lord had promised that all nations would be blessed in Abraham. Cornelius became the open door of the blessing of Abraham coming upon the Gentiles through Jesus Christ. In this baptism of the Holy Spirit, the Lord chooses to personally baptize the Gentiles without the hands of the Jewish apostles. A precedent is set that later ensures that the Jewish church (based in Jerusalem) could never hold sway over the Gentile church—the body of Christ was one new man.

Remember, Jerusalem, before its destruction by Titus in AD 70, had not only become a Christian stronghold but a religious one as well. Even certain of the apostles had been affected by the religious fervor of the Christian Jews in that ancient city. In AD 70, Jerusalem was destroyed, and the religious church was scattered. This event began the age of Christianity in the hands of the Gentiles. Before the Roman destruction of Jerusalem, we see the hand of God plant like seeds, both Peter and Paul, into Rome to empower this new direction of Christianity and its global mission.

My final thought pertains to the force of the praise coming out of the Gentiles. Truly hearing Romans speaking in tongues was a sign to these Jerusalem-based apostles, but to hear them shouting and praising God was just as real—this was truly a sign and a wonder to these Jews who had already believed upon Christ.

17. JOHN THE BAPTIST AND JESUS

Acts 11:15–16

"And as I began to speak, the Holy Ghost fell on them, as on us at the beginning. Then remembered I the word of the Lord, how that he said, John indeed baptized with water; but ye shall be baptized with the Holy Ghost."

Note: When the angel Gabriel declared to Mary, *"The Holy Spirit shall come upon you and the power of the Most High shall overshadow you and this holy child, born of thee, shall be called the Son of God,"* she had no idea what this meant, she just believed (Luke 1:35). We are given more insight into this operation of the Holy Spirit when Mary greeted Elizabeth, and the power of God filled both Elizabeth and John the Baptist (Luke 1:41). At that time, Jesus, the Word of God, was only an embryo—and yet the presence of the Holy Spirit upon Him was working mightily. It is no wonder that John the Baptist preached that Jesus would baptize His followers in the Holy Spirit (Matthew 3:11).

In this passage, the Holy Spirit was reminding Peter of what Jesus had said. It is important to note, as stated above, that both John the Baptist and Jesus preached the same message about the baptism of the Holy Spirit. It is also important to note that what took place in Acts chapter two, as well as with Cornelius and the Gentiles in Acts chapter twelve, was the manifestation of what these two prophets were declaring. For truly, in the mouth of two or three witnesses, every word is established—and in this passage, it was established for the Gentiles.

18. BARNABAS, A MAN FULL OF THE HOLY SPIRIT

Acts 11:24

"For he was a good man, and full of the Holy Ghost and of faith: and many people were added unto the Lord."

Note: The recipe for effective witness is found in the word *"full."* Barnabas was full of the Holy Spirit and full of faith. It is important to note that many years had passed since we saw the introduction of Barnabas in Chapter four. Barnabas lived a life that cherished what God gave the church on the day of Pentecost and proved that one could maintain a spirit-filled life over the course of many years. The promise of the Father, which is the baptism of the Holy Spirit with tongues, did not pass away in Barnabas' life nor has it waned for believers alive today. We must cherish this tremendous gift.

(To the Uttermost Parts of the Earth)

19. PAUL CONFRONTS A SORCERER

Acts 13:9

"Then Saul, (who also is called Paul,) filled with the Holy Ghost, set his eyes on him."

Note: As mentioned earlier, the world is full of wicked people who are full of demonic power. In dealing with these demonic spirits, God has provided for us to be *"filled"* with the Holy Spirit and power. Paul was baptized in the Holy Spirit in chapter 9, and here in chapter 13, he received a fresh filling (refilling) to equip him in confronting Elymas. This demonstration of power and authority caused the deputy to turn to the Lord. This concept of a refilling is expressed best in Paul's writing to the Ephesians when he commands them to *"keep being filled"* with the Holy Spirit.

"But be filled (continually) with the Spirit."
Ephesians 5:18

20. FILLED WITH JOY AND THE HOLY SPIRIT

Acts 13:52

"And the disciples were filled with joy, and with the Holy Ghost."

Note: The life of communion with the Lord brings us into seasons of refreshing in His presence. In this account, we see these believers possessing a joy and fullness about them that empowered them to live their lives in blessing and spiritual fullness.

21. SPEAKING IN TONGUES IS THE FOREMOST SIGN

Acts 15:8

"And God, which knoweth the hearts, bare them witness, giving them the Holy Ghost, even as he did unto us."

Note: The greatest sign of the baptism of the Holy Spirit is and always will be speaking in other tongues. On the day of Pentecost, the nations present heard the disciples speaking in other tongues. At the baptism of Samaria, Simon the Sorcerer was amazed at how people received the Holy Spirit by the laying on of hands—and how they began to speak in other tongues. Remember, the baptism of the Holy Spirit is both what you see and hear (Acts 2:33). So, it is in this passage when Peter explained that the Gentiles received the baptism of the Holy Spirit exactly as they had, which means they were baptized personally by Jesus without the assistance of man's hands being laid upon them, and they also prayed in other tongues.

22. APOLLOS BAPTIZED IN THE HOLY SPIRIT

Acts 18:26

"And he began to speak boldly in the synagogue: whom when Aquila and Priscilla had heard, they took him unto them, and expounded unto him the way of God more perfectly."

Note: In this account, we find a man who believed and followed the Lord, but who had only been baptized with John's baptism of repentance. Jesus' life and teachings affected thousands upon thousands who were not all living in Jerusalem on the day of Pentecost. In this account, we find a man with a teaching gift who was both fervent and diligent in teaching the things of the Lord through the lens of the baptism of John. When Aquila heard this man, he was touched by the gift of God in operation through him. Then Paul's trusty helpers realized that Apollos needed something more. There are no accounts given in the book of Acts that leave the door open to whether the baptism of the Holy Spirit is an option. This baptism, spoken by Jesus, was preached equally with salvation. To the Jewish mind, if God is going to build a temple, He is also going to glorify it. The result of this baptism enhancement was a new level of boldness which enabled Apollos to *"mightily"* (Greek *Eutonos "with power"*) convince the Jews that Jesus was the Christ.

23. TWELVE ARE BAPTIZED IN THE HOLY SPIRIT

Acts 19:6

"And when Paul had laid his hands upon them, the Holy Ghost came on them; and they spake with tongues, and prophesied."

Note: This is that last account in the book of Acts of the baptism of the Holy Spirit. Here we find other disciples, men who likely had been taught by Apollos, who needed to receive the baptism in the Holy Spirit. What is profound about this account is that these men were living in Gentile lands. Thus, the Holy Spirit demonstrates that this power of God can be administered outside the boundaries of Israel.

In conclusion, not only has the gospel been preached around the globe, but so has this holy baptism. The families of the earth (nations) are now being blessed in faithful Abraham, just as the Lord had declared. Currently, there are more people living on planet earth than ever before who have received the gift of the Holy Spirit with the corresponding sign of speaking in other tongues.

Throughout the book of Acts, there is never an example given of a person not being granted this holy baptism. It is important to note that in many examples throughout the book of Acts, the word *"all"* is used to describe the reception of this holy submersion. Even in the dedication of Solomon's temple, all of it was clothed in the shekinah glory—not some of it! Thus, Satan seeks through religious tradition, fear, and unbelief to limit born-again believers in their reception of this commanded blessing.

The administration of the baptism of the Holy Spirit in the book of Acts was never a point of division but one of unifying the church, comprised of people from all nations and tribes, in the power of the Holy Spirit.

"For the earnest expectation of the creature waits for the manifestation of the sons of God."
Romans 8:19

THE GIFTS OF THE HOLY SPIRIT

THE DEFINITIONS OF

THE GIFTS OF THE HOLY SPIRIT

REVELATION POWER INSPIRATION

"But the manifestation of the Spirit is given to every man to profit withal."
1 Corinthians 12:7

INTRODUCTION TO THE GIFTS OF THE HOLY SPIRIT

In approaching the subject of the gifts of the Holy Spirit, I would admonish the reader to study Howard Carter's book entitled *Questions and Answers on Spiritual Gifts*. Howard Carter, from London, England, was given such tremendous revelation on all nine spiritual gifts, and in my opinion, his writings on the gifts of the Holy Spirit set the standard for a proper understanding of the ministry of the Holy Spirit to the church and through the church.

In studying these nine special graces, it does not take long before the student realizes the masterful fingerprint of God upon each, as well as how they group together into groups of three.

In the English language when the word trinity is heard, it invokes a reverential acknowledgment of the triune (three-part) nature of God—being Father, Son, and Holy Spirit. On the other hand, in its basic definition, the word trinity means a group of three. Throughout creation, we find this special creative stamp of three. For example, man, created in the image of God, has three parts—spirit, soul, and body. Concerning geographical locations, the Bible only mentions three—heaven, earth, and hell. Even with electricity, which is crucial to life on this planet, we find a positive, negative, and a neutral charge. All three are the key functioning parts of electricity. The search for the number three in creation is an inexhaustible study.

With this basic understanding of the number three, we can now approach the nine gifts of the Holy Spirit. With these nine special graces of God, we identify a further subcategorization of three groups consisting of three gifts each.

With the assistance of Howard Carter's book on *Questions and Answers on Spiritual Gifts*, these three groups can be appropriately labeled: 1) Revelation, 2) Power, and 3) Inspirational Utterance. The quick definitions that would govern these three categories could be stated: 1) gifts that see, 2) gifts that do, and 3) gifts that speak encouragement and comfort.

THE GIFTS OF THE HOLY SPIRIT

"Now concerning spiritual** (spiritual things pertaining to the Holy Spirit) **gifts** (gifts not in Greek text), **brethren, I would not have you ignorant. Now there are diversities of gifts** (Greek Charisma: divine grace operating—favor given as a gift), **but the same Spirit. And there are differences of administrations** (Apostles, Prophets, Evangelists, Pastors, Teachers, Elders, Deacons, All Members of the Church) **but the same Lord. And there are diversities of operations, but it is the same God which worketh all in all. But the manifestation of the Spirit is given to every man to profit withal** (to get the advantage)**. For to one is given by the Spirit [the word of wisdom]; to another [the word of knowledge] by the same Spirit; To another [faith] by the same Spirit; to another [the gifts of healing(s)] by the same Spirit; To another [the working of miracles]; to another [prophecy]; to another [discerning of spirits]; to another [divers kinds of tongues]; to another [the interpretation of tongues]: But all these worketh that one and the selfsame Spirit, dividing to every man severally as he will."

1 Corinthians 12:1,4–11

As you progress further into this study, it would be proper to understand that though many modern language translations call these grace operations *"gifts,"* the actual Greek New Testament doesn't call them *"gifts"* as we understand the term. A proper understanding of these nine grace operations would be better defined as *"spirituals or the things that pertain to and of the Holy Spirit."* Because God freely bestows these *"spirituals,"* therefore we call them gifts. To make this point clearer, a person that is hired by a company will receive a desk, a computer, and maybe a car to use in their accomplishing the duties of their job. Though those things are a blessing and often a sign of favor, they are not really gifts in our traditional definition of the term gift. In the truest sense, they are tools given to get the job done. So, it is with the Holy Spirit. These diverse favors belong to the Spirit of God, and they are added to ministries or manifested at times in our individual lives to accomplish the will of the Lord and to give us the advantage in certain situations of need.

"Through mighty signs and wonders, by the power of the Spirit of God; so that from Jerusalem, and round about unto Illyricum (Albania), I have fully preached the gospel of Christ."

Romans 15:19

Paul so desired that all believers (throughout all generations) would understand the necessity of the power of God and understand the functioning of these grace operations in the church. With all that Paul accomplished in the preaching of the gospel, he prefaced it with these five words, *"Through mighty signs and wonders."* As you study the three revelation gifts, the three power gifts, and the three inspirational gifts, make room in your heart to desire them so that you also will change the world through the power of the Holy Spirit.

REVELATION GIFTS

WORD OF WISDOM
WORD OF KNOWLEDGE
DISCERNING OF SPIRITS

REVELATION GIFT 1

THE WORD OF WISDOM

"For to one is given by the Spirit the word of wisdom."
1 Corinthians 12:8

"The word of wisdom might be defined as a supernatural revelation of the mind and purpose of God communicated by the Holy Spirit."
Howard Carter. Questions and Answers. Page 19

"There is nothing greater than the revelation of the mind and purpose of God. The word of wisdom transports one to the very council chamber of the Almighty and affords a participation, however infinitesimal, in the government of the universe."
Howard Carter. Questions and Answers. Page 36

"In the gift of the word of God's wisdom, God gives forth a small segment or portion of information from His vast storehouse of wisdom. Wisdom has to do with that which is unborn, or of the future. When God gives a word of His wisdom, He is revealing something that has not yet come to pass."
Lester Sumrall. The Gift and Ministries of the Holy Spirit. Page 59

As stated above, the word of wisdom is a supernatural revelation into the mind and purpose of God. This gift in operation is not to be confused with natural wisdom, or wisdom for daily living, as seen in the book of Proverbs. Solomon was greatly blessed with natural wisdom for life and godliness. The gift of the word of wisdom is a revelatory gift given as the Holy Spirit wills. It gives insight into the future or of things that pertain to the will of God. Messianic prophesies in the Old Testament are prime examples of this gift in operation. We also see this gift in operation when the Lord reveals doctrine, whether in the Old or New Testament so that men could know how to live and approach God. The word of wisdom differs from natural wisdom in that a person who receives a word, or a piece of God's purpose or mind, may not always fully understand what was revealed; such was the case when Isaiah the prophet declared that a virgin would conceive and bring forth a son (Isaiah 7:14). When he spoke that word some 700 years before Mary was born, he knew it was from God but had no idea what it meant—or when it would be fulfilled. On the other hand, natural wisdom for daily living, of which we are admonished to seek and ask for, comes from above and is first pure, then peaceful, and easy to put into operation (James 3:17). This type of wisdom helps the one desiring it to make quality decisions. Both are called *"wisdom"* but differ in purpose. Clearly stated, the gift of the word of wisdom operates on a higher level of God's wisdom, manifesting as the Holy Spirit wills. The wisdom for daily living, on the other hand, operates according to man's desire and his searching for it. One operation is God to man, while the other is man to God.

An appropriate example of this gift of foretelling the future is when Peter tells Sapphira that she will die for her actions (Acts 5:9). The word of wisdom revealed—not present tense information, but a prediction of the future. God revealed that Sapphira would be judged with the same judgment that her husband received. Another wonderful example is when Peter was on the housetop receiving a vision (Acts 10:10–19). When the vision was complete, the Holy Spirit revealed the will of God to Peter concerning the cleansing of the Gentiles. With this revelation into New Testament doctrine, the Holy Spirit then gave Peter direction into the will of God, *"go with them."* In my opinion, this gift would be classified as the chief of the nine gifts of the Holy Spirit. Revelation into the will of God and seeing into the future has turned the course of nations and empires without the use of military might, as seen with Joseph in Egypt and Daniel in Babylon. We are commanded to desire this gift.

The references listed below are divided into two parts which show the operations of the Holy Spirit within the boundaries of Israel as well as how He worked outside those boundaries as the gospel went forth to the ends of the earth.

THE WORD OF WISDOM
A DEFINITIVE LOOK

(Jerusalem, Judea, Samaria)

1. **WORD OF WISDOM: Jesus to His disciples**
   Acts 1:5
   "For John truly baptized with water; but ye shall be baptized with the Holy Ghost not many days hence."

   Note: Jesus reveals two fragments or pieces of revelation concerning what is about to happen. First, you will be (*future tense*) baptized in the Holy Spirit. Second, soon! Both John the Baptist and Jesus had been teaching about the promise of the Father, and now Jesus continues to prepare them to receive it. The simple phrase *"you shall be"* is the key phrase that denotes the operation of this gift in this verse. It is also important to note that with this simple word or phrase, Jesus was laying the foundation of New Testament doctrine concerning the Holy Spirit's work in the church. In short, this gift of the Holy Spirit reveals both future events as well as the mind of the Lord pertaining to doctrine.

2. **WORD OF WISDOM: Jesus to His disciples**
   Acts 1:8
   "But ye shall receive power, after that the Holy Ghost is come upon you: and ye shall be witnesses unto me both in Jerusalem, and in all Judaea, and in Samaria, and unto the uttermost part of the earth."

Note: The Lord reveals what it is they are about to receive when the Holy Spirit comes upon them—which is power. The baptism of the Holy Spirit is not to be confused with the Holy Spirit's work in salvation. In salvation, through repentance and faith in Jesus Christ as the Son of God, we receive our adoption into the kingdom of God. The Holy Spirit cleanses us and makes us a temple of His presence, residing within us, confirming our sonship (Romans 8:14–16).

The baptism of the Holy Spirit, mentioned in this passage, is what Jesus received after being baptized by John in the river Jordan. Remember, Jesus, the Word of God made flesh, was in fellowship with the Holy Spirit prior to His ministry baptism. The difference is that when Jesus was baptized in the Holy Spirit, He was released into His earthly ministry. In like manner, Jesus commands His disciples to receive this mantle of power to continue His ministry. The doctrinal word in this revelation is *"upon."* This baptism is one that comes upon, in contrast to the indwelling of the spirit of adoption.

In this passage Jesus reveals that this baptism is one of *"power,"* which also reveals New Testament doctrine concerning the work of the Holy Spirit through the church. Jesus continues to reveal the purpose of this Holy Spirit soaking, *"you will be my witnesses."*

Finally, He lays out the perimeters of their calling, *"Jerusalem, Judea, Samaria, and the ends of the Earth."* This revelation concerning the proclamation of the gospel differed from the Jewish understanding of salvation. To the devout Jew, Jerusalem is at the center or hub, and the nations were to come to her. Not so in the New Testament or church age. With this Holy Spirit baptism, the preaching and witnessing began in Jerusalem and then, from there, proceeded outward to the ends of the earth. Once again, this revelation not only foretold future events but established New Testament doctrine concerning the mission of the church.

3. **WORD OF WISDOM: Angels to disciples**
   Acts 1:11
   "Which also said, Ye men of Galilee, why stand ye gazing up into heaven? this same Jesus, which is taken up from you into heaven, shall so come in like manner as ye have seen him go into heaven."

Note: Here, we see that a word of wisdom (revelation into doctrine or of future events) can be spoken by angels. The disciples watched the Lord being taken up by a cloud and then removed from their sight. In this example, the angels had been instructed to declare to the church the doctrine of the Lord's return. The word was simple, *"He is coming back just as you saw Him go!"* How dramatic it must have been to watch Jesus taken up by a cloud of glory and then to watch Him vanish from sight. Thus, at such an emotional moment, those revelatory words spoken by the angels etched a message of hope concerning the Lord's return into the hearts of those disciples present and into the lives of every believer who was to come. The doctrine of the Lord's return, although declared in the first chapter of the book of Acts, is dealt with more thoroughly in the epistles, especially in the writings of Paul.

4. **WORD OF WISDOM: Peter to the crowd**
   Acts 2:39
   "For the promise is unto you, and to your children, and to all that are afar off, even as many as the Lord our God shall call."

   Note: Peter, through this revelation, was making known to all present that this gift of the Lord's power was to all, even to those who were *"far off."* Unknowingly, Peter was speaking of the Gentiles that would come into the body of Christ. We see the depth of this revelation fully manifest in Acts chapter 10 with the conversion of Cornelius and his household. Thus, making Peter's statement at this point in his life and ministry even more profound.

5. **WORD OF WISDOM: Peter talking about the Church age**
   Acts 3:21
   "Whom the heaven must receive until the times of restitution of all things, which God hath spoken by the mouth of all his holy prophets since the world began."

   Note: Peter once again begins to flow in a word of wisdom pertaining to times and seasons. Even though Peter had heard the Lord declare that He would go away and then return, he did not understand that the restitution of all things while the Lord is in heaven included the Gentiles being saved. Also, the word *"until,"* which deals with the boundaries of times and seasons is key to this revelation.

   "He said unto them, It is not for you to know the times or the seasons, which the Father hath put in his own power."
   Acts 1:7

6. **WORD OF WISDOM: Peter declares that it was sent to the Jews first and then to the nations**
   Acts 3:26
   "Unto you first God, having raised up his Son Jesus, sent him to bless you, in turning away every one of you from his iniquities."

   Note: We know that Peter did not have full revelation at this time concerning the gospel being preached *"first"* to the Jews. It was after Cornelius' conversion and his baptism in the Holy Spirit that Peter and the other apostles understood the mind of God concerning the far-reaching power of salvation. In short, Peter, by revelation, made it clear that it was to the Jews first. Paul, in his epistles, makes this truth clearer (Romans 1:16). Because this operation of revelation comes from the Spirit of God to the spirit of a man, it is possible to speak without your natural mind understanding the fullness of what was spoken. This was obvious in this verse with Peter as it was with Isaiah concerning many of the things he declared.

7. **WORD OF WISDOM: Peter declaring salvation only in Jesus' name**
   Acts 4:12
   "Neither is there salvation in any other: for there is none other name under heaven given among men, whereby we must be saved."

   Note: Only by revelation could Peter preach this sermon. Can you imagine the revelation Moses was receiving from heaven as the Lord wrote the ten commandments into stone tablets? It was no different for Peter as he preached that salvation was only by faith in Jesus' name. The Jews had been sacrificing animals for over a thousand years and now Peter, through the power of the Holy Spirit, was changing a key aspect of the doctrine of forgiveness and cleansing. This truly was a new thing being established by the Lord. Also, it was the power in the name of the Lord that carried God's saving grace to the ends of the earth.

   "And that repentance and remission of sins should be preached in his name among all nations, beginning at Jerusalem."
   Luke 24:47

8. **WORD OF WISDOM: Peter dealing with Sapphira**
   Acts 5:9
   "Then Peter said unto her, How is it that ye have agreed together to tempt the Spirit of the Lord? behold, the feet of them which have buried thy husband are at the door, and shall carry thee out."

   Note: Peter, through this gift of revelation, foretold of a coming event and what it would be. First, Sapphira would be judged, and second, the judgment would be the same as her husband's.

9. **WORD OF WISDOM: The angel gives specific direction to the apostles**
   Acts 5:20
   "Go, stand and speak in the temple to the people all the words of this life."

   Note: The normal response to having broken out of prison is to flee. In this passage, the Lord gives specific orders to the apostles concerning His will, *"Go, stand, and speak in the temple!"* This gift gives revelation for direction into the will and purposes of God.

10. WORD OF WISDOM: An angel speaks to Philip, giving direction
Acts 8:26
"And the angel of the Lord spake unto Philip, saying, Arise, and go toward the south unto the way that goeth down from Jerusalem unto Gaza, which is desert."

Note: In this example, Philip was only given a fragment of information pertaining to the physical direction into the will of God. In this word, Philip was given both the direction (*south*) and which road to travel on. That was all! Once again, the Lord was revealing His will to Philip, though not all His will, just a word of it.

11. WORD OF WISDOM: The Holy Spirit gives Philip more information
Acts 8:29
"Then the Spirit said unto Philip, Go near, and join thyself to this chariot."

Note: Very often, the Lord will only give us an initial word or piece of direction. However much He gives; it is always enough for us to activate our faith towards obedience. Remember, without faith, it is impossible to please God. Then, as we obey, walking in the realm of faith, He gives us more information or direction. In this case, once Philip arrived, the next piece of information was then given. This is a classic example of how the Lord uses this gift in our lives. In short, it is simply a *"word"* or a piece of information that supernaturally points us in the direction of God.

12. WORD OF WISDOM: Jesus gives direction to Paul
Acts 9:6
"And he trembling and astonished said, Lord, what wilt thou have me to do? And the Lord said unto him, Arise, and go into the city, and it shall be told thee what thou must do."

Note: The Lord answers Paul's prayer, *"Arise and go into Damascus."* The Lord raises his expectancy in knowing that while he is in Damascus, it *"shall be"* told him what to do. This gift gives revelation into coming events.

13. WORD OF WISDOM: Ananias receiving direction
Acts 9:11
"And the Lord said unto him, Arise, and go into the street which is called Straight, and inquire in the house of Judas for one called Saul of Tarsus: for, behold, he prayeth,"

Note: A word of wisdom is sometimes just a word. The Lord's will was revealed in this passage by the words, *"Arise and go."* With these words Ananias had enough information to begin moving by faith into the directional will of God. As the Lord was revealing His will, he then, through the word of knowledge, revealed the present tense details needed to find Saul. Many times, the word of wisdom and the word of knowledge work together.

14. **WORD OF WISDOM: Paul receiving revelation of what is going to happen**
    Acts 9:12
    "And hath seen in a vision a man named Ananias coming in, and putting his hand on him, that he might receive his sight."

    Note: Ananias through the operation of the word of knowledge was given information concerning Paul's vision. The simple phrase *"that he might receive his sight"* to Ananias is an operation of the word of knowledge (present tense) but to Paul it is an operation of the word of wisdom (future tense). Through this revelation Paul was given hope for his future.

15. **WORD OF WISDOM: Jesus revealing Paul's future to Ananias**
    Acts 9:15–16
    "But the Lord said unto him, Go thy way: for he is a chosen vessel unto me, to bear my name before the Gentiles, and kings, and the children of Israel: For I will show him how great things he must suffer for my name's sake."

    Note: Ananias is seeing into the future concerning Paul's life and ministry. Also, though not mentioned here, the Lord is revealing to Ananias that He will give Paul the same revelation.

16. **WORD OF WISDOM: The Will of God will be revealed through Peter's preaching**
    Acts 10:6
    "He lodgeth with one Simon a tanner, whose house is by the seaside: he shall tell thee what thou need to do."

    Note: The whole purpose of this vision was to direct Cornelius into the plan of God. This word, or piece of God's wisdom, left Cornelius expectant upon the Lord.

17. **WORD OF WISDOM: Peter receives New Testament doctrine**
    Acts 10:15
    "And the voice spake unto him again the second time, What God hath cleansed, that call not thou common."

    Acts 10:28
    "And he said unto them, Ye know how that it is an unlawful thing for a man that is a Jew to keep company, or come unto one of another nation;

but God hath showed me that I should not call any man common or unclean."

Note: Up until this time, the gospel had only been preached to the Jews and Samaritans. The Jerusalem, Judea, and Samaria part of the Lord's commission was being fulfilled. Now, through this vision, the Lord reveals doctrine to Peter pertaining to the cleansing of the Gentiles. The key phrase is found in verse 28, *"God hath showed me."*

18. **WORD OF WISDOM: Peter receives direction to go with these unknown men**
    Acts 10:20
    "Arise therefore, and get thee down, and go with them, doubting nothing: for I have sent them."

    Note: This word of revelation gives insight into the direction of God's will. The simple phrase *"Go with them"* was the direction of God's will. With this revelation, Peter was expected to obey, moving forward in faith. (For further study, reference the gift of faith in this passage)

19. **WORD OF WISDOM: Agabus foretells of a famine**
    Acts 11:28–29
    "And there stood up one of them named Agabus, and signified by the Spirit that there should be great famine throughout all the world: which came to pass in the days of Claudius Caesar. Then the disciples, every man—according to his ability, determined to send relief unto the brethren which dwelt in Judea."

    Note: Jesus taught His disciples that one aspect of the Holy Spirit's ministry would show them things to come (John 16:13). Agabus was a prophet, or a seer. He was used by God in revelation gifts to help the church navigate through coming events. In this case, the Lord revealed a coming famine. The result of the manifestation of this gift enabled believers around the region to mobilize the first humanitarian outreach. Since this event, Christians have led the way globally in reaching out to help lift the burdens of man's need by the love of Christ.

(To the Uttermost Parts of the Earth)

20. **WORD OF WISDOM: Prophets in Antioch speaking to Paul and Barnabas**
    Acts 13:2
    "As they ministered to the Lord, and fasted, the Holy Ghost said, Separate me Barnabas and Saul for the work whereunto I have called them."

Note: The Holy Spirit revealed purpose and direction. The word *"separate me"* is a very strong command. Their duties in Antioch had come to an end, and a new direction was unfolding. This direction from the Lord would require complete focus and reliance upon the Lord who was charting their destiny into Gentile lands—opening a new chapter in church history.

21. WORD OF WISDOM: Paul tells Elymas that the judgment is for a season

Acts 13:11

"And now, behold, the hand of the Lord is upon thee, and thou shalt be blind, not seeing the sun for a season. And immediately there fell on him a mist and a darkness; and he went about seeking some to lead him by the hand."

Note: Paul, through the word of wisdom, reveals to Elymas that the judgment was for a season and thus would end. This word of wisdom not only demonstrates that there is no God like Jehovah who controls the future, but it also gave Elymas hope that the judgment would end. Thus, God gave Elymas an opportunity to mend his ways. Remember Saul (Paul) in a similar situation repented!

22. WORD OF WISDOM: The Lord to Paul and Barnabas

Acts 13:47

"For so hath the Lord commanded us, saying, I have set thee to be a light of the Gentiles, that thou shouldest be for salvation unto the ends of the earth."

Note: This is an Old Testament word of wisdom fulfilled in Jesus (Isaiah 49:6). Fulfilled in Christ, it became a present tense operation of the will of God for Paul and Barnabas concerning their future ministry. Therefore, it is a word of wisdom in operation for them. Very often, we receive similar words of encouragement or even words of direction from the Holy Spirit when reading the Bible. Words that were spoken concerning a different time can become present tense direction and inspiration to us by the Holy Spirit. There is no book like the Bible that continually speaks.

23. WORD OF WISDOM: Paul receiving direction of where not to go

Acts 16:6

"Now when they had gone throughout Phrygia and the region of Galatia, and were forbidden of the Holy Ghost to preach the word in Asia,"

Note: Here, we see this operation of revelation work in a different manner. Jesus had commanded His disciples to go into *"all"* the world and preach the gospel. As Paul endeavored to go into Asia, the Holy Spirit forbade them—blocking their direction. This revelation gave them new direction by knowing *"where not"* to go. Remember, the word of wisdom is sometimes only a word; and sometimes the word is *"no."*

24. WORD OF WISDOM: Direction of where not to go

Acts 16:7

"After they were come to Mysia, they assayed to go into Bithynia: but the Spirit suffered them not."

Note: Once again, there are times when a simple word *"no"* concerning direction is an example of this gift. The word no in this verse is revelation. There are times by knowing what the will of the Lord is not, that we receive encouragement to press forward, seeking out His will with a confidence that He will show us. That is why this word *"no"* is full of Holy Spirit ability.

25. WORD OF WISDOM: Paul's Macedonian call

Acts 16:10

"And after he had seen the vision, immediately we endeavored to go into Macedonia, assuredly gathering that the Lord had called us for to preach the gospel unto them."

Note: Spiritual visions, dreams, and trances are often used as tools to release revelation into the will of God. This is a great example of the discerning of spirits and the word of wisdom working together.

26. WORD OF WISDOM: The Lord speaks to Paul about His people in the city

Acts 18:9–10

"Then spake the Lord to Paul in the night by a vision, Be not afraid, but speak, and hold not thy peace: For I am with thee, and no man shall set on thee to hurt thee: for I have much people in this city."

Note: In this passage, we see the Lord revealing to Paul His will concerning staying in Corinth and not being afraid to speak. The Lord needed Paul to build the church there, and therefore He had to speak very clearly to him. The Lord commanded him to *"speak."* Paul knew that when he opened his mouth, persecution usually followed. Because of the continual threat of persecution and death, the Lord had to step in and supernaturally give him revelation into his calling to build the church there. In this, the Lord tells Paul that no harm would come to him in Corinth. In this chapter of Acts, the townspeople did take hold of Paul as if to harm him, but Jesus, through this gift, had already revealed (future tense) that the final outcome would be his safety. In the end, no harm came to Paul—just as Jesus said.

27. WORD OF WISDOM: Paul reveals his direction from the Lord
Acts 19:21
"After these things were ended, Paul purposed in the spirit, when he had passed through Macedonia and Achaia, to go to Jerusalem, saying, After I have been there, I must also see Rome."

Note: Paul had received revelation concerning his direction. There had been much persecution of the Jews in Rome, and the desire to go there could only have come from the Lord.

28. WORD OF WISDOM: Paul speaking about future persecution
Acts 20:23
"Save that the Holy Ghost witnesseth in every city, saying that bonds and afflictions abide me."

Note: The Holy Spirit continually reminded Paul of what lay before him. In this case, persecution was continually a part of Paul's life and ministry. I am sure that Paul never forgot the Christians he imprisoned, even consenting to the death of some. He also never forgot the power of Jesus' face that burnt his eyes on the road to Damascus. These two memories were at the core of God's grace that enabled Paul to endure.

"Are they ministers of Christ? I (speak as a fool) I am more; in labors more abundant, in stripes above measure, in prisons more frequent, in deaths oft. Of the Jews five times received I forty stripes save one. Thrice was I beaten with rods, once was I stoned, thrice I suffered shipwreck, a night and a day I have been in the deep; In journeyings often, in perils of waters, in perils of robbers, in perils by mine own countrymen, in perils by the heathen, in perils in the city, in perils in the wilderness, in perils in the sea, in perils among false brethren; In weariness and painfulness, in watchings often, in hunger and thirst, in fastings often, in cold and nakedness. Beside those things that are without, that which cometh upon me daily, the care of all the churches."
2 Corinthians 11:23–28

29. WORD OF WISDOM: Paul to the disciples
Acts 20:25
"And now, behold, I know that ye all, among whom I have gone preaching the kingdom of God, shall see my face no more."

Note: Paul, through revelation, states that this would be their final meeting together. Such loving affection was released in those moments that most assuredly, the memory of it was carried with Paul for the rest of his days on earth.

30. WORD OF WISDOM: Paul warns the church of what will come
Acts 20:29–30
"For I know this, that after my departing shall grievous wolves enter in among you, not sparing the flock. Also of your own selves shall men arise, speaking perverse things, to draw away disciples after them."

Note: The Holy Spirit, through Paul, was revealing what was going to happen to the church in Ephesus after his departure. The purpose of this revelation was to exhort them to be diligent in protecting the work there. In reading the book of Revelation, the Lord commends the Ephesian church for being fervent in proving those who said they were apostles, thus knowing those who were not. They took seriously Paul's warnings. Of course, they ultimately failed in their first love for the Lord. This is a warning to us all. We were never called to place the business of church over our deep love of the Lord. This is illustrated clearly with the powerful Ephesian church, which by the way, does not exist today—just as the Lord said.

31. WORD OF WISDOM: Disciples warn Paul
Acts 21:4
"And finding disciples, we tarried there seven days: who said to Paul through the Spirit, that he should not go up to Jerusalem."

Note: Paul knew by the Holy Spirit that he was to go to Jerusalem. But in this passage, the disciples, by the same Holy Spirit, warn Paul not to go to Jerusalem. The Holy Spirit was fine-tuning Paul's direction. In analyzing this, you realize that timing was of the essence. Though the Holy Spirit was directing Paul towards Jerusalem, there were other things that needed to happen first. Therefore, Paul diverted to the house of Philip the evangelist. The Lord clearly wanted to slow Paul down to minister to him before he entered Jerusalem. The encouragement Paul received at the house of Philip came through people, which stresses the importance of fellowship. This special time at the house of Philip marked an end of Paul's ministry as a free man. Paul was entering the final stage of his ministry, which ultimately would plant the Christian base of apostolic authority into Europe, where he would give his life as a martyr in Rome.

32. WORD OF WISDOM: Agabus to Paul
Acts 21:10–11
"And as we tarried there many days, there came down from Judaea a certain prophet, named Agabus. And when he was come unto us, he took Paul's girdle, and bound his own hands and feet, and said, Thus saith the Holy Ghost, So shall the Jews at Jerusalem bind the man that owneth this girdle, and shall deliver him into the hands of the Gentiles."

Note: Here, we see a very important piece of revelation given by the Holy Spirit through the prophet Agabus. Paul knew that persecutions awaited him in every city where he would go and preach. But in this passage, the Holy Spirit reveals to those present that Paul would be taken by the Jews. Then, the last piece of revelation was that after the Jews bound him, he would be handed over to Rome. For further understanding, reference Acts 20:22, *"And now, behold, I go bound in the spirit unto Jerusalem, not knowing the things that shall befall me there."* Paul knew that persecutions (in general) awaited him, but in verse 22, he makes it clear that he does not specifically know what will happen in Jerusalem. Therefore, in this passage, Agabus, as a prophet, revealed by a word of wisdom what would happen in Jerusalem. As it was revealed, it came to pass that when the Roman captain in Jerusalem took Paul from the Jews, he was never free again (Acts 21:33).

33. WORD OF WISDOM: Direction to get out of Jerusalem
Acts 22:18
"And saw him saying unto me, Make haste, and get thee quickly out of Jerusalem: for they will not receive thy testimony concerning me."

Note: In this passage, Paul gives us more information concerning his first visit to Jerusalem after his conversion. In this revelation, Paul learns through a word of knowledge that his testimony will not be received—no matter how powerful it is. Then the word of wisdom reveals direction for him to leave Jerusalem quickly.

34. WORD OF WISDOM: Jesus reveals to Paul his calling to nations
Acts 22:21
"And he said unto me, Depart: for I will send thee far hence unto the Gentiles."

Note: Paul receives revelation that his calling is to the Gentiles. Here we have a Jew of Jews, a Pharisee of Pharisees, receiving revelation that his calling is to bring the Gentiles into Christ. One keyword in this revelation is the word *"far."* His call of God was going to touch the Gentiles—far and wide. Ultimately, through his epistles, he has touched the entire world—generation after generation. Paul's calling was to fulfill what Jesus spoke in the Gospel of John.

> *"And other sheep I have, which are not of this fold: them also I must bring, and they shall hear my voice; and there shall be one fold, and one shepherd."*
> *John 10:16*

35. WORD OF WISDOM: The Lord reveals Paul's destiny concerning Rome

Acts 23:11

"And the night following the Lord stood by him, and said, Be of good cheer, Paul: for as thou hast testified of me in Jerusalem, so must thou bear witness also at Rome."

Note: The Lord reveals direction to Paul. Paul had been through much, and the Lord came close to him, strengthening his heart and reminding him of the will of God for his life.

36. WORD OF WISDOM: Jesus to Paul

Acts 26:16–18

"But rise, and stand upon thy feet: for I have appeared unto thee for this purpose, to make thee a minister and a witness both of these things which thou hast seen, and of those things in the which I will appear unto thee; Delivering thee from the people, and from the Gentiles, unto whom now I send thee, To open their eyes, and to turn them from darkness to light, and from the power of Satan unto God, that they may receive forgiveness of sins, and inheritance among them which are sanctified by faith that is in me."

Note: Paul gives more detail concerning what the Lord revealed to him during his conversion experience in Acts chapter nine. The Lord quotes Isaiah 42:6 as Paul's calling (future tense) to the Gentiles.

37. WORD OF WISDOM: Paul to the owner and Centurion

Acts 27:10

"And said unto them, Sirs, I perceive that this voyage will be with hurt and much damage, not only of the lading and ship, but also of our lives."

Note: It was God's will for Paul to go to Rome. Direction into the will of God does not mean that there will not be dangerous obstacles along the way. Paul was sensitive to the big picture direction and to the steps needed to fulfill the plan. In this case, Paul was a prisoner in the hands of Rome and had to submit to Rome's commands. Though Paul, through this gift of revelation, warned them not to leave the Fair Havens, he had no authority to stop them. Therefore, the Lord, in His mercy (through the operation of the gift of faith), protects Paul in the storm—as well as all other travelers onboard.

38. WORD OF WISDOM: Paul exhorts the people with hope concerning their near future
Acts 27:22
"And now I exhort you to be of good cheer: for there shall be no loss of any man's life among you, but of the ship."

Acts 27:24
"Saying, Fear not, Paul; thou must be brought before Caesar: and, lo, God hath given thee all them that sail with thee."

Acts 27:26
"Howbeit we must be cast upon a certain island."

Note: Here, we see several pieces of revelation given to Paul concerning the lives of those onboard and concerning his calling to stand before Caesar. This is the first time where it is revealed to Paul that the purpose of his calling to Rome is to stand before Caesar. Up until this point, it has been about going to Rome. Paul also reveals that they will wash up on a certain island.

39. WORD OF WISDOM: Paul to the Centurion
Acts 27:31
"Paul said to the centurion and to the soldiers, Except these abide in the ship, ye cannot be saved."

Note: At the beginning of the voyage, Paul warns the owner and the centurion not to continue because of certain dangers. Because Paul was a prisoner, he was ignored. Now in this passage, as certain members of the crew were planning their escape, Paul reveals more information directly to the centurion, *"if they go, you cannot be saved."* The Holy Spirit, through Paul, was giving this stern decree and warning due to the centurion's earlier decision to disregard Paul's warning. Through the gifts of the Holy Spirit, God had given Rome into the hands of Paul. Now, this sea-soaked apostle was giving the orders. The earth is a place of life and death. How many storms could have been avoided if only we had perceived and not merely supposed? Paul was called by God to stand before Caesar, and that boat was a part of his calling.

40. WORD OF WISDOM: Paul declares that the Gentiles will hear (receive) the gospel
Acts 28:28
"Be it known therefore unto you, that the salvation of God is sent unto the Gentiles, and that they will hear it."

Note: Paul, through the word of wisdom, speaks concerning the future of the church in the hands of the Gentiles. Once again, this operation of revelation into the future is called a word of wisdom. In this passage, Paul declares one simple truth, *"they will hear it."* The first gift of the Holy Spirit manifested in the book of Acts was the word of wisdom. The last gift to be manifested in the book of Acts was also the word of wisdom. These two facts help this student of the Bible believe that the greatest of the gifts of the Holy Spirit is this gift—the word of wisdom.

REVELATION GIFT 2

THE WORD OF KNOWLEDGE

"To another the word of knowledge by the same Spirit."
1 Corinthians 12:8

"The word of knowledge is a supernatural revelation of the existence, or nature, of a person or a thing, or the knowledge of some event, given to us by the Holy Spirit for a specific purpose...Through this gift has been revealed the creation of the world, and the forming of man from the dust of the earth."
Howard Carter. Questions and Answers. Page 39, 55

"The gift of the word of knowledge is when God reveals to one of His servants something that now exists or did exist on the earth. Knowledge is a fact—a reality."
Lester Sumrall. The Gifts of the Holy Spirit Study Guide. Page 49

The word of knowledge is a supernatural revelation concerning facts, details, or events in either the present or past tense. The books of Genesis, Job, as well as the gospels, are examples of books written through the operation of this gift. Only the Holy Spirit could give such precise detail of the creation of the world as described in the first chapter of the Bible. Only through this gift could the writer of Genesis describe genealogies of the first families as well as life on this planet before Noah built the ark. The word of knowledge does not reveal the future to any degree. In contrast, the prophetic books of the Old Testament were written through the operation of the word of wisdom.

An appropriate example of the word of knowledge is when Peter revealed before the congregation that Ananias had kept back *"part"* of the price. Peter did not know how much Ananias sold his property for—nor did he care. As Ananias brought his offering before the Lord and stood before Peter, the Holy Spirit revealed the truth about the sale of the property—which exposed the lie. Another New Testament example of this gift is when Peter, while on the housetop, is told that three men were seeking him. Peter was caught up in a wonderful spiritual experience and was not interested in any other thing. While caught up in this glorious experience, the Holy Spirit interrupted him and revealed that men were at the door seeking him. This little piece of information is a true operation of the word of knowledge.

THE WORD OF KNOWLEDGE
A DEFINITIVE LOOK

(Jerusalem, Judea, Samaria)

1. **WORD OF KNOWLEDGE: Peter dealing with Ananias**
   Acts 5:3–4
   "But Peter said, Ananias, why hath Satan filled thine heart to lie to the Holy Ghost, and to keep back part of the price of the land?
   While it remained, was it not thine own? and after it was sold, was it not in thine own power? why hast thou conceived this thing in thine heart? thou hast not lied unto men, but unto God."

   Note: As we draw close to the Lord, He draws close to us. When dross comes near fire, the fire will begin to purge it. In this example, these two wealthy people were seeking more than the Lord that Sunday. It seems they were seeking prominence in the eyes of the congregation, otherwise known as self-promotion. This self-promotion was wrapped in a lie—though hidden from man's eyes, it was completely exposed to the omniscience of God. Through the word of knowledge, Peter knew that what Ananias had promised was different from what was being presented—thus making their approach to the altar that day unclean. The congregation also learned that offerings were holy. As Aaron's sons died before the presence of the Lord in the Old Testament, even so with Ananias and his wife in the New Testament—the altar of the Lord is holy (Leviticus 10:1,2).

2. **WORD OF KNOWLEDGE: Peter speaks of the young men returning**
   Acts 5:9
   "Then Peter said unto her, How is it that ye have agreed together to tempt the Spirit of the Lord? behold, the feet of them which have buried thy husband are at the door, and shall carry thee out."

   Note: Peter is inside the building, and the Holy Spirit reveals that the young men are about to enter. Peter was caught up in the glory of the Lord and had no way in the natural to see who was approaching the door. This simple word of knowledge brought a further depth of God's holiness upon the people. With God, all things are known!

3. **WORD OF KNOWLEDGE: Jesus to Ananias**
   Acts 9:11–12
   "And the Lord said unto him, Arise, and go into the street which is called Straight, and inquire in the house of Judas for one called Saul, of Tarsus: for, behold, he prayeth, And hath seen in a vision a man named Ananias coming in, and putting his hand on him, that he might receive his sight."

Note: This passage is a wonderful example of the word of knowledge. Here the Lord reveals the name of the street, the name of the owner of the house, who is in the house, and what Saul is doing. The Lord also reveals to Ananias that Paul is having a vision. It always amazes me that God chose to use a simple Christian man to pray for Paul and not an apostle from Jerusalem. In this operation, we see the power of the new creation in Christ that makes all believers, such as Ananias, able ministers of the gospel.

4. **WORD OF KNOWLEDGE: Paul is given Ananias' name**
   Acts 9:12
   "And hath seen in a vision a man named Ananias coming in, and putting his hand on him, that he might receive his sight."

   Note: In this passage Ananias, through the word of knowledge, is given (present tense) information about what is happening with Paul (Saul). Through the word of knowledge, it is revealed that Paul, through the manifestation of the discerning of spirits, is having a vision, and in that vision, he is receiving information concerning the future. Slowly meditate on this! This is one of the greatest examples of all three revelation gifts working together. In closing, the Lord felt the need to reveal to Ananias Paul's vision. It must have been somewhat of a relief for Ananias to know that Paul has seen him in a vision and already knows his name.

5. **WORD OF KNOWLEDGE: Angel speaking to Cornelius**
   Acts 10:5–6
   "And now send men to Joppa, and call for one Simon, whose surname is Peter: He lodgeth with one Simon a tanner, whose house is by the sea side: he shall tell thee what thou oughtest to do."

   Note: In this passage the angel reveals the name of the town and Simon's name, even his surname Peter. The angel also reveals the house, who owns the house and where it is located. The word of knowledge simply reveals past or present tense information. In many cases this gift operates through the ministry of angels. Remember, angels are servants of the Lord who also operate in the power of the Holy Spirit. The difference is that they come directly from the throne of God which makes them mighty. But we are the children of God, which in the future makes us even mightier.

   "Are they not all ministering spirits, sent forth to minister for them who shall be heirs of salvation?"
   Hebrews 1:14

6. **WORD OF KNOWLEDGE: Peter about Cornelius' men**
   Acts 10:19
   "While Peter thought on the vision, the Spirit said unto him, Behold, three men seek thee."

Note: Peter was up on the roof having a spiritual experience and was not attending to who was knocking at the door. He did not care about what was happening downstairs. The Holy Spirit interrupted him and revealed that *"three"* men were seeking him.

7. **WORD OF KNOWLEDGE: An angel removes a king**
   Acts 12:23
   "And immediately the angel of the Lord smote him, because he gave not God the glory: and he was eaten of worms and gave up the ghost."

   Note: In this occurrence, we would assume that the writer of the book of Acts was not physically present at Herod's judgment. Most likely, the people present did not see the angel either. The Bible is a book given by inspirational revelation, and in this case, Luke, the writer of the book of Acts, was given an extra piece of information concerning the administration of Herod's judgment.

(To the Uttermost Parts of the Earth)

8. **WORD OF KNOWLEDGE: Paul pleads with the jailor**
   Acts 16:28
   "But Paul cried with a loud voice, saying, do thyself no harm: for we are all here."

   Note: When the power of God fell upon the jail, no one moved from their dark cells. It was by revelation that Paul pleaded with the jailor to not kill himself. God was fishing for the soul of a man. The bait was an earthquake that shook not only the prison but the jailor himself. Also, note, the jailor called for a light because of the darkness, thus reinforcing Paul's knowing (supernaturally) to plead with the man to not kill himself.

9. **WORD OF KNOWLEDGE: The Lord speaks to Paul about His people in the city**
   Acts 18:9–10
   "Then spake the Lord to Paul in the night by a vision, Be not afraid, but speak, and hold not thy peace: For I am with thee, and no man shall set on thee to hurt thee: for I have much people in this city."

   Note: Jesus revealed to Paul that He had *"many"* followers in Corinth. This word was a piece of information that Paul did not know. This account reminds me of when the Lord revealed to Elijah that He had reserved seven thousand in Israel who had not bowed their knees to Baal. If the Lord knows the number of hairs on the head of one of His children, then how much more does He know the number of His servants on the earth and where they are located. This piece of revelation comforted Paul's heart.

10. WORD OF KNOWLEDGE: Heart attitudes

Acts 22:18

"And saw him saying unto me, Make haste, and get thee quickly out of Jerusalem: for they will not receive thy testimony concerning me."

Note: Paul, in relating his testimony, gives information that is not mentioned earlier. In this example, the Holy Spirit revealed that Jerusalem's religious leaders would not at that time receive Paul's testimony of the Lord. This is a tremendous and needed revelation for Paul to know. Paul probably thought that his new testimony of Jesus as well as the dynamic way it happened would change things in Jerusalem. The Lord needed to correct Paul's thinking. Therefore, the Lord gave him much-needed information. The religious leaders had seen Jesus' face and still rejected Him. How much more would they reject Paul, who testified that he had seen the Lord. In short, the Lord was giving Paul information concerning the present tense attitude of their hearts.

11. WORD OF KNOWLEDGE: Sailors about to flee

Acts 27:30–31

"And as the shipmen were about to flee out of the ship, when they had let down the boat into the sea, under colour as though they would have cast anchors out of the foreship, Paul said to the centurion and to the soldiers, Except these abide in the ship, ye cannot be saved."

Note: This is the last example of the word of knowledge in the book of Acts. The sailors were afraid and decided to deceptively depart. Paul, not being a sailor, would not have been able to discern what certain crew members were doing. The Holy Spirit revealed to Paul what was happening and the reality of their demise if they were free to proceed.

REVELATION GIFT 3

THE DISCERNING OF SPIRITS

"To another discerning of spirits"
1 Corinthians 12:10

"The discerning of spirits is a gift of the Holy Spirit by which the possessor is enabled to see into the spirit world. By this insight he can discern the similitude of God, or of the risen Christ, or the Holy Spirit, or cherubim, seraphim, archangels or the hosts of angels, or Satan and his legions."
Howard Carter. Questions and Answers. Page 146

"The discerning of spirits gives members of the body of Christ insight into the spirit world, a realm that their five physical senses–feeling, hearing, seeing, smelling, tasting cannot enter. The telescope can reveal the amazing stars in space. The microscope can bring to light the intricate mysteries of microscopic life. But it takes the gift of discerning of spirits to penetrate to the dividing of soul and spirit within a person."
Lester Sumrall. The Gifts and Ministries of the Holy Spirit. Page 76–77

The discerning of spirits gives revelation into spiritual operations. In short, this gift is a *"seeing"* gift and, in many cases, operates through visions, dreams, or trances. In some situations, the Holy Spirit uses this gift to reveal spiritual influences in a human heart. Jesus saw into Nathaniel's heart (John 1:47). Peter saw into Ananias' heart (Acts 5:3). Nathaniel had no guile, while Ananias had the obscurity of Satan. New Testament examples of this gift in operation would be when Jesus looked at Peter and rebuked Satan (Matthew 16:23). Peter, in a similar situation, discerned that Simon, who once worked as a magician, was yielding to Satan out of a root of bitterness. Peter had no way of knowing this through his natural senses. The Holy Spirit showed him (Peter) Simon's heart. Another example is found when Stephen looked up and saw into heaven. Remember, this gift is a seeing gift. Stephen, in this operation, declared that he saw the Lord standing at the right hand of God. The discerning of spirits opened Stephen's eyes to see what the natural eye could never see. Remember, the distance is far too great, and heaven is in another realm. Though this gift carries a diversity of purpose, it most likely is the key gift given by the Holy Spirit to help keep the church clean morally and its doctrine strong spiritually.

My final thought pertains to the church in Ephesus and this gift. Before Paul left the Ephesian believers in Acts 20:29, he warned them of wolves who would endeavor to come into the church to devour the flock. He was preparing them to stand guard and fight for the church. In Revelation chapter two, Jesus commends the Ephesian church for its stance against false apostles—yes, the very ones that Paul saw coming. I cannot believe that their success in keeping these wicked people out of the church was without the assistance of this seeing gift called the discerning of spirits.

THE DISCERNING OF SPIRITS
A DEFINITIVE LOOK

(Jerusalem, Judea, Samaria)

1. **DISCERNING OF SPIRITS: Peter dealing with Ananias**
   Acts 5:3
   "But Peter said, Ananias, why hath Satan filled thine heart to lie to the Holy Ghost, and to keep back part of the price of the land?"

   Note: Here, we see the discerning of spirits in operation. The Holy Spirit revealed to Peter that Ananias was yielding to demonic council. Ananias' greed opened a door for Satan to fill his heart. This gift in operation opened the spiritual eyes of Peter to see what was working in Ananias' spirit. We understand through this passage how important this gift is to the body of Christ. As Ananias approached the altar of blessing, he, in fact, was exalting himself through deception and greed. The Bible teaches that as we draw near to God, He draws near to us. In this case, Ananias was drawing close to the Almighty, who is a fire from His loins up and a fire from His loins down (Ezekiel 8:2, Hebrews 12:2). Therefore, holy fire was drawing close to Ananias as he approached the altar where Peter was standing (James 4:8).

   The Bible makes this point further in that *"great grace"* was upon them all. This great grace was the manifest glory of the Lord. No person present knew what Ananias was doing except the Holy Spirit. This portion of scripture reveals the subtlety of how Satan works against the local congregation to keep it from rising in the glory of God—which ultimately is to be a light to the local community. It is these hidden operations of evil that affect the local church and its leaders, bringing them into a place of weakness, thus covering their light with a bushel (Matthew 5:15). This gift, manifesting through Peter that day, helped deliver the local church from satanic obscurity operating in the hearts of two congregational members.

2. **DISCERNING OF SPIRITS: Stephen looking up into Heaven**
   Acts 7:55–56
   "But he, being full of the Holy Ghost, looked up stedfastly into heaven, and saw the glory of God, and Jesus standing on the right hand of God, And said, Behold, I see the heavens opened, and the Son of man standing on the right hand of God."

   Note: Gifts of revelation reveal something. These revelatory operations of the Holy Spirit are like taking the lid off a jar to see into it. The word of wisdom reveals insight into the will of God, the plan of God, or a coming event. The word of knowledge reveals informational knowledge of things

DISCERNING OF SPIRITS

past or present. The discerning of spirits reveals or *"takes the lid off"* the spirit realm, thus allowing the recipient to see something that cannot be seen by the natural eye or the eye of natural reasoning. In this example, Stephen sees a spiritual vision of heaven and Jesus standing at the right hand of God. The key phrase is, *"I see."* Because this is a spiritual operation, there is no limit on physical distance. Stephen was seeing into heaven, which is too far for the natural eye to see, not to mention it is in another realm. This gift is a unique operation of the Holy Spirit. To further explain this truth, we will need to look at 2 Kings 5:26, when the prophet Elisha said, *"Did not my heart go with you?"* Elisha knew that Gehazi had gone after Naaman to take his gifts—which had been denied moments before by the prophet. This is not a word of knowledge because Elisha talks about seeing it happen rather than knowing it is happening. Just as Stephen saw into heaven, Elisha saw the whole transaction between Naaman and Gehazi. Both the word of knowledge and the discerning of spirits are revelation gifts and can accomplish, *in certain cases,* the same result. The difference is how they operate.

3. **DISCERNING OF SPIRITS: Peter to Simon**
   Acts 8:23
   "For I perceive that thou art in the gall of bitterness, and in the bond of iniquity."

Note: Peter, through the gift of the discerning of spirits sees into Simon's heart. The Holy Spirit revealed the root of bitterness operating in Simon and how it was bringing him into iniquity. It appears that Simon humbled himself after this encounter. It is correct to note that in many cases, the gifts of the Holy Spirit, when manifested, bring the fear of the Lord upon cities, congregations, and individuals.

The fear of the Lord is one of the seven spirits of the Lord that stand before the throne of God (Isaiah 11:2, Revelation 4:5, 5:6). These seven spirits of Jehovah are the eyes of the Lord that are sent into the earth to show Himself strong on behalf of those who fear the Lord (2 Chronicles 16:9). In the gospels we see this same holy presence of reverential awe come upon many through the ministry of Jesus.

Through this gift and the corresponding rebuke from Peter, the fear of the Lord fell on Simon. It is also proper to note the measure of authority Peter walked in, as well as this gift of the discerning of spirits that operated through him. Philip had healings and miracles working in his ministry, but Philip was not a chief apostle who had been given charge to watch and care over the church of the living God. The gift of the working of miracles (which operates in power) is not the same as the authority to care for (feeding) and to watch over (guarding) the body of Christ. Remember, Stephen was full of faith and power, but his job in the church was to feed widows. There is great need for further teaching on the word *power,* which is the Greek word *dunamis*, in contrast to the word *authority*, which is the Greek word *exousia*. There is a difference between the two, and it is important to discern the operation of both.

On many occasions, I have been aware of these two principles in operation during an anointed time of congregational worship. The difference is discerned as the pastor or leader of the meeting walks up into the pulpit. As the leader stands before the congregation, there should be a deepening in the presence of God due to the Lord's authority upon the pastor—an authority that the worship leader is rarely given unless he or she stands before the Lord as one of the five governing anointings found in Ephesians 4:11. Worship leaders can be very anointed, but they are not given the authority to watch over and govern the local assembly. Many anointed helpers have fallen prey to the wicked one by not understanding their position of ministry before the Lord's presence. Simply put, do what the Lord has asked you to do and be thankful.

4. **DISCERNING OF SPIRITS: Philip has a vision of an angel**
Acts 8:26
"And <u>the angel of the Lord spake unto Philip</u>, saying, Arise, and go toward the south unto the way that goeth down from Jerusalem unto Gaza, which is desert."

Note: There are occasions in the Bible when the angel of the Lord was physically manifested, as in the case with Elijah. Elijah was tired, depressed, and wanting to die. The Lord sent an angel to minister to him by cooking him a meal (1 Kings 19:5–8). In Elijah's case, no discerning of spirits was necessary. In this account with Philip, the Bible does not give clarity on whether the angel was manifested through a vision or if he was physically present. I took the liberty to include Philip's discerning him as an operation of this gift. The reason I included this was to stir the holy imagination of the student to think and pray and to reach their own conclusion. If the angel came to Philip through a vision or dream, then this gift of *"seeing"* would have been necessary. The third option is that the writer of the book of Acts (Luke), through a word of knowledge, knew that it was an angel—meaning that Philip only heard (spiritually received) the angel's command—a command which came to Philip under the anointing of the Holy Spirit. Slowly meditate!

5. **DISCERNING OF SPIRITS: Paul sees Jesus**
Acts 9:3–5
"And as he journeyed, he came near Damascus: and suddenly there shined round about him a light from heaven: And he fell to the earth, and heard a voice saying unto him, Saul, Saul, why persecutest thou me? And he said, Who art thou, Lord? And the Lord said, <u>I am Jesus</u> whom thou persecutest: it is hard for thee to kick against the pricks."

Note: As the glory of the Lord fell upon Paul's traveling band of persecutors, they all found themselves on the ground before the Lord. They all saw the light, they all fell, they all heard the initial voice that said, *"Saul, Saul, why persecutes thou me?"* But only Paul saw the Lord and heard His voice. The difference between what Paul's friends experienced and what Paul experienced came through the operation of the discerning of spirits. Paul saw Jesus and heard Jesus—his associates did not!

6. **DISCERNING OF SPIRITS: Ananias has a vision**
   Acts 9:10
   "And there was a certain disciple at Damascus, named Ananias; and to him said the Lord in a vision, Ananias. And he said, Behold, I am here, Lord."

   Note: A vision from the Lord is an operation of this gift.

7. **DISCERNING OF SPIRITS: Paul seeing a vision**
   Acts 9:11–12
   "And hath seen in a vision a man named Ananias coming in, and putting his hand on him, that he might receive his sight."

   Note: Paul, while in Damascus, had a vision of Ananias coming to him and praying for him (both the discerning of spirits and the word of wisdom working together). Remember, the discerning of spirits is a *"seeing"* gift of revelation that operates in visions. The interesting note is that Ananias (in real-time) was receiving a word of knowledge concerning Paul having a vision that included him (Ananias) coming to minister to Paul. Amazing! (Slowly meditate)

8. **DISCERNING OF SPIRITS: Cornelius' vision of an angel**
   Acts 10:3
   "He saw in a vision evidently about the ninth hour of the day an angel of God coming to him, and saying unto him, Cornelius."

   Note: This gift is an operation that sees. The key to this verse is found in the words *"he saw in a vision."* All visions from the Lord operate by this gift. This is the first noted operation of a gift of the Holy Spirit coming upon a Gentile in the book of Acts. The word of wisdom operating with the discerning of spirits has done more to change nations and the course of history than we will ever know. The hearts of kings and military leaders are in the hand of the Lord, and many times these two gifts are used to direct these men of earthly authority into the plans and purposes of God.

9. DISCERNING OF SPIRITS: Peter on the rooftop
Acts 10:10,11
"And he became very hungry, and would have eaten: but while they made ready, he fell into a trance, And saw heaven opened, and a certain vessel descending unto him, as it had been a great sheet knit at the four corners, and let down to the earth:"

Note: Once again, a trance or a vision is an operation of this gift. It is also important to note the words *"saw heaven opened."* The gift of the discerning of spirits is a seeing gift. Peter and the apostles were so engrained in Jewish thinking that the Lord had to use a trance to break down the walls of religious and culturally wrong thinking so that salvation could flow out to the Gentiles. This truth encourages us to pray for our leaders so that they also will not be blocked by wrong thinking. Once again, this gift in operation moves the river of God (Psalms 65:9) into new lands, lands that are dry (Isaiah 41:17,18), where people thirst for living water (John 5:3).

(To the Uttermost Parts of the Earth)

10. DISCERNING OF SPIRITS: Paul to the sorcerer, Elymas
Acts 13:9–10
"Then Saul, (who also is called Paul,) filled with the Holy Ghost, set his eyes on him, And said, O full of all subtlety and all mischief, thou child of the devil, thou enemy of all righteousness, wilt thou not cease to pervert the right ways of the Lord?"

Note: Here, we see a certain characteristic in the operation of the baptism of the Holy Spirit. Paul had already been baptized in the Holy Spirit and fire, but we see that after the first filling, there are re-fillings. This filling with the Holy Spirit prepared Paul for a confrontation with darkness. Paul, through the discerning of spirits, reveals that it is satanic power operating in Elymas. The key to this passage is in the phrase, *"set his eyes on him."* Paul was seeing spiritually concerning the wickedness of Elymas.

11. DISCERNING OF SPIRITS: Paul discerned the spirit of faith in the man's heart for healing
Acts 14:9–10
"The same heard Paul speak: who stedfastly beholding him, and perceiving that he had faith to be healed, Said with a loud voice, Stand upright on thy feet. And he leaped and walked."

Note: Here, the Holy Spirit reveals the operation of faith in the man's heart. Faith cannot be seen except by works. In this case, the cripple man's faith needed assistance. Therefore, the Holy Spirit revealed to Paul the spirit of faith operating in the man's heart—a faith that was hungering for corresponding action (James 2:14–26). With such heavenly authority, Paul commands, and the man obeys—and the power of God manifested. This miracle of healing was aided by the manifestation of the discerning of spirits.

"But the manifestation of the Spirit (all nine gifts) is given to every man to profit withal (get the advantage)."
1 Corinthians 12:7

12. DISCERNING OF SPIRITS: Paul's vision
Acts 16:9–10
"And a vision appeared to Paul in the night; There stood a man of Macedonia, and prayed him, saying, Come over into Macedonia, and help us. And after he had seen the vision, immediately we endeavored to go into Macedonia, assuredly gathering that the Lord had called us for to preach the gospel unto them."

Note: As stated earlier, a vision is an operation of the Holy Spirit that causes the recipient to see into the realm of the spirit. Paul's eyes were opened into the realm of the spirit to see the man from Macedonia. Once again, we see the importance of this gift manifesting to assist the church in moving forward in its obedience to the great commission.

13. DISCERNING OF SPIRITS: Lydia opens her house to Paul
Act 16:15
"And a certain woman named Lydia, a seller of purple, of the city of Thyatira, which worshipped God, heard us: whose heart the Lord opened, that she attended unto the things which were spoken of Paul. And when she was baptized, and her household, she besought us, saying, If ye have judged me to be faithful to the Lord, come into my house, and abide there. And she constrained us."

Note: When Lydia invited these men to her house, she had no idea that it was soon to become the base of operation for Christianity in that region. I would have to think that the discerning of spirits came upon Lydia to know she could trust these men, that these were good men—men sent from God. When she opened her house to them—she was loaning her house to the Lord.

14. DISCERNING OF SPIRITS: Paul to the demon-possessed girl
Acts 16:18
"And this did she many days. But Paul, being grieved, turned and said to the spirit, I command thee in the name of Jesus Christ to come out of her. And he came out the same hour."

Note: In this case, either gift of revelation (discerning of spirits or the word of knowledge) could have been used to reveal to Paul the source behind the young girl's words. Whether it was the discerning of spirits or the word of knowledge, we do know that it was revelation given by the Holy Spirit that released Paul to minister to the young girl. I personally favor that the discerning of spirits was the grace used in this case. Ultimately, this study is to make the student hungry to search out these truths, thus not being ignorant of spiritual gifts—which is the utmost goal of this study.

15. DISCERNING OF SPIRITS: Paul's vision
Acts 18:9–10
"Then spake the Lord to Paul in the night by a vision, Be not afraid, but speak, and hold not thy peace: For I am with thee, and no man shall set on thee to hurt thee: for I have much people in this city."

Note: The discerning of spirits is always involved in a vision given by the Lord.

16. DISCERNING OF SPIRITS: Paul sees a vision in the temple
Acts 22:17
"And it came to pass, that, when I was come again to Jerusalem, even while I prayed in the temple, I was in a trance."

Note: As stated in prior examples, the Lord uses this gift in visions, trances, and dreams.

17. DISCERNING OF SPIRITS: Paul is aware that the Lord is standing by him
Acts 23:11
"And the night following the Lord stood by him, and said, Be of good cheer, Paul: for as thou hast testified of me in Jerusalem, so must thou bear witness also at Rome."

Note: Paul discerned the Lord standing by him, bringing much-needed comfort and encouragement. Two thousand years later, we have little understanding of the price that many have paid to bring the gospel to us. In the midst of it all, the Lord promised to never leave or forsake us, and through the discerning of spirits, Paul was encouraged by the reality of this promise.

18. DISCERNING OF SPIRITS: Paul sees the angel
Acts 27:23
"For there stood by me this night the angel of God, whose I am, and whom I serve,"

Note: Nobody saw the angel except Paul. As stated earlier, a vision from the Lord operates with this gift. This is the final operation of the discerning of spirits in the book of Acts—but not the final operation of this tremendous gift in church history. We must fervently desire this gift.

POWER GIFTS

GIFT OF FAITH
GIFTS OF HEALINGS
WORKING OF MIRACLES

POWER GIFT 1
THE GIFT OF FAITH

"To another faith by the same Spirit."
1 Corinthians 12:9

"The gift of faith is a supernatural operation of the Holy Spirit in the experience of the possessor, which enables him to sustain an unwavering trust in God for his personal protection, and for the provision of his needs... it would seem that in some very exceptional instances it enables its possessor to trust God for bodily transportation or it may be used for the pronouncement of some special blessing upon another."

Howard Carter. Questions and Answers. Page 59

"We observe the gift of faith in operation when God, through the power of the Holy Spirit, performs supernatural exploits for a human when there is no human strength or intelligence involved. In this gift, God does something supernaturally for you."

Lester Sumrall. The Gifts of the Holy Spirit study guide. Page 57

The gift of faith is the first of the three gifts of power. The primary operation of this gift in the recipient is to receive God's ability working on their behalf. Biblical examples of this gift in operation have brought supernatural supply such as manna in the wilderness or bread and flesh flown in by ravens. Also, a widow's meal never ran out because of a command that came from heaven and not from the prophet.

"And it shall be, that thou shalt drink of the brook; and I have commanded the ravens to feed thee there."
1 Kings 17:4

Throughout scripture, it would seem that the primary purpose of this gift of power is for protection and or for deliverance. Obviously, supernatural provision would fall into either of these two categories. Concerning protection, we see the three Hebrew children not delivered from the fiery furnace but rather protected while in it (Daniel 3:20–25). In this case, God's provision of protection was so perfect that their clothes did not smell of smoke, nor was their hair singed by fire. In fact, they had to be invited to come out of the furnace. The danger that confronted these three young men was beyond what their personal trust in God could have handled. Therefore, God's special faith, administrated by the angel, came with great power and glory, preserving their lives. Though their faith in God was operating, it was God's special faith that came down upon them and quenched the violence of the fire.

"Who through faith ... Quenched the violence of fire."
Hebrews 11:33–34

Concerning Elijah, it was noted of him that there had been certain occasions when the Spirit of the Lord carried him away. This catching away, while Ahab searched for him, would be classified as a deliverance from evil. Elijah had no ability to translate himself—he simply received it done.

"It shall come to pass, as soon as I am gone from thee, that the Spirit of the LORD shall carry thee whither I know not."
1 Kings 18:12

A further example of the gift of faith is clearly seen in the life of Daniel. Daniel, when thrown into the den of lions, received God's power protecting him. On the other hand, Samson, when confronted by a lion, received God's power to kill it. Daniel was operating in the gift of God's special faith (receiving), while Samson was operating in the working of miracles (doing).

Is there a difference between the fruit of faith mentioned in Galatians 5:22 and the gift of God's special faith mentioned in 1 Corinthians 12:9? Yes, by virtue of their names. The fruit of faith is a faith that is built by hearing the Word of God and allowing His Word to grow in us, developing our trust in Him. This type of faith has a process to it and is likened to a seed planted. Once planted, it begins to grow, and as it matures, it ripens with fruit.

Scripture references four kinds of faith the believer has access to as they endeavor to please the Lord. The first would be *saving* faith (Ephesians 2:8). The second is the *fruit* of faith (Romans 10:17). The third type of faith comes by *association.* Paul reminded Timothy of the faith he received from his grandmother and his mother (2 Timothy 1:5–7). The fourth operation of faith is the gift or *charisma* of the Holy Spirit called *"faith,"* which, in this study I will often refer to it as God's special faith. This faith comes directly from God and operates as the Holy Spirit wills (1 Corinthians 12:4,11). It comes perfect and mature and full of power. This special faith is given to accomplish a specific purpose, and in certain situations, angels are assigned to its operation.

"Are they not all ministering spirits, sent forth to minister for them who shall be heirs of salvation?"
Hebrews 1:14

The gift of faith has no time barrier associated with it. In comparison to the working of miracles, the gift of faith can operate instantly, like a lightning flash at the rapture of the church (Matthew 24:27, 1 Corinthians 15:52), or over a determined scope of time, such was the case with the provision of manna for forty years in the wilderness.

In the Old Testament, we see the impartation of blessing, empowered by God's special faith in Abraham by the priest Melchizedek. This blessing, wrapped in the power of God, has carried the Jewish nation over the course of thousands of years and is still at work today. On the other hand, Christ, who is a type of

Melchizedek, through this special operation of faith, administers this blessing to His body as a double blessing of power (Isaiah 61:7, John 1:16, Galatians 3:14). This New Testament blessing, on both Jewish and Gentile believers, is the key facet denoting the church age. At the rapture of the church, this charisma operation of faith (God's special faith) will catch the church up to the Lord in the air—in an atomic second. In my opinion, of the three gifts of power, this operation is the greatest.

THE GIFT OF FAITH
A DEFINITIVE LOOK

(Jerusalem, Judea, Samaria)

1. **GIFT OF FAITH: Jesus received up into heaven**
   Acts 1:9
   "And when he had spoken these things, while they beheld, he was taken up; and a cloud received him out of their sight."

   Note: In this operation, Jesus simply received the power of the Holy Spirit translating Him back to the throne of God. He was *"taken,"* and a cloud *"received"* Him! Jesus received the power of the Holy Spirit, removing Him from their sight and seating Him back at the right hand of God. Remember, with the gift of faith, God's power is received and not worked. Heaven works—we receive. In this passage, a cloud of glory took Jesus up. The angels then said to the disciples, *"as He went, so shall He come."* It is this operation or gift of God's special faith that will rapture the church in a twinkling of an eye. Just as He went, in the power of the glory of God's special faith working, so shall He come and catch away the church.

   "In a moment, in the twinkling of an eye, at the last trump: for the trumpet shall sound, and the dead shall be raised incorruptible, and we shall be changed."
   1 Corinthians 15:52

2. **GIFT OF FAITH: Jesus baptizes 120 disciples in the Holy Spirit**
   Acts 2:4
   "And they were all filled with the Holy Ghost, and began to speak with other tongues, as the Spirit gave them utterance."

   Note: On the first day of the church, this baptism of power was administered by Christ Himself to His body—no man was involved. One operation of the gift of faith is in the impartation of blessing. Just as the priest Melchizedek blessed Abraham, so now Christ, our high priest after the order of Melchizedek, blesses (spiritually empowers) the church.

GIFT OF FAITH

My final thought, when Israel crossed the Red Sea, it became a type of baptism—both of water and of the Holy Spirit (1 Corinthians 10:2). The Bible says that the Lord looked out from the cloud and the pillar of fire and began fighting on Israel's behalf (Exodus 14:24). He was there in the cloud, present with them. So it must have been on the day of Pentecost. As the cloud of glory filled the *"upper room,"* I believe that Jesus stepped into their midst and began to lay His hands upon them—saturating them in the promise of the Father (John 20:19–23).

3. GIFT OF FAITH: Church in prayer receives boldness
Acts 4:31
"And when they had prayed, the place was shaken where they were assembled together; and they were all filled with the Holy Ghost, and they spake the word of God with boldness."

Note: Acts chapter four introduces the first episode of persecution against the church. When confronted with such hatred and threats, the apostles decided not to back away in timidity from the Lord's commission to preach. They took their stand in prayer, and when they had finished praying, the power of God fell upon that place. The Lord was standing with them, and when His power fell, the house where they had gathered shook, and they were all filled with fresh boldness.

So many miracles we forsake when we back away from the gospel as opposition arises. The gift of faith is an operation of the Holy Spirit that imparts such blessing of bold power to Christ's followers facing such tremendous opposition or danger. The gift of faith, releasing such bold confidence as seen in this passage, is a part of the blessing that Jesus declared upon those who are persecuted for His name's sake (Matthew 5:11). I believe that this operation of power is actively working in the church, flowing from the constant intercession of Christ for His people.

"That your faith fail not."
Luke 22:32

4. GIFT OF FAITH: This operation of God's power removes lack
Acts 4:33–34
"With great power gave the apostles witness of the resurrection of the Lord Jesus: and great grace was upon them all. Neither was there any among them that lacked: for as many as were possessors of lands or houses sold them, and brought the prices of the things that were sold,"

Note: In the wilderness, the children of Israel had no need to provide their own food. They simply received it done for them; daily over the course of forty years. It was the operation of God's special faith that provided for their every need. As it was in the Old Testament, so it is in the New Testament—the Lord changes not. The books of Exodus and Acts have many correlations of how God manifested His power on behalf of those He redeems. The key to this passage is the phrase, *"great grace was upon them all."* This grace operates under the power of God's special faith. It is also important to note that certain gifts or graces can be imparted to the whole and not just the one. This congregation corporately carried this operation of faith—not just the apostles. The goal of church is not just to have anointed preachers who have gifts and operations of God working in and through them, but rather to have congregations of people that house these special graces and carry them to a lost and dying world. The latter is truly a greater threat to darkness than the individual minister could ever be.

"For I long to see you, that I may impart unto you some spiritual gift, to the end ye may be established."
Romans 1:11

5. **GIFT OF FAITH: Deliverance from prison**
   Acts 5:19–21
   "But the angel of the Lord by night opened the prison doors, and brought them forth, and said, Go, stand and speak in the temple to the people all the words of this life. And when they heard that, they entered into the temple early in the morning, and taught. But the high priest came, and they that were with him, and called the council together, and all the senate of the children of Israel, and sent to the prison to have them brought."

   Note: The gift of faith is a manifestation of God's power that brings into operation the powers of the world to come, where the ministry of angels and man meet. In this passage, the apostles did nothing; they simply received the power of God opening prison doors. Also, this gift empowered Peter to go, with confidence, back to the temple and preach Christ. Remember, God is faithful and would not have sent them back without having imparted supernatural boldness to do so.

6. **GIFT OF FAITH: Philip—Preaching with boldness**
   Acts 8:6–7
   "And the people with one accord gave heed unto those things which Philip spake, hearing and seeing the miracles which he did.
   For unclean spirits, crying with loud voice, came out of many that were possessed with them: and many taken with palsies, and that were lame, were healed."

   Note: So far, the Book of Acts has been focused on Jerusalem and its surroundings. Now, a new chapter in church history opens from the effects of religious persecution. Jesus had declared that the power of the Holy Spirit would make them witnesses in Jerusalem, Judea, Samaria, and the uttermost parts of the earth. As the persecution intensified in Jerusalem, those who loved the Lord found themselves scattered to places like Samaria. As they fled, they preached. In an indirect way, Saul, later known as the Apostle Paul, was being used to advance the missionary ministry of the church into new lands—obviously from the wrong side of the equation.

In this example with Philip, there had to be an operation of supernatural confidence (which comes from the gift of faith) to boldly declare the word of the Lord into Samaria. In this example, Philip was in complete control, possessing such boldness as he preached. Then, as the people listened, the Holy Spirit began manifesting miracles and healings.

7. **GIFT OF FAITH: Samaritans are baptized in the Holy Spirit**
   Acts 8:17
   "Then laid they their hands on them, and they received the Holy Ghost."

   Note: I am sure that Peter was astonished as he watched the power of God fall upon Samaria. He probably remembered back to his time there with Jesus when the Lord ministered to the lady at the well. As a Jew, he witnessed such hunger for God there amongst those who were deemed as undesirables. Now, through the operation of God's special faith, Peter was watching the Lord touch Samaria again.

   It is also important to note that Simon, the magician, watching the apostles pray and lay their hands on people to receive the baptism of the Holy Spirit, wanted this power. He obviously was impacted by witnessing his friends and neighbors speaking in new languages. Though Philip had performed many miracles and signs, it seems that the baptism of the Holy Spirit with speaking in tongues grabbed Simon's attention the most. Once again, the Holy Spirit ministers this blessing of power through the operation of special faith.

8. **GIFT OF FAITH: Philip translated by the Holy Spirit**
   Acts 8:39
   "And when they were come up out of the water, the Spirit of the Lord caught away Philip, that the eunuch saw him no more: and he went on his way rejoicing."

   Note: Translation, which is supernatural relocation, occurs throughout the Bible. Enoch was taken (Genesis 5:24). Elijah was taken (1 Kings 18:12, 2 Kings 2:1,11). Ezekiel was carried (Ezekiel 37:1). Jesus and the disciples immediately arrived at the other side (John 6:21). Jesus was taken back to heaven (Acts 1:9). Also, the church being *"caught away"* is another operation of this gift of God's faith energizing in power. Remember, in this operation of power, the recipient *"receives"* and does not *"do."* In this example, Philip was likely prepared to go back to Ethiopia to disciple the eunuch and preach Christ. Philip was not prepared to be translated.

The Holy Spirit simply snatched him away. Upon returning home, the Ethiopian had an amazing story to tell. Also, we see a type of rapture of the church. Philip was busy doing the work of an evangelist, and then, in a twinkling of an eye, he was gone. He had been taken!

9. GIFT OF FAITH: Ananias ministering to Paul
Acts 9:17
"Ananias went his way, and entered into the house; and putting his hands on him said, Brother Saul, the Lord, even Jesus, that appeared unto thee in the way as thou camest, hath sent me, that thou mightest receive thy sight, and be filled with the Holy Ghost."

Note: In this example, we see that the baptism of the Holy Spirit can be administered by the hands of a layman. So far in the book of Acts, we have seen the baptism of the Holy Spirit administered directly by the Lord as well as by the Lord through the hands of His apostles. Now, with this example, we learn that all members of the body of Christ have been made able ministers of the gospel. Ananias, a non-apostle, was a great example of this truth.

10. GIFT OF FAITH: Peter raises Tabitha from the dead
Acts 9:40
"Peter put them all forth, and kneeled down, and prayed; and turning him to the body said, Tabitha, arise. And she opened her eyes: and when she saw Peter, she sat up."

Note: I would have to imagine that it is the operation of faith, the same as in translation, that put her spirit back into her body. She was a believer and most likely was already seeing heaven. To be absent from the body is to be present with the Lord (2 Corinthians 5:8). I am sure that after she was raised back to life, she had some wonderful stories to tell about heaven. These stories most likely caused many to turn to Christ. This operation of God's faith, full of glorious power, can take a person to heaven or, in reverse, take a person from heaven putting them back into their body—causing them to live again.

11. GIFT OF FAITH: Gentiles—a new door of faith
Acts 10:20
"Arise therefore, and get thee down, and go with them, doubting nothing: for I have sent them."

Note: In this passage, Peter and the Jewish church find themselves confronted with the enormity of a new door being opened—namely, the salvation of the Gentiles. The opposition to this new direction would be enormous, and the enemy was no doubt already working to oppose this door from being fully opened. In this passage, I can envisage Peter standing in the boat (Matthew 14:28), determining if he will step out and walk onto the storm-tossed sea to go to Jesus. As Peter stepped out into the miraculous, his natural mind soon became distracted by the wind and the waves. As Peter sank, Jesus quickly took hold of him, questioning where his faith was. In this passage, the simple phrase *"doubting nothing"* is when heaven deposited a gift of faith into Peter to assist him in merging this new direction of God in the earth. God had cleansed the Gentiles, and Peter was on the threshold of witnessing this first-hand. This new step of faith would obviously, at some point, encounter wind and waves, and Peter had to be prepared to boldly move forward in the plan of God.

12. **GIFT OF FAITH: Cornelius and household**
Acts 10:44–45
"While Peter yet spake these words, the Holy Ghost fell on all them which heard the word. And they of the circumcision which believed were astonished, as many as came with Peter, because that on the Gentiles also was poured out the gift of the Holy Ghost."

Note: The key to this chapter is found in one little phrase spoken by Peter in Acts 10:37, *"That word, I say, you know."* Peter knew that Cornelius had heard about Jesus. Cornelius was also knowledgeable about how the church in the region was growing *(remember Philip the evangelist lived in the same town)*. Also, to further this truth, Paul in Acts 26:26 declares that the life and death of Jesus were not done in a corner and that Agrippa had full knowledge of it. This passage leans toward the fact that Cornelius had already come into faith in Jesus Christ and that Peter had been sent to place the seal of acceptance on their faith. As Peter spoke, without laying his hands upon those present, the Holy Spirit moved in a sovereign way—baptizing them in the Holy Spirit with the evidence of speaking in other tongues.

The Roman Cornelius and the Gentiles present received the baptism of the Holy Spirit with new tongues just as dramatically as the apostles did. Because of how the Lord administered this baptism of power personally, the Jewish church could never hold influence over Gentile believers pertaining to *'who laid hands on who'* for the reception of this blessing. God was declaring that all men were cleansed through faith in Christ. He also demonstrated that the baptism of the Holy Spirit was for all as well. When John the Baptist proclaimed that Jesus, *"the Lamb of God,"* would baptize men with the Holy Spirit and fire, no one ever considered the Gentiles, especially the Romans, as a part of this fulfillment. All men were equally unclean through sin, and all men were equally cleansed through the cross. This Holy Spirit baptism can be seen and heard and is administered by the Lord through the operation of the gift of God's faith energizing in power. The gift of God's special faith is truly a powerful gift.

13. GIFT OF FAITH: Peter supernaturally delivered from prison

Acts 12:7

"And, behold, the angel of the Lord came upon him, and a light shined in the prison: and he smote Peter on the side, and raised him up, saying, Arise up quickly. And his chains fell off from his hands."

Note: Peter, thinking he was having a vision, did nothing to make this deliverance happen. The only thing Peter did was to put on his clothes and follow the angel. In the operation of the gift of faith, angels are commonly involved, such as with Daniel in the lion's den or the three Hebrew children in the fiery furnace. Peter was receiving his deliverance from harm through this operation of power.

(To the Uttermost Parts of the Earth)

14. GIFT OF FAITH: Paul and Barnabas—bold to confront, power to turn

Acts 13:46

"Then Paul and Barnabas waxed bold, and said, It was necessary that the word of God should first have been spoken to you: but seeing ye put it from you, and judge yourselves unworthy of everlasting life, lo, we turn to the Gentiles."

Note: As the devil's servants were filled with envy, God's servants received a fresh filling of power to confront them. With this boldness, the gift of God's special faith empowered a complete turning towards Paul's high calling—the Gentiles.

15. GIFT OF FAITH: Paul and Barnabas speaking boldly in the Lord

Acts 14:3

"Long time therefore abode they speaking boldly in the Lord, which gave testimony unto the word of his grace, and granted signs and wonders to be done by their hands."

Note: The gospel must be spoken forth with boldness, a boldness that comes from the Spirit of the Lord and not from the flesh. Paul asked the Ephesians to pray for him in order that he would receive this boldness to speak forth the gospel (Ephesians 6:18–20). The key to this passage is the phrase, *"in the Lord."* This bold confidence that they were operating under was not a normal boldness that one can stir up within themselves, but rather an operation of the gift of God's special faith that was empowering their speech. When they spoke, faith was released, and signs and wonders followed their words. This truly is a wonderful example of the gift of faith operating. How we need this gift!

16. GIFT OF FAITH: A door of faith

Acts 14:27

"When they were come, and had gathered the church together, they rehearsed all that God had done with them, and how he had opened the door of faith unto the Gentiles."

Note: Every major transition in the book of Acts came through the manifestation of the gifts of the Holy Spirit. In this passage the wording is once again crucial to help understand the operations of God in the harvest. In Matthew 9:38, Jesus taught His disciples to pray to the Lord of the harvest to send forth laborers into His harvest. The Greek word for sending in this passage is the word *ekballo*, meaning to thrust forth violently. Because of the demonic resistance to the gospel, it takes power likened to a gust of wind, to insert laborers into their assigned fields. Thus, on the day of Pentecost, the Holy Spirit came as a violent, mighty wind.

To further this point, a door of faith is a door the Lord opens. When the Lord opens a new direction, He will also supply the faith power to move laborers into position, or in this case, to walk through the door—with confidence. With this faith door also comes supernatural provision to sustain the natural needs that arise in the spiritual work of the Lord. Therefore, the gift of God's special faith will always be in operation to assist and protect those who are laboring in those fields. Thus, it is important not to be ignorant of these grace gifts.

17. GIFT OF FAITH: Paul and Barnabas

Acts 15:12

"Then all the multitude kept silence, and gave audience to Barnabas and Paul, declaring what miracles and wonders God had wrought among the Gentiles by them."

Note: The phrase *"God had wrought"* opens the door to all three operations or *"gifts"* of power: 1) the gift of faith; 2) gifts of healings; and 3) the working of miracles. Considering other examples in the book of Acts, when the Gentiles believed, the apostles prioritized praying for them to receive the baptism of the Holy Spirit with the evidence of other (prayer) tongues. This baptism with speaking in other tongues is definitely a *"wonder."* Remember, it wasn't only Philip's miracles that captured Simon's attention, but rather the ministration of the baptism of the Holy Spirit with the evidence of speaking in other tongues. When Gentiles watched their friends and neighbors begin speaking in new languages, it truly was a wonder.

Also, because the gift of faith energizes the servants of the Lord with boldness and brings supernatural protection, I took the liberty to include the gift of faith in this passage. How exciting it must have been to experience a move of God like this. Equally, how exciting it must have been to sit and listen to Paul share his stories of walking with God. Just as

Adam walked with God before the fall of man, now, through the gospel of Christ, we can walk with God in the earth.

18. GIFT OF FAITH: Paul casts out the devil
Acts 16:18
"And this did she many days. But Paul, being grieved, turned and said to the spirit, I command thee in the name of Jesus Christ to come out of her. And he came out the same hour."

Note: I believe this gift of God's special faith gave Paul boldness (at the right moment) to deal with the devil in the young lady. This same Holy Spirit confidence also was imparted to preserve Paul through the coming persecution (and beating) that followed this act of God's deliverance. This special faith most certainly was in manifestation.

"The manifestation of the Spirit is given to every man to profit withal (To get the advantage)."
1 Corinthians 12:7

19. GIFT OF FAITH: Paul and Silas receive supernatural deliverance from jail
Acts 16:26
"And suddenly there was a great earthquake, so that the foundations of the prison were shaken: and immediately all the doors were opened, and every one's bands were loosed."

Note: As Paul and Silas prayed and sang praises, the power of God came down upon the prison. Paul and Silas did nothing; they simply received God's power working on their behalf. If Paul had torn the bars off the wall, like Samson, it would be classified as the working of miracles. In this passage, Paul and Silas sat back (so to speak) and received God's power working in their situation. We are commanded to desire this gift.

20. GIFT OF FAITH: Ephesian believers
Acts 19:6
"When Paul had laid his hands upon them, the Holy Ghost came on them; and they spake with tongues, and prophesied."

Note: Once again, the baptism of the Holy Spirit is administered through the operation of this gift of God's faith. Just as the priest (Hebrews 7:1) Melchizedek blessed Abraham, so Jesus, our high priest, administers the blessing of Abraham as a double blessing into and upon the church. The impartation of blessing or *"spiritual empowerment"* is one of the operations of the gift of God's special faith.

21. GIFT OF FAITH: Paul's ministry

Acts 19:20

"So mightily grew the word of God and prevailed."

Note: The Greek word for *"mightily"* has to do with the power of God in demonstration. It was the preaching of the Word of God with mighty operations of power that caused the church to increase. Therefore, I took the liberty to list all three power gifts in demonstration, which would include the gift of God's special faith.

22. GIFT OF FAITH: Paul raises the dead

Acts 20:10

"Paul went down, and fell on him, and embracing him said, "Trouble not yourselves; for his life is in him."

Note: The atmosphere in that meeting must have been electric as the great apostle taught into the night, testifying of the power of God that bore witness to the word he preached. Suddenly people began to stir, causing Paul to realize that something bad had happened. There outside, lying on the ground, was a dead young man who had fallen out of the top window. Paul, walking in such tangible power, fell upon the boy. When he did, the gifts of power went into operation, breaking death's hold and restoring the spirit of the lad back into him. Then finally, the gifts of healings restored his body from the damage received from the fall. All three gifts of power would have been in operation in this resurrection.

23. GIFT OF FAITH: Paul in the storm

Acts 27:23

"For there stood by me this night the angel of God, whose I am, and whom I serve,"

Acts 27:25

"Wherefore, sirs, be of good cheer: for I believe God, that it shall be even as it was told me."

Note: Just as it had been with Daniel in the lion's den, the angel of the Lord stood with Paul, protecting him. Paul did not calm the storm but rather, through the operation of this power gift, received protection from it. Oh, death, where is your sting! This gift of power comes perfect in operation and is often administered by the presence of an angel. Even to the three Hebrew children in the furnace, their deliverance was so perfect that the smell of smoke could not touch them. Remember, they had to be invited to come out of the furnace. We are commanded to desire these gifts!

24. GIFT OF FAITH: Paul overcomes the snake bite
Acts 28:5
"He shook off the beast into the fire and felt no harm."

Note: In this passage, Paul simply received the power of God's faith, preserving him from death. The presence of the angel brought divine protection to Paul in the storm; and so it was here. The special operation of protection around Paul, ensuring his course to Rome, kept the venom of the snake from harming him. Also, it is proper to note that in the great commission, the Lord declares that His servants will take up serpents and not be harmed. This is a clear example of what the Lord meant in His commission to the disciples. In conclusion, this is the final operation of the gift of God's special faith in the book of Acts, but by no means is it the final manifestation of it in church history. Earnestly desire this gift!

POWER GIFT 2

THE GIFTS OF HEALINGS

"To another the gifts of healings by the same Spirit."
1 Corinthians 12:9

"The gifts of healing are manifestations of the Holy Spirit in the sphere of disease."
Howard Carter. Questions and Answers. Page 97

"One of the most exciting gifts from heaven, the gifts of healing, have to do with the supernatural imparting of God's healing power to human beings."
Lester Sumrall. The Gifts of the Holy Spirit study guide. Page. 64

The gifts of healings are spiritual endowments that heal. In John chapter 5, verse 4, we see a wonderful example of God (Jehovah Rapha—the Lord our healer Exodus 15:26), sending an angel who ministered the Lord's healing power into a pool of water. In this special operation, only one person, the person responding first, was made whole of their affliction. The gifts of healings, in Jesus' ministry, unlike the operation of special healings at the pool of Bethsaida, healed every sickness and disease among the people (Matthew 9:35). We see these same operations, though in a more limited fashion, in the ministry of Peter, whose shadow brought healing to those lining the streets of Jerusalem (Acts 5:12–16), as well as with Paul, who prayed over handkerchiefs (Acts 19:11–12). The anointing in this gift seems to be tangible and can be stored in fabric, such as Jesus' garments, Paul's handkerchiefs, and even deposited into a pool of water.

The actual Greek words for this *charisma* operation are in the plural—meaning gift(s) and healing(s). Howard Carter described this gift as a clump likened to grapes on a vine[2]. Simply meaning that the clump was healings, and the individual grapes of the clump were for specific ailments. I like this description. Therefore, in this healing operation, there are gifts that heal specific categories of disease. I personally have been in meetings where an evangelist prayed in faith for all desiring healing but seemed to possess extra special confidence towards specific sicknesses or maladies. Along the same lines, I have been in other meetings where a different minister demonstrated a certain boldness with success towards other ailments. In each of these cases, both ministers prayed for the sick, but their specific healing gifts differed, carrying greater boldness towards differing groups of ailments. Therefore, looking at how this gift is described in the plural, I personally lean toward a composite gift approach that is given as the

[2] *Spiritual Gifts and their Operations. Howard Carter. Radiant Books. Gospel Publishing House, Springfield, MO. ISBN 0-88243-593-0 Page: 48 Paragraph 3.*

Holy Spirit wills. I cannot explain everything about the Holy Spirit and how He ministers, but the purpose of this book is to stir you up to hunger to know the Lord and to be a student of His Word and of His ways. This gift is the epitome of God's mercy for human affliction. My final thought before launching into this study concerns the Lord's healing mercy. Jesus is our healer who always responds to faith and trust in Him. He heals our bodies in a variety of ways, not just through the gifts of healings. The Psalmist declared, *"He sent His Word and healed them, delivering them from destruction" (Psalms 107:20)*. Healing flows from Jesus, the Word of God, and this study focuses on the ministry of the Holy Spirit and His gifts of healings.

THE GIFTS OF HEALINGS
A DEFINITIVE LOOK

(Jerusalem, Judea, Samaria)

1. **GIFTS OF HEALINGS: Apostles minister to a crowd**
   Acts 2:43
   "And fear came upon every soul: and many wonders and signs were done by the apostles."

   Note: The book of Acts does not give specifics in this passage concerning the signs and wonders done. What we do know is that the church, a few verses before, had been submerged into the power of God. Jesus promised to never leave or forsake them, and the outpouring of the Holy Spirit with signs and wonders was one aspect of His presence being with them. Signs and wonders are a part of the package of the power gifts of the Holy Spirit. Miracles and healings, as gifts of the Holy Spirit, are gifts that *"do"* something. Whereas the gift of faith, though equally a power gift, simply receives God's power operating on one's behalf. In view of the wording in this passage, the Lord's apostles were *"doing,"* which would exempt the gift of faith in this example. Remember, the one who receives the gift of faith receives the power of God operating on their behalf. Healings and miracles, on the other hand, are administered by the Lord's servants in an outward flow of the Holy Spirit.

2. **GIFTS OF HEALINGS: Crippled man healed**
   Acts 3:6–7
   "Then Peter said, Silver and gold have I none; but such as I have give I thee: In the name of Jesus Christ of Nazareth rise up and walk.
   And he took him by the right hand, and lifted him up: and immediately his feet and ankle bones received strength."

   Acts 3:16
   "And his name through faith in his name hath made this man strong,

whom ye see and know: yea, the faith which is by him hath given him this perfect soundness in the presence of you all."

Note: In the first chapter of Acts, Jesus commissioned His disciples to wait in Jerusalem until they received the promise of the Father. In chapter two, we witness the birth of the church through the outpouring of the Holy Spirit. Now in chapter three, we see the power and authority given to the church through the name of Jesus. This chapter is crucial for the doctrine of the name of Jesus and its place in the lives of believers. Through faith in the name of Jesus, a crippled man was restored to health. This man had no faith of his own to receive healing, but rather through the gifts of healings operating through Peter and John's faith in the Lord, the mercy of God raised him up as a testimony to all.

3. **GIFTS OF HEALINGS: Apostles to the crowds**
   Acts 4:33
   "And <u>with great power gave the apostles witness</u> of the resurrection of the Lord Jesus: and great grace was upon them all."

   Note: In this operation the apostles were actively working in the power of God. They were not receiving supernatural provision, protection, or blessing but rather administrating this power into the harvest. Therefore, we would have to assume that the great power in demonstration was both in healings and miracles. Remember, the gift of faith receives, while healings and miracles do. A further point is that this power was given by God to confirm His Word as a witness of Christ's resurrection—thus stirring great fear into the hearts of Jerusalem's religious order.

4. **GIFTS OF HEALINGS: Through the hands of the Apostles**
   Acts 5:12
   "And <u>by the hands of the apostles were</u> many signs and wonders wrought among the people; and they were all with one accord in Solomon's porch."

   Note: Here, again, we see the power of God flowing from the apostles as they laid their hands upon people. These apostles followed Jesus for three years, watching Him minister to the multitudes. Now, they were doing what Jesus had taught them to do. All three gifts of power can operate through the laying on of hands. In this example, we are not given any specifics, but we are supplied with needed information that continues to reinforce our faith in the ministry of the Holy Spirit in and through the church.

5. GIFTS OF HEALINGS: Peter and the Apostles

Acts 5:15

"Insomuch that they brought forth the sick into the streets, and laid them on beds and couches, that at the least the shadow of Peter passing by might overshadow some of them."

Note: Peter, who had been trained by Jesus for three years, was very familiar with the healing ministry of Jesus. In this passage, we see the Holy Spirit manifesting healing in some very unusual ways. If Jesus hasn't changed, then why would a healing shadow be any more unique than spitting, making clay, and rubbing it into a man's eyes? These miracles were never about the apostles or the church but about a living Jesus who was actively working with them as they obeyed and went forward in faith. They truly went out preaching and healing as lambs sent out into the midst of wolves. These disciples were staying close to their Great Shepherd, and He was turning the world upside down through them.

6. GIFTS OF HEALINGS: Multitudes—everyone

Acts 5:16

"There came also a multitude out of the cities round about unto Jerusalem, bringing sick folks, and them which were vexed with unclean spirits: and they were healed everyone."

Note: In this passage, we are given further insight into the healing ministry of Jesus through the church. Jesus has never changed and will never change. How He ministered on the earth, He so desires to continue through His body—the church. Also, the casting out of demons is a part of the healing ministry of Jesus. In conclusion, it must have given Jesus such great joy to see the plan of God, through the redeeming power of the cross, continue to heal the multitudes that gathered in His name. These simple words, *"I am with you always"* Matthew 28:20, must have been stirring in the hearts of the apostles as they watched the cripples walk, the deaf hear, and the blind see. Everyone loves to see the power of God operate, but those disciples probably gleaned more from His presence being with them than by the actual signs and wonders being done before their eyes. They had known Jesus in the flesh and missed Him greatly and were learning to walk by faith.

7. GIFTS OF HEALINGS: Stephen to the multitudes

Acts 6:8

"Stephen, full of faith and power, did great wonders and miracles among the people."

Note: Stephen was full of the Holy Spirit and power doing the works of Jesus. As mentioned earlier, the power in demonstration by Stephen is given in a general context and not with specific examples. It is also proper to note that this chapter gives insight into the importance of being full of faith and of the Holy Spirit. Stephen was a deacon, and his job was to be an extension of the hands of the apostles. Because the apostles had given themselves to prayer, the power of God flowed through these holy servants as they set tables and served widows. The secret of Stephen's success was the flow of prayer coming from the apostles, which resulted in a fullness of the Holy Spirit in their lives as well as upon the church. Stephen, by faith, connected the apostle's prayer life to the tables of the widows, and the power of God began to flow. The other healing that was taking place in this passage was the ethnic division that existed between two different groups of Jews—those being Hebrew in culture and those who saw themselves as Greeks.

8. **GIFTS OF HEALINGS: Paralyzed and lame healed**
Acts 8:7
"And the people with one accord gave heed unto those things which Philip spake, hearing and seeing the miracles which he did.
For unclean spirits, crying with loud voice, came out of many that were possessed with them: and many taken with palsies, and that were lame, were healed."

Note: Therefore, if Jesus is the same yesterday, today, and forever, so is the Holy Spirit. In this passage, we see the healing mercy of Jesus continue to heal the crippled and lame through the power of His Spirit upon Philip. As Philip preached Christ, the anointed one, a cloud of glory fell upon those listening. As he preached, the gifts of healing(s) flowed like a river, delivering and healing without Philip touching them. This passage alludes to the sounds of people being healed and restored. It is possible the bones of the lame were heard cracking while popping back into place. I am sure that people cried out as demons were leaving and then cried for joy when they were gone. There are sounds that accompany the healing ministry of Jesus. In this operation of glory, as the power of God's faith fell upon the crowd, demonic powers began to be removed while gifts of healings were restoring what had been broken. This truly was a sovereign outpouring of the Holy Spirit upon a region. What an event!

9. **GIFTS OF HEALINGS: Peter ministering to Aeneas**
Acts 9:34
"And Peter said unto him, Aeneas, Jesus Christ maketh thee whole: arise, and make thy bed. And he arose immediately."

Note: The gifts of healings heal! Also, in this example, we see Peter making it clear who the healer was as he used the name of Jesus with authority and faith.

10. GIFTS OF HEALINGS: Peter raising Tabitha back to life
Acts 9:40
"But Peter put them all forth, and kneeled down, and prayed; and turning him to the body said, Tabitha, arise. And she opened her eyes: and when she saw Peter, she sat up."

Note: In raising the dead, it is needed in most cases for the gifts of healings to restore the body from the sickness or disease that originally caused the death.

11. GIFTS OF HEALINGS: Disciples preaching in Antioch
Acts 11:21
"And the hand of the Lord was with them: and a great number believed, and turned unto the Lord."

Note: Throughout scripture, the phrase *"the hand of the Lord"* denotes supernatural operation. Though a specific event is not listed, it does reveal that God's power was moving during the preaching of the gospel. I have taken the liberty, considering scripture, to list both the gifts of healings and the working of miracles as the result of the hand of the Lord being with them. In conclusion, as we seek the face of God, we must equally desire His hand to move as we go forth in His name.

(To the Uttermost Parts of the Earth)

12. GIFTS OF HEALINGS: Paul and Barnabas
Acts 14:3
"Long time therefore abode they speaking boldly in the Lord, which gave testimony unto the word of his grace, and granted signs and wonders to be done by their hands."

Note: Here, we see the operation of God's power through the apostles. There is no specific case given, but I would conclude that miracles and healings were the signs and wonders done through them. It is also important to note how they spoke in the Lord. The gospel of Christ, who is alive, was never intended to be preached without heavenly boldness. Heaven supplies the boldness to accompany the declaration of the eternal truth of God's saving grace.

13. GIFTS OF HEALINGS: Paul commands a man to walk
Acts 14:9–10
"The same heard Paul speak: who stedfastly beholding him, and perceiving that he had faith to be healed,
Said with a loud voice, Stand upright on thy feet. And he leaped and walked."

Note: I have taken the liberty to categorize this healing under the gifts of healings. Though it is possible for a man to be healed by faith in the Word of God being preached, I would have to assume that this man did not have his own knowledge of healing faith but rather was moved upon by the dynamics of Paul's gifts energizing through his preaching. The gifts of healings are often used to capture the attention of people who have never heard the gospel. In this passage, the whole city was affected by this healing miracle, which opened the door for them to hear the gospel. Is it possible that this healing was not a specific gift of healing but rather an operation of the man's faith? Perhaps. In our approach to documenting these operations of God, we will honestly admit that we do not have complete knowledge of everything listed. Remember, the purpose of this study is to encourage the student to hunger for the gifts and operations of God and to ultimately not be ignorant of them.

14. **GIFTS OF HEALINGS: Paul stoned and left for dead**
    Acts 14:19–20
    "And there came thither certain Jews from Antioch and Iconium, who persuaded the people, and, having stoned Paul, drew him out of the city, supposing he had been dead. Howbeit, as the disciples stood round about him, he rose up, and came into the city: and the next day he departed with Barnabas to Derbe."

    Note: The Jews only supposed that Paul had died. Though still alive, it was evident that the stoning had left him greatly injured. As the disciples stood around him and prayed, the power of God came down upon Paul and healed him. That place became a *"pool of Bethesda"* for Paul (John 5:1–4).

15. **GIFTS OF HEALINGS: Paul and Barnabas testify of God's power**
    Acts 15:12
    "Then all the multitude kept silence, and gave audience to Barnabas and Paul, declaring what miracles and wonders God had wrought among the Gentiles by them."

    Note: The phrase *"God had wrought"* opens the door to all three operations of power: 1) the gift of faith; 2) gifts of healings; and 3) working of miracles. How exciting it must have been to experience a move of God like this. Equally, how exciting it must have been to sit and listen to Paul share his stories of walking with God. Remember, Adam walked with God in the garden, and now in Christ, we can walk with God to every corner of the earth.

16. GIFTS OF HEALINGS: Paul's handkerchiefs and aprons

Acts 19:12

"So that from his body were brought unto the sick handkerchiefs or aprons, and the diseases departed from them, and the evil spirits went out of them."

Note: The healing anointing is tangible. We see the same principle in the ministry of Jesus when multitudes sought to touch His garments (Luke 6:19). Paul, through the gifts of healings, was laying hands upon handkerchiefs and saturating them in the healing presence of Jesus.

17. GIFTS OF HEALINGS: Paul's ministry

Acts 19:20

"So mightily grew the word of God and prevailed."

Note: The Greek word for *"mightily"* is the word *kratos*. *Kratos* is defined by Strong's dictionary as a mighty work of power. The New Testament Greek scholar Kenneth Wuest defines this word as God's power in demonstration[3]. It was the preaching of the Word of God with demonstrating might that caused the gospel to prevail in the hearts of the people. Truly the Lord was working with them, confirming His Word with signs and wonders following. Finally, because the wording is generic, I took the liberty to list all three power gifts for this passage which includes the gifts of healings.

18. GIFTS OF HEALINGS: Paul raises the dead

Acts 20:10

"And Paul went down, and fell on him, and embracing him said, Trouble not yourselves; for his life is in him."

Note: Raising the dead is probably the greatest of all miracles. In this miracle of resurrection, we see all three operations of power working together through Paul. Notably, in this case, the gifts of healings restored the young man's body from the injury that killed him.

19. GIFTS OF HEALINGS: Paul ministers to the Father of Publius

Acts 28:8–9

"And it came to pass, that the father of Publius lay sick of a fever and of a bloody flux: to whom Paul entered in, and prayed, and laid his hands on him, and healed him."

Note: Paul had survived the storm and the serpent's bite through the operation of God's special faith. Now, the gifts of healings restore

---

[3] *Word Studies from the Greek New Testament, for the English Reader. Volume One: Ephesians. By Kenneth S. Wuest. Page 54.*

Publius' father. These gifts are truly the Lord's healing mercy extended to all men—both believer and unbeliever.

20. GIFTS OF HEALINGS: Paul ministers to the sick on the island.
Acts 28:8–9
"When this was done, others also, which had diseases in the island, came, and were healed."

Note: Though the islanders may not have had faith to be healed, for they knew nothing of Jesus, they did have an expectation which ultimately opened the door to their receiving from the Lord. Though Paul was still considered a prisoner, he was in complete control. I often wonder about the effect Paul's life of faith had upon both the centurion and others who sailed with him on that voyage. They witnessed the peace of God in Paul's life during a life-threatening storm. They watched him pray to his God and bless the food before they ate. Then, after washing up upon an island, they realized they had all lived; not one was lost, which was exactly as Paul had said. Paul then escapes the poison of the serpent's bite, and now they watch him minister to the sick. From Roman soldiers guarding prisoners to the sailors and their captain to all other passengers, everyone on that trip was eternally impacted by a man of faith. This, of course, is the final reference to the gifts of healings in the book of Acts—but it is not the final occurrence throughout the course of church history, thank God.

POWER GIFT 3

THE WORKING OF MIRACLES

"To another the working of miracles."
1 Corinthians 12:10

"The working of miracles is the supernatural demonstration of the power of God by which the laws of nature are altered, suspended, or controlled, (excepting in the sphere of disease). Miracles demonstrate the power of God and healings demonstrate His love and compassion."

Howard Carter. Questions and Answers. Page 82–83

"The gift of the working of miracles denotes a supernatural intervention by God in the ordinary course of nature. In this gift, God works through a man or through some instrument."

Lester Sumrall. The Gifts of the Holy Spirit study guide. Page. 62

The working of miracles needs to be defined by its Greek translation. The best definition of this gift would be (in my opinion), *"The energizing of miraculous ability—put forth into a purpose or direction."* This operation of power differs from the gift of faith in that this grace gift enables the possessor to enact or do the miraculous. Both gifts manifest the power of the Holy Spirit, but in execution, they differ. The best example to contrast these two gifts of power would be in the lives of Samson and Daniel. Both servants of God had to deal with lions. Samson, under the operation of miracles, killed the lion. In the natural, no man has the strength to overcome a hungry lion. Daniel, on the other hand, simply trusted God. He did not kill the lions but rather rested in God's power, receiving supernatural protection from them.

In contrast, after Daniel's release, the operation of God's power in the pit changed. God's special faith that had been protecting Daniel turned miraculous, coming upon the lions, enabling them to do the impossible. The Bible says that when the (corrupt) officials of the king were thrown into the den, Daniel's docile lions broke every bone in the bodies of the officials, their wives, and their children before they hit the ground. This truly was a visual definition of miraculous power—energizing! I am sure that the guards never forgot what they saw in the lion's den that day.

In the New Testament, Peter asked Jesus to command him to walk on the water. Jesus spoke, and Peter, by faith, stepped out into the operation of miracles. Another clear contrast between the gift of faith and miracles can be seen in the lives of Joshua and Elijah. Joshua, after praying, spoke to the sun to stand still. Joshua enacted upon creation with this gift. The result was that the sun and most likely all of creation stood still until the children of God gained complete victory. Elijah on the other hand, primarily operated under the gift of faith. In confronting the priests of Baal, he simply left the act of power in God's hands, while knowing through revelation what God was going to do. He stated, *"Let the God who answers with fire be God!"* He did not enact or speak forth for fire to fall; he simply received it done. Both gifts are powerful but in function they operate differently.

THE WORKING OF MIRACLES
A DEFINITIVE LOOK

(Jerusalem, Judea, Samaria)

1. **WORKING OF MIRACLES: Apostles to crowd**
   Acts 2:43
   "And fear came upon every soul: and many wonders and signs were done by the apostles."

   Note: The book of Acts doesn't give specifics in this passage as to the signs and wonders, except that they were done by the apostles. Both miracles and healings are gifts that *"do"* something. It is also important to note that the word *"signs"* literally means a mark or a sign that demonstrates the manifest presence of God. The word *"wonders"* is best defined as an act done that demands attention. God was manifesting His tangible presence, demanding their attention, as the apostles preached the gospel.

2. **WORKING OF MIRACLES: Apostles to the crowds**
   Acts 4:33
   "And with great power gave the apostles witness of the resurrection of the Lord Jesus: and great grace was upon them all."

   Note: In this operation, the apostles were actively working in the power of God. They were not receiving supernatural provision, protection, or blessing but rather administrating this power outward into the harvest. Therefore, we would have to assume that the great power in demonstration was both in healings and miracles.

3. **WORKING OF MIRACLES: Through the hands of the Apostles**
   Acts 5:12
   "And by the hands of the apostles were many signs and wonders wrought among the people; (and they were all with one accord in Solomon's porch)."

   Note: In this passage, we have no specifics of what happened, other than many signs and wonders were done by the hands of the apostles. The term *"working of miracles"* in the Greek language simply means miraculous power energizing. Samson killed a lion under the operation of this gift. Jesus walked on water through the function of this gift. As these apostles went forward teaching and preaching in the name of Jesus, declaring His resurrection, this power began to energize. It was the Lord present with them, just as He said, confirming His word with signs following. Those precious words, *"I will never leave you,"* must have been surging through the hearts of these apostles as they watched Jesus minister to the needy through their hands. As Peter lay in bed that night, thinking back over the three wonderful years of training with Jesus, he must have been so encouraged to know experientially that Jesus was still with them—and very close to them through the presence of the Holy Spirit.

4. WORKING OF MIRACLES: Stephen to the multitudes
Acts 6:8
"And Stephen, full of faith and power, <u>did</u> great wonders and miracles among the people."

Note: This chapter demands much study. A man functioning as a deacon, a simple helper, was also walking in the miraculous power of God. Remember, Jesus commanded His disciples to receive the baptism of the Holy Spirit. He also clarified that this baptism would be a saturation of the power of God upon them. Stephen, as a deacon serving widows, was proof that every member of the body of Christ is an able minister of the New Testament (2 Corinthians 3:6). This truth must have shaken the religious world as Jerusalem's leaders were hearing of non-apostles doing miracles. This also shook the demonic kingdom, realizing that the church and all its members were now demonstrating the wisdom of God through the power of the gospel. In this passage, Stephen *"did"* rather than *"received"* concerning the power of God. The gift of faith is a receiving operation, while the working of miracles is a doing operation. To further clarify, when Jesus was sleeping in the boat, He was receiving God's protection from a terrible storm (Mark 4:37,38). After being awakened, He then enacts upon the storm and stills it. One operation is faith, while the other is the working (energizing) of miracle power. Think about this, it is not normal for a man to change a weather system. Jesus changed the storm by enacting upon it. Both examples are manifestations of the power of God, though in function they differ.

5. WORKING OF MIRACLES: Seeing the miracles which <u>he did</u>
Acts 8:6–7
"And the people with one accord gave heed unto those things which Philip spake, hearing and seeing the miracles which he did.
For unclean spirits, crying with loud voice, came out of many that were possessed with them: and many taken with palsies, and that were lame, were healed."

Note: Philip, a fellow deacon with Stephen, fled Jerusalem, leaving the widows and their tables behind. Filled with the power of God, and yet undoubtedly still mourning the loss of his friend, He finds himself now heading towards his destiny in none other than the land of Samaria—which would have been unthinkable to the Jewish mind. On the first day, as Philip preached, the power of God fell. The Bible notes that both healings and miracles were being demonstrated by this former Jerusalem table waiter. Truly the Lord works in mysterious ways.

6. **WORKING OF MIRACLES: Philip doing great miracles**
   Acts 8:13
   "Then Simon himself believed also: and when he was baptized, he <u>continued</u> with Philip, and wondered, beholding the <u>miracles and signs</u> which were done."

   Note: The key to this passage is found in the word *"continued."* Samaria was shaken by the power of God. In this example, Simon, who had earlier used magic to control the minds of the people, was also shaken—to the point of believing. His magic show was now over, and a new strongman named Philip had appeared—full of the Holy Spirit and miracles. It is important to note that miracles proclaim the presence of God, and Philip's *"God declaring miracles"* were not a one-day event but continued during his time in Samaria.

7. **WORKING OF MIRACLES: Peter raises Tabitha back to life**
   Acts 9:40
   "But Peter put them all forth, and kneeled down, and prayed; and turning him to the body said, <u>Tabitha, arise</u>. And she opened her eyes: and when she saw Peter, she sat up."

   Note: Peter was called to come and interject himself into this tragedy. While standing over the lifeless body of a very loved saint of God, Peter turns his attention to prayer. As the peace of God filled Peter's heart, he then turned to Tabitha and spoke. In one sense, he was using his faith to speak to the mountain of death to move. Remember, the working of miracles is simply, in Greek, defined as *"miraculous power energizing."* This miraculous power of God went into Tabitha and broke the power of death—it drove it out. As stated earlier, death will one day be thrown into the lake of fire, so until then, we must actively resist it and believe God to overturn it in the earth.

8. **WORKING OF MIRACLES: Disciples preaching in Antioch**
   Acts 11:21
   "And <u>the hand of the Lord was with them</u>: and a great number believed, and turned unto the Lord."

Note: Throughout scripture, the phrase *"the hand of the Lord"* denotes supernatural operation. Though a specific event is not listed, it does reveal that God's power was flowing like a river during the preaching of the gospel. I have taken the liberty, in light of scripture, to list both the gifts of healings and the working of miracles as the result of the hand of the Lord being with them. In one sense, we could list all nine gifts of the Holy Spirit for this verse, but because it is tied to the concept of people turning to the Lord, I will limit my focus to the two primary gifts that work through the ministry of the evangelist—which are healings and miracles.

(To the Uttermost Parts of the Earth)

9. **WORKING OF MIRACLES: Paul and Barnabas**
Acts 14:3
"Long time therefore abode they speaking boldly in the Lord, which gave testimony unto the word of his grace, and granted signs and wonders to be done by their hands."

Note: In the Old Testament, Moses laid his hands upon Joshua and the power of God filled him, giving him wisdom. The Bible has many examples of hands being used to impart the power of God. Jesus often used His hands to heal and bless multitudes. The disciples learned the importance of using their hands in the performance of ministry from watching Jesus. Jesus never changed, and in the book of Acts, He was using their hands, which brought pleasure to the heart of the Father. In this account, there is no specific case given of miracles, but I would conclude that miracles and healings were the signs and wonders done through them.

10. **WORKING OF MIRACLES: Paul and Barnabas**
Acts 15:12
"Then all the multitude kept silence, and gave audience to Barnabas and Paul, declaring what miracles and wonders God had wrought among the Gentiles by them."

Note: The simple words *"God wrought"* opens the door to all three operations of power: 1) the gift of faith; 2) gifts of healings; and 3) the working of miracles. How exciting it must have been for those believers to hear firsthand from Paul concerning such a move of God like this.

11. **WORKING OF MIRACLES: Paul's ministry**
Acts 19:20
"So mightily grew the word of God and prevailed."

Note: The Greek word kratos or *"mightily"* has to do with strength or God's power in demonstration. It was the preaching of the Word of God with these mighty operations of power that caused the plan of God to prevail. Therefore, I took the liberty to list all three power gifts in demonstration—which includes the working of miracles.

12. WORKING OF MIRACLES: Paul raises the dead
Acts 20:10
"And Paul went down, and fell on him, and embracing him said, Trouble not yourselves; for his life is in him."

Note: The raising of the dead is probably the greatest of all miracles. If we only knew how much Jesus hates death. Everything about Jesus is life. His life is so prevailing and strong that death itself could never have held Him. Because of sin, the spirit of death has rights to the fleshly body of every man and woman on this planet—believer or non-believer. As we wait for the redemption of our physical bodies, living in the shadow of death, there is still a power that comes upon the sons of God to demonstrate against this wickedness called death on the earth. Jesus Christ is the same yesterday, today, and forever (Hebrews 13:8). He raised the dead during His earthly ministry and commanded His disciples to do the same. In the book of Acts, we see both Peter, the apostle to the Jews, and Paul, the apostle to the Gentiles, demonstrate this mighty operation of God's power against death.

INSPIRATIONAL GIFTS

PROPHECY
TONGUES
INTERPRETATION OF TONGUES

INSPIRATIONAL GIFT 1

PROPHECY

"To another prophecy."
1 Corinthians 12:10

"Prophecy is the first of the three gifts of inspiration. It is a simple gift, and has often been greatly misunderstood, because the term "prophecy," like so many other terms is used both generally and specifically. Prophecy may be defined as the simplest form of inspired utterance."
Howard Carter. Questions and Answers. Pages. 121, 124

"Prophecy is speaking unto men supernaturally"
Lester Sumrall. The Gifts of the Holy Spirit study guide. Page. 28

Paul, writing under the inspiration of the Holy Spirit, admonished the church in Corinth to desire spiritual gifts. When he wrote to them about prophecy, he urged them to desire this gift, *"even more so."* The definition of New Testament (inspirational) prophecy is found in 1 Corinthians 14:3 where Paul writes, *"he that prophesies (being a specific charisma gift) speaks unto men to edification, exhortation, and comfort."* Each of these characteristics of prophecy is ministered by the Holy Spirit to encourage and build the heart of believers—it truly is a heart-building gift. In approaching this charisma gift of the Holy Spirit, we must distance ourselves from the generic use of the term *"prophecy,"* which is used to define any divine utterance. In the New Testament, however, this gift of the Holy Spirit is called, in a specific sense, *"prophecy."*

To further this point, the gift of New Testament (inspirational) prophecy is not a revelatory gift likened to the word of wisdom, the word of knowledge, or the discerning of spirits. These three revelation gifts are the keynote operations that mark the ministry of a prophet of the Lord. Therefore, in this study, we will endeavor to place clear lines of delineation between the office of a prophet who sees spiritually versus the specific operation of New Testament (inspirational) prophecy—which is a simple gift of speech with profound possibilities.

An appropriate example between the ministry of a prophet or seer and the function of New Testament prophecy (exhortation, comfort, and edification) is in the life of Paul. In Acts 21, while Paul was en route to Jerusalem, he received through revelation a directional detour to Caesarea to the house of Philip the evangelist. Philip had four daughters who prophesied. They were not prophets but rather were used by the Holy Spirit to speak forth words of edification, exhortation, and comfort. Paul was heading into the biggest storm of his life, and the Lord wanted to strengthen his heart. After these daughters were used to minister through the gift of prophecy, a prophet named Agabus arrived and began, through revelation or *"seeing gifts,"* to tell Paul what was about to happen to him in Jerusalem. Agabus was speaking divinely by the Holy Spirit, and we would say correctly, in a general sense, that Agabus was prophesying over Paul. But concerning the actual New Testament charisma gift, only the daughters of Philip functioned in that grace.

Paul's heart needed exhortation, edification, and comfort to strengthen him for what was coming. Though on the other hand, Paul's natural understanding needed revelation from God on what lay before him. In short, the word of wisdom revealed the future through a prophet, while the gift of New Testament prophecy imparted strength and comfort to Paul, preparing his heart to have victory in the midst of what was coming.

Now we understand why Paul urged believers to desire this gift so that the church would be edified and strengthened. I am sure that Paul appreciated the ministry of Agabus, but even more so, he cherished the edification and comfort of the Holy Spirit imparted into his heart through this simple gift of utterance called New Testament (inspirational) prophecy.

PROPHECY
A DEFINITIVE LOOK

(Jerusalem, Judea, Samaria)

1. **PROPHECY: Rest, edified, and comforted in the Holy Ghost**
   Acts 9:31
   "Then had the churches rest throughout all Judaea and Galilee and Samaria, and were edified; and walking in the fear of the Lord, and in the comfort of the Holy Ghost, were multiplied."

   Note: The persecution by Saul and others against the church had been great. Many believers had been jailed while others had been put to death. Yet, through the power of the Holy Spirit, this onslaught against Christ's followers had been dealt a major blow through the conversion of Saul. During His teaching at the last supper, Jesus called the Holy Spirit the *"comforter"* (John 14:16). One of the greatest operations of comfort in the church comes from New Testament (inspirational) prophecy, which edifies, exhorts, and comforts. With the intense persecution the church had experienced, it would be within acceptable bounds to assume that prophecy, with tongues and the interpretation of tongues, had been operating in the assemblies during this time.

2. **PROPHECY: Church in Antioch**
   Acts 11:26
   "When he had found him, he brought him unto Antioch. And it came to pass, that a whole year they assembled themselves with the church, and taught much people. And the disciples were called Christians first in Antioch."

Note: The word *"called"* in the original Greek is *"chrematizo,"* which means *"a divine utterance."* The New Testament definition of prophecy is a divine utterance that edifies, exhorts, and comforts (1 Corinthians 14:3). Here, in this passage, the Lord through edification and comfort calls the church a name that characterizes who they follow and the miraculous presence in them and upon them. The Lord loves to give names, and when He does—the name He gives will last. The name Christian and how it came through prophecy both comforted and edified the church in Antioch and is still the principal name for believers today—used globally some 2000 years later.

(To the Uttermost Parts of the Earth

3. **PROPHECY: Judas and Silas strengthened the church**
   Acts 15:32
   "And Judas and Silas, being prophets also themselves, <u>exhorted</u> the brethren with <u>many words</u>, and <u>confirmed</u> (strengthened) them."

Note: The key words in this passage are *"exhorted, with many words, and confirmed."* Let us take this verse step by step. First, Judas and Silas were called prophets. They ministered to the body of Christ through gifts of revelation *(word of wisdom, word of knowledge, discerning of spirits)*, which are gifts that spiritually *"see."* Being ministers with a sensitivity to the Holy Spirit, they were used in this example to exhort the brethren with *"many"* words. Let me clarify, a person who is a prophet with gifts of revelation can also be used in the simple gift of inspirational prophecy.

As stated earlier, Paul urged the Corinthians to desire the gift of prophecy above all. Why? Because this gift imparts the needed nutrients of faith, hope, and love into the hearts of God's people. These two prophets were used in this verse to speak with edification, exhortation, and comfort into the corporate life of the church as well as to the individual hearts of the believers. The word in this passage *"confirmed"* is better defined by the word established, strengthened, or placed firmly, which is the very purpose of the gift of prophecy operating in the local church.

Remember, this is a simple gift with profound possibilities, for through this gift, Peter's fearful heart was changed so that he stepped out of a boat and walked on water—walking in the miraculous. In closing, this passage is a wonderful example that brings clarity on how a prophet (or a seer) who is used in revelation gifts can also be used in the inspirational gift called prophecy.

4. **PROPHECY: Lydia hearing Paul**
   Acts 16:14
   "A certain woman named Lydia, a seller of purple, of the city of Thyatira, which worshipped God, heard us: whose heart the Lord opened, that she attended unto the things which were spoken of Paul."

   Note: As Paul spoke, Lydia listened, and the words he spoke were unlike any she had ever heard. The gift of prophecy, which is equal in outcome to the two other inspirational gifts known as tongues and the interpretation of tongues, accomplishes three objectives: 1) to edify; 2) to exhort; 3) to comfort. In this passage, as Paul was speaking, so was the Holy Spirit. Reference 1 Corinthians 14:24–25: *"But if all prophesy, and there come in one that believeth not, or one unlearned, he is convinced of all, he is judged of all: And thus are the secrets of his heart made manifest; and so falling down on his face he will worship God, and report that God is in you of a truth."* I have included this passage, in line with 1 Corinthians 14:24–25 under prophecy, due to how the Bible states the Lord opened Lydia's heart as she listened. There is no gift like prophecy that can open the human heart, bringing life-changing conviction.

5. **PROPHECY: The Lord Encourages and Comforts Paul**
   Acts 18:9–10
   "Then spake the Lord to Paul in the night by a vision, Be not afraid, but speak, and hold not thy peace: For I am with thee, and no man shall set on thee to hurt thee: for I have much people in this city."

   Note: There is nothing like the voice of the Lord speaking into the hearts of His people. Paul's road was not an easy one; therefore, there was great need for continual encouragement and comfort. Here, in this passage, we have multiple gifts working alongside the simple gift of prophecy, such as the word of wisdom and the word of knowledge. The simple words, *"be not afraid... I am with you,"* set Paul's heart to rest (strengthened and comforted) as he went forward in the direction of the Lord.

6. **PROPHECY: Twelve Ephesians**
   Acts 19:6
   "And when Paul had laid his hands upon them, the Holy Ghost came on them; and they spake with tongues, and prophesied."

   Note: Once again, the baptism of the Holy Spirit is both seen and heard. That day, outside the boundaries of the land of Israel, these men experienced the reality of being in Christ. As the Holy Spirit descended upon them, divine utterance began to flow out—both in foreign tongues as well as words of edification, exhortation, and comfort. I am sure these twelve men never forgot the day Paul came to town.

7. **PROPHECY: Daughters of Philip to Paul**
Acts 21:9
"And the same man had four daughters, virgins, which did prophesy."

Note: In this passage, we see the purpose for which the Holy Spirit diverted Paul's trip to Caesarea. The Lord needed to fortify Paul's heart before going to Jerusalem. Obviously, Paul was about to enter one of the greatest storms of his life and ministry as the winds of the Holy Spirit began to blow—moving the great apostle towards Rome. There is nothing like the operation of prophecy, which edifies, exhorts, and comforts the human heart. The essence of this gift brings the voice of the Father into the home of the human heart, and the result is always miraculous. It is not hard to understand why Paul urged the church to fervently desire this gift above all others.

8. **PROPHECY: The Lord comforts Paul's heart**
Acts 23:11
"And the night following the Lord stood by him, and said, Be of good cheer, Paul: for as thou hast testified of me in Jerusalem, so must thou bear witness also at Rome."

Note: The Lord spoke such comfort into Paul's heart by declaring, *"be of good cheer."* It is the entrance of His word that brings light, life, joy, peace, and everything good. This simple gift carries with it the assurance of the ever-watchful care of our great shepherd.

"For God, who commanded the light to shine out of darkness, hath shined in our hearts, to give the light of the knowledge of the glory of God in the face of Jesus Christ. But we have this treasure in earthen vessels, that the excellency of the power may be of God, and not of us. We are troubled on every side, yet not distressed; we are perplexed, but not in despair; Persecuted, but not forsaken; cast down, but not destroyed"
2 Corinthians 4:6–9

9. **PROPHECY: Comfort spoken into Paul's heart**
Acts 27:23–24
"For there stood by me this night the angel of God, whose I am, and whom I serve, Saying, Fear not, Paul; thou must be brought before Caesar: and, lo, God hath given thee all them that sail with thee."

Note: Their being in the storm was not a part of God's original plan. Paul warned them, but they ignored him. Now Paul, en route to somewhere, is beginning to wonder whether God's plan has been ruined by the men who had been given charge over him. Probably the devil was sitting there, day and night, telling Paul that this was the end for him. This all changed when the angel appeared and spoke simple words of comfort into Paul's heart,

"Fear not!" I am reminded of the disciples in a similar situation on the sea of Galilee. Jesus was walking on the water, and the disciples, full of fear, thought He was a ghost. Jesus simply spoke, *"Fear not, it is I."* These simple words changed the atmosphere in Peter's heart and launched him into the realm of miracles. Peter, because of what happened in his heart, was now enabled to get out of the boat and walk on water—actually water with waves.

Never underestimate the importance of prophecy. Simple words spoken can change the atmosphere in a man's heart from fear to faith. One final thought concerning this passage is that different gifts can work together at the same time. As simple words of prophecy were released to Paul's heart, then came the word of wisdom, confirming that his destination would be Caesar.

10. PROPHECY: Paul uses the word of wisdom in a prophetic operation to encourage their hearts

Acts 27:34–37

"Wherefore I pray you to take some meat: for this is for your health: for there shall not an hair fall from the head of any of you. And when he had thus spoken, he took bread, and gave thanks to God in presence of them all: and when he had broken it, he began to eat. Then were they all of good cheer, and they also took some meat. And we were in all in the ship two hundred threescore and sixteen souls."

Note: Only a supernatural gift of inspiration can change the atmosphere in the hearts of 276 desperate, exhausted, and hungry men. Paul, under an anointing of the Holy Spirit, uses revelation from the word spoken earlier to encourage the hearts of all those listening. The inspiration gifts, which carry a measure of the glory of the Lord, exhort and comfort the hearts of men, even in certain cases where men are not Christians. The Lord's compassion was for all, not just for Paul.

The chief gift in this operation was the gift of faith, being administered by the presence of the angel of the Lord. The word of wisdom and the simple words of prophecy were hooked into this overriding operation of God's faith as the wind of the Holy Spirit was propelling Paul to Rome.

INSPIRATIONAL GIFT 2

TONGUES

"To another divers (different) kinds of tongues."
1 Corinthians 12:10

"One might say, then, that a definition of this gift is the power to speak supernaturally by the Holy Spirit, in a language not known to the one possessing the gift. The speaking with tongues, therefore, is an amazing miracle of utterance."

Howard Carter. Questions and Answers. Page. 166.

The *"sign gift"* of different kinds of tongues is when God speaks directly to man through man such as on the day of Pentecost (Acts 2:4–8).
To understand tongues further we must accept one important, unchanging truth—the truth being that all languages come from God.

When the Lord breathed life into Adam, his eyes opened. The first thing Adam saw was the face of God. Adam saw God's smile. Then Adam heard the Lord's voice for the first time. After a short pause, Adam spoke, and God heard Adam's voice for the first time. As man spoke, creation itself rejoiced in this new relationship of Father and son. It is in this special creation called man that language finds itself at the core of who man is, created in the image of God to fellowship with God. In the new birth, man is restored to sonship, and with this restored position of authority comes a new language of communion, flowing in unlimited speech upward to the throne of God. This prayer language, empowered by the baptism of the Holy Spirit, enables God and man to pray together the perfect will of God.

Paul wrote in 1 Corinthians 14:4 that he who speaks (prays) in tongues edifies himself, while they that prophesy (which includes the gift of tongues and the interpretation of tongues) edifies the church. It becomes clear in studying chapter 14 that there is both a place for unlimited communion through prayer to God in tongues as well as the Holy Spirit using tongues in a directional change to speak outward to man.

In approaching this wonderful gift of the Holy Spirit, we must move forward slowly, step by step, so that a firm foundation is laid in our hearts. The goal is to *"not be ignorant"* of this gift. Therefore, *"tongues"* is a New Testament operation of speech that is composed of 1) a personal prayer language—speaking to God, and 2) a *charisma* gift of the Spirit—where the Holy Spirit speaks outward to men. In studying Paul's writings, it becomes clear that Paul saw tongues as tongues, and the difference between the two operations would be the directional flow of how they are used.

This speaking characteristic of the Holy Spirit in the life of a New Testament believer was noted by Jesus in John 4:14. Jesus likened salvation to a well of water springing up into everlasting life and then turned around in John 7:38,39, declaring that out of the same believer's belly would gush forth a river of living water. One operation is heavenward, while the other operation is manward.

The prayer language called tongues is the foundational gift of tongues that is imparted into a believer when he or she is baptized in the Holy Spirit. Remember, the book of Acts is not a suggestive picture of what the Lord desires for His church but rather a living blueprint that was designed to govern the church throughout the ages. In our communion with the Lord, the Holy Spirit in us can empower a change in our speaking in tongues, just as you and I can turn the cold water on at the sink and then quickly change to hot water by turning a different handle. The water is coming from the same source, but hot water carries a specific modification in it—heat. So it is with tongues, and there is a noticeable difference in how this flow of inspiration can change from upward to outward. Please note that the charisma gift of *tongues* found in 1 Corinthians 12:10 is controlled by the Holy Spirit (as He wills) and not by man—man simply yields to this flow of grace.

In my closing thought, the three inspirational gifts of the Holy Spirit accomplish the same task of 1) encouragement, 2) edification, and 3) comfort. In one sense, it is as if the Lord split prophecy into two divisions (prophecy on one side with tongues and the interpretation of tongues on the other).

"For with stammering lips and another tongue
will he speak to this people. To whom he said,
This is the rest wherewith ye may cause the weary to rest;
and this is the refreshing: yet they would not hear."
Isaiah 28:11–12

You may ask, *"why does God use the gift of tongues with the interpretation of tongues when He can accomplish the same result through the gift of prophecy?"* Good question. First, He does it because He is God and finds pleasure in what He creates. Remember, it is God who created us and not we who created God! Second, God is gathering what He scattered at the Tower of Babel. It is a full circle from the Tower to the Upper Room. One act of bestowing languages was to scatter, while the second act was to gather all nations (Acts 2).

TONGUES
A DEFINITIVE LOOK

(Jerusalem, Judea, Samaria)

1. **TONGUES: 120 (Apostles and other disciples including Mary)**
   Acts 2:4
   "They were all filled with the Holy Ghost, and began to speak with other tongues, as the Spirit gave them utterance.

   Acts 2:6–8
   "When this was noised abroad, the multitude came together, and were confounded, because that every man heard them speak in his own language. And they were all amazed and marveled, saying one to another, Behold, are not all these which speak Galileans? And how hear we every man in our own tongue, wherein we were born?"

   Note: The gift of tongues on certain occasions does not need the actual sister gift of the interpretation of tongues. In this example, the interpretation was not needed because the gift of tongues was being manifested in the actual languages of those present. Of course, the miracle was found in that the disciples had never spoken in those languages. In conclusion, prayer tongues and the gift of tongues are still tongues. Both are miraculous in operation, and in the hands of the Holy Spirit, the Lord can speak to mankind in a very edifying way. This is the reason why Satan has fought both operations of tongues so viciously.

(To the Uttermost Parts of the Earth)

2. **TONGUES: Ephesian believers.**
   Acts 19:6
   "When Paul had laid his hands upon them, the Holy Ghost came on them; and they spake with tongues, and prophesied."

   Note: In this passage, we will put our focus on the words *"spake with tongues and prophesied."* This simple phrase and the depth contained therein are further explained in 1 Corinthians 14. These Ephesian believers had no understanding of tongues. Yet when hands were laid on them, they began to speak in new languages like the apostles did when they spoke in tongues on the day of Pentecost. It is also important to note that this baptism took place outside the land of Israel, thus showing the power of the gospel was not limited to the geographical boundaries of the Holy Land. Both the great commission to preach to the lost and the baptism of the Holy Spirit function on a global scale. As these Ephesian believers were experiencing the fulness of the Holy Spirit for the first time, tongues and prophecy were the result.

The reason I listed this passage as a demonstration of the gift of tongues is that when you have tongues being spoken mixed with prophecy, it is very likely that the *"gift of tongues and interpretation of tongues"* are (or could be) operating as well. Remember, these two gifts manifested are equal in result to prophecy. The only difference is in functionality. You may ask, *"how are tongues and the interpretation of tongues equal to prophecy?"* On the day of Pentecost, as the disciples spoke in new tongues, those watching and listening had no need for the gift of the interpretation of tongues. To those speaking, it was an operation of the gift of tongues. But to those listening, it was no different than prophecy. To put it a different way, the interpretation of tongues, which is spoken in the known language of those listening, is no different than prophecy, except that it was preceded by an operation of the gift of tongues. These three languages gifts, or language operations of the Holy Spirit, are truly the blessing of God; the same God who gave man languages at Babel as a type of judgment, who now, through Christ gives believers this same ability, but as an act of blessing.

Tongues are a further sign to the unbeliever of the indwelling presence of a living Christ. This is the last reference in the book of Acts to tongues, but it was not the end of this precious operation of the Holy Spirit in the lives of believers. I personally have received this wonderful gift of communion prayer. I have also experienced the power of God coming upon me as a gift, changing my prayer tongue to perfect Ukrainian. When this happened, a group of newly arrived immigrants from Ukraine received a personal word from the Lord. Though speaking in perfect Ukrainian, I, of course, understood nothing. I was simply enjoying the presence of God that had come upon me as I yielded to the gift of tongues. We must desire this gift!

INSPIRATIONAL GIFT 3

THE INTERPRETATION OF TONGUES

"To another the interpretation of tongues."
1 Corinthians 12:10

"The interpretation of tongues is, of course, simply the ability to translate into a known tongue what has been spoken in an unknown tongue. The one possessing the gift will be in the Spirit at the time when the utterance in other tongues is given, so that the words will be registered on his spirit and he will feel the urge to speak what God gives him."

Howard Carter. Questions and Answers. Page. 179,180

The interpretation of tongues is a *"charisma"* gift of the Holy Spirit that corresponds with its sister gift called *"tongues."* This gift brings an interpretation (message) of an unknown tongue into the realm of man's understanding through the vehicle or message in a known language. Though, there are times when the Holy Spirit uses a tongue to speak to someone (usually a guest to a particular group) who does not speak in the principal language of those leading the meeting. Therefore, when this happens the gift of the interpretation of tongues would not be needed in that the message was understood by the intended hearer—even though the person operating under this gift had no knowledge of what they had said.

When praying in our personal prayer language of tongues, we are admonished to desire to interpret what we pray. But, for the most part, we pray and trust what the Word of God says, *"the understanding is unfruitful"* (1 Corinthians 14:14). The gift of the interpretation of tongues is the answer or message that accompanies the supernatural gift called tongues. The interpretation will always be in the language of the audience for which the Spirit of God is seeking to comfort, edify, and encourage. Tongues and the interpretation of tongues equal prophecy and were added to the New Testament as a sign of the inward presence of the Holy Spirit in the body of Christ. Tongues, in either operation, prayer language, or gift, are a sign to the unbeliever.

In closing, these three gifts of utterance bring the voice of the Father into the house of the human heart to stabilize and bring assurance to the children of God. Prophecy edifies. Tongues and the interpretation of tongues edify. Last, but not least, the individual in communion with the Lord, while praying in other tongues, is also edified. All these operations produce the fruit of edification and comfort. In reading 1 Corinthians 14, one can hear Paul's deep desire for the body of Christ to be edified, and with this plea, he admonished them to *"forbid not"* speaking in other tongues (1 Corinthians 14:39).

THE INTERPRETATION OF TONGUES
A DEFINITIVE LOOK

(To the Uttermost Parts of the Earth)

1. **INTERPRETATION OF TONGUES: Ephesian believers**
   Acts 19:6
   "When Paul had laid his hands upon them, the Holy Ghost came on them; and they spake with tongues, and prophesied."

   Note: As stated earlier, the reason I listed this passage as a demonstration of the gift of the interpretation of tongues is that when you have tongues being spoken with prophecy, it is very likely that the *"interpretation of tongues"* is (or could be) operating as well. Remember, these two gifts manifested are equal in result to prophecy. The only difference is in functionality. I have been in strong prayer meetings where prophecy began to be spoken forth, and because those attending had been speaking in other tongues, only the Lord knew whether the prophecy was with or without the initial gift of the Holy Spirit called tongues. Put more simply, prophecy and the interpretation of tongues are the same operation, except the interpretation of tongues is released through the operation of its sister gift called *"tongues."* Also, a minister in charge of a meeting, providing he is spiritually matured, will discern a change in the operation of the Holy Spirit when these gifts come into manifestation.

   Though prophecy and the interpretation of tongues are the same, it is the manifestation of the gift of tongues *(which precedes the interpretation of tongues)* that is also used as an additional sign to the unbeliever. Remember, the Holy Spirit is God, and He can operate how He desires. His thoughts are not our thoughts, neither are His ways our ways (Isaiah 55:10).

   We must desire this gift! We are commanded to desire all these gifts.

DOCUMENTED
HARVEST

"SAY NOT, THERE ARE YET FOUR MONTHS, AND THEN COMETH HARVEST? BEHOLD, I SAY UNTO YOU, LIFT UP YOUR EYES, AND LOOK ON THE FIELDS; FOR THEY ARE WHITE ALREADY TO HARVEST."

JOHN 4:35

DOCUMENTED HARVEST

A DEFINITIVE LOOK AT HARVEST IN THE BOOK OF ACTS

"And Jesus said unto them, Come ye after me, and I will make you to become fishers of men."
Mark 1:17

"Then saith he unto his disciples, The harvest truly is plenteous, but the labourers are few; Pray ye therefore the Lord of the harvest, that he will send forth labourers into his harvest."
Matthew 9:37–38

"Be patient therefore, brethren, unto the coming of the Lord. Behold, the husbandman waiteth for the precious fruit of the earth, and hath long patience for it, until he receive the early and latter rain."
James 5:7

PREFACE

When Jesus stepped into Peter's boat and requested him to push out from shore, Peter had no idea that he was embarking into his destiny. As Jesus finished teaching the multitudes, He turned to Peter and commanded him to thrust out into deeper water. Peter, who had been fishing all night, was tired but, in his tiredness, he could not deny the fire burning in his heart as Jesus taught. He had never heard words like these. With holy fire burning in Peter's heart, he obeyed and thrust the boat out further. Now in deeper water, Jesus spoke again, bringing new conflict between Peter's natural intellect and the burning sensation in his heart. With eyes full of love for this headstrong fisherman, Jesus commanded, *"throw out your nets for a catch."* With natural tiredness from fishing all night mixed with the reality of the foolishness of the request, Peter obeyed, stating, *"at your word I will let down the net."* Once the net was brought in, almost sinking the boat from the weight of the catch, Peter fell at Jesus' feet and repented, requesting Jesus to depart from him. Jesus then spoke new words to Peter, *"fear not, from now on you will catch men!"* These words not only charted the course of Peter's destiny but the book of Acts as well. The book of Acts is a book of harvest, the harvest of all nations.

HARVEST
QUICK REFERENCE

Reference	Description of Harvest
(Jerusalem, Judea, Samaria)	
1. Acts 2:41	About 3000 souls
2. Acts 2:47	The Lord added daily
3. Acts 4:4	5000 men
4. Acts 5:12,14	Multitudes of men and women
5. Acts 6:7	Disciples greatly multiplied in Jerusalem
6. Acts 6:7	A great company of priests
7. Acts 8:12,14	Samaria broken open by the power of God
8. Acts 8:13	Simon the Sorcerer
9. Acts 8:37,38	An Ethiopian
10. Acts 9:18	Saul who became Paul
11. Acts 9:31	Churches multiplied
12. Acts 9:35	All Sharon and Lydda
13. Acts 9:42	Many in Joppa
14. Acts 10:44–48	Cornelius, his family, and friends (Gentiles)
15. Acts 11:21	A great number
16. Acts 11:24	Many People
17. Acts 12:24	Grew and multiplied
(To the Uttermost Parts of the Earth)	
18. Acts 13:12	Deputy Sergius Paulus
19. Acts 13:43	Many Jews and religious proselytes
20. Acts 13:48	Many
21. Acts 14:1	A great multitude of Jews and Greeks
22. Acts 16:5	Increased in number daily
23. Acts 16:15	Lydia and her household
24. Acts 16:30–34	Keeper of the jail and his household
25. Acts 17:4	Some Jews
26. Acts 17:4	Great multitude of Greeks
27. Acts 17:4	Chief women
28. Acts 17:12	Many Jews in Berea
29. Acts 17:12	Honorable Greek women and men
30. Acts 17:34	Dionysius, Damaris, and others
31. Acts 18:8	Crispus and his household
32. Acts 18:8	Many Corinthians
33. Acts 19:5–7	About twelve of John's disciples
34. Acts 19:18	Many
35. Acts 28:24	Some believed
36. Acts 28:28	Gentiles

HARVEST
A DEFINITIVE LOOK

(Jerusalem, Judea, Samaria)

1. **ABOUT 3000 SOULS**
   Acts 2:41
   "Then they that gladly received his word were baptized: and the same day there were added unto them about three thousand souls."

   Note: Jesus shocked His disciples one day when He declared that He was returning to His Father and that the result of His returning to heaven would bring an empowerment upon them to do *"even greater works"* than He had done. The disciples had grown accustomed to hearing Jesus speak words they didn't understand. This was another such case, in that they had watched Jesus give sight to the blind, cause cripples to walk and even raise the dead—regardless of how long they had been dead. Those two words *"greater works"* must have totally shocked them. But standing before the multitudes on the day of Pentecost, Peter entered into a type of ministry that Jesus had never demonstrated during His time with them on earth.

   As he preached to the multitude gathered, something new began to stir in their hearts. Finally, the crowd called out to Peter, *"what must we do?"* Peter proceeded to give the first altar call for men to be saved by faith in the name of Jesus. On that first day of the church, roughly 3000 souls were born again. Peter had a front row seat in watching the power of the Holy Spirit change men from death to life, from darkness to light. As Peter stood there, he must have thought back to his first fishing experience with Jesus. From a boat sinking load of fish to now this, Jesus had done it again!

   Was Peter alone in this operation of harvest? No. As the power of God was poured out upon Jerusalem, there were three recorded gifts of the Holy Spirit manifested that affected this harvest of souls. How we need the gifts and operations of the Holy Spirit!

2. **THE LORD ADDED DAILY**
   Acts 2:47
   "And the Lord added to the church daily such as should be saved."

   Note: Salvation is not a work of man, though we are commanded to preach the gospel. In our preaching, we are empowered to plant and to water, but the increase comes from the Lord (1 Corinthians 3:6). Paul, in writing to the Corinthians tells them that it is the Lord who sets the members in the church. As the apostles preached, the Lord confirmed His word with signs, wonders, and miracles. Though no specific manifestation of the Holy Spirit is documented in this verse, we do know that God's power was flowing through the ministry of the apostles. Would this harvest have been the same without the gifts of the Holy Spirit in operation?

3. **5000 MEN**
   Acts 4:4
   "Many of them which heard the word believed; and the number of the men was about five thousand."

   Note: Everyone who went to the temple most likely had seen this man. This miracle performed at the temple, the very epicenter of Jewish worship, catapulted the church into the forefront of Jewish society through the demonstration of the name of Jesus! That day the Lord, by healing a crippled man, established his authority to forgive sin through faith in His name (Mark 2:1–12). The effect of this healing saw over 5000 people turn to the Lord.

4. **MULTITUDES OF MEN AND WOMEN**
   Acts 5:12
   "And by the hands of the apostles were many signs and wonders wrought among the people; and they were all with one accord in Solomon's porch."

   Acts 5: 14
   "And believers were the more added to the Lord, multitudes both of men and women."

   Note: The judgment upon Ananias and Saphira brought a fear of the Lord upon all who heard the story. The multiple operations of the Holy Spirit in this judgment had a definite effect upon the people (both believers and non-believers). The church, without the fear of the Lord in their midst, is handicapped from certain aspects of the harvest. It is also clear that the apostles, through the laying on of their hands, were actively working in the power of God. Such power, such harvest!

5. **DISCIPLES GREATLY MULTIPLIED IN JERUSALEM.**
   Acts 6:7
   "And the word of God increased; and the number of the disciples multiplied in Jerusalem greatly; and a great company of the priests were obedient to the faith."

   Note: The Bible does not list a specific example of the gifts of the Holy Spirit in operation in this harvest. What we do understand is that when the church made necessary adjustments to how it was operating structurally, a corresponding flow of grace was released into the harvest. It would also be correct to link the effect of Stephen's miracles to this harvest, even though this passage does not specifically reveal how long Stephen's ministry lasted before his death. In closing, it is necessary to note that how the church thinks and operates affects the flow of the Holy Spirit out into the harvest.

6. **A GREAT COMPANY OF PRIESTS**
   Acts 6:7
   "And the word of God increased; and the number of the disciples multiplied in Jerusalem greatly; and a great company of the priests were obedient to the faith."

   Note: The adjustments made by the Jerusalem church, by appointing Holy Spirit-filled deacons, not only affected multitudes of people but it also had a direct effect on the priesthood. When these priests witnessed ordinary men ministering in the power of God, and not just the apostles, it convinced them of the authority that is in the gospel of Christ. A new tier of miracle workers was a sign and wonder as well as a threat to the religious and pagan world of their day. This rock of revelation was moving in the earth, and it was breaking to pieces the idols of Jewish religious culture. In closing, I would attribute this harvest to the fresh flow of God's power that came through structural adjustments by church leadership.

7. **SAMARIA BROKEN OPEN BY THE POWER OF GOD**
   Acts 8:12, 14
   "But when they believed Philip preaching the things concerning the kingdom of God, and the name of Jesus Christ, they were baptized, both men and women. Now when the apostles which were at Jerusalem heard that Samaria had received the word of God, they sent unto them Peter and John:"

   Note: The Lord was working with Philip, confirming the word he preached with signs and wonders. The signs manifested God's sovereign presence, and the wonders demanded Samaria's attention. These signs and wonders done by Philip were called *"miracles"* in a general sense. In a more specific understanding, we know that the gifts of healings were in operation because of the various illnesses that were cured. God had captured their attention; He was reaffirming His great love for them through the preaching of the gospel. The result was another boat sinking load of fish—of the humankind.

8. **SIMON THE SORCERER**
   Acts 8:13
   "Then Simon himself believed also: and when he was baptized, he continued with Philip, and wondered, beholding the miracles and signs which were done."

HARVEST

Note: There is nothing like the power of God in manifestation. Though Pharoah's magicians performed magic, it was the power of God in Moses' staff that devoured any competing demonstration of miracles before the king that day. In this example, Simon was getting a taste of real holy power, and it caused him to believe.

9. AN ETHIOPIAN

Acts 8:37, 38

"And Philip said, If thou believest with all thine heart, thou mayest. And he answered and said, I believe that Jesus Christ is the Son of God. And he commanded the chariot to stand still: and they went down both into the water, both Philip and the eunuch; and he baptized him."

Note: God saw the heart of a man that was hungering for righteousness and truth. When the poor and needy seek water, and there is none, God declared that He not only hears them but will also open a river in high places to satisfy them (Isaiah 41:17–20). These gifts of the Holy Spirit manifested in Philip's ministry opened a river of living water that not only satisfied the Eunuch but watered Ethiopia as well. Without the operation of the gifts of the Holy Spirit directing Philip, this man from a foreign nation may never have heard the gospel. This passage of scripture deserves much time in study and in prayer. Without the manifestation of the power of God and the ministry of angels, is the church truly fulfilling the great commission?

10. SAUL, WHO BECAME PAUL

Acts 9:18

"And immediately there fell from his eyes as it had been scales: and he received sight forthwith, and arose, and was baptized."

Note: The power of God manifested in Paul's conversion was soon to be manifested through Paul—shaking the world through the gospel that he preached.

11. CHURCHES MULTIPLIED

Acts 9:31

"Then had the churches rest throughout all Judaea and Galilee and Samaria, and were edified; and walking in the fear of the Lord, and in the comfort of the Holy Ghost, were multiplied."

Note: The operations of the Holy Spirit at work in Paul's turning to the Lord had a direct effect upon the harvest listed here. Also, people had witnessed how the church had been treated, and still, during such persecution, they had an undeniable peace about them. This tangible comfort upon the church was key to their multiplication.

12. ALL OF SHARON AND LYDDA

Acts 9:35

"And all that dwelt at Lydda and Sharon saw him, and turned to the Lord."

Note: One operation of the gifts of healings caused two villages to turn to the Lord.

13. MANY IN JOPPA

Acts 9:42

"It was known throughout all Joppa; and many believed in the Lord."

Note: The harvest in Joppa was the result of Dorcas being raised from the dead. This resurrection testimony was the result of the power gifts of the Holy Spirit operating in Peter's life. I would also imagine that when Dorcas opened her eyes, she had some wonderful stories to tell. Her testimony of heaven would also have had a great effect upon this harvest of souls.

"We are confident, I say, and willing rather to be absent from the body, and to be present with the Lord."
2 Corinthians 5:8

14. CORNELIUS, HIS FAMILY AND FRIENDS (GENTILES)

Acts 10:44–48

"While Peter yet spake these words, the Holy Ghost fell on all them which heard the word. And they of the circumcision which believed were astonished, as many as came with Peter, because that on the Gentiles also was poured out the gift of the Holy Ghost. For they heard them speak with tongues, and magnify God. Then answered Peter, Can any man forbid water, that these should not be baptized, which have received the Holy Ghost as well as we? And he commanded them to be baptized in the name of the Lord. Then prayed they him to tarry certain days."

Note: In this salvation testimony of Cornelius and his household, we see nine gifts of the Holy Spirit in operation. Without these supernatural operations of God, Jewish Peter and Roman Cornelius would never have come together for this harvest. Not only was Cornelius and his household saved, but the door to the Gentiles had been opened—and it stayed open.

15. A GREAT NUMBER

Acts 11:21

"And the hand of the Lord was with them: and a great number believed, and turned unto the Lord."

Note: The phrase, *"the hand of the Lord"* refers to supernatural operations of the Holy Spirit. Because the hand of the Lord in this passage is associated with great numbers of people coming to faith, I would credit both evangelistic power gifts of healings and miracles to be the ones responsible for breaking open the spiritual atmosphere and binding the strongman. Once the demonic strongman was bound, the harvest of souls began to come forth (Matthew 12:29, Mark 3:27).

16. MANY PEOPLE

Acts 11:24

"For he was a good man, and full of the Holy Ghost and of faith: and much (many) people was (were) added unto the Lord."

Note: Being full of the Holy Spirit and faith is the key to fruitful evangelism. The secret to this fullness was the strength of a church given to prayer. The New Testament Acts church fervently prayed that the Lord would stretch out His hand to heal, performing signs and wonders. They believed that the future of Christianity depended on evangelistic prayer mixed with the preaching of the gospel.

17. GREW AND MULTIPLIED

Acts 12:24

"But the word of God grew and multiplied."

Note: Though there are no specific gifts of the Holy Spirit in operation in this account of harvest, it is undeniable that the miraculous judgment upon Herod, which was administered by the angel, was critical to the church having peace. In conclusion, it was the strong corporate praying of the church that released the authority of the throne of God to change civil government—thus paving a way for souls to be saved.

(To the Uttermost Parts of the Earth)

18. DEPUTY SERGIUS PAULUS

Acts 13:12

"Then the deputy, when he saw what was done, believed, being astonished at the doctrine of the Lord."

Note: In this passage, we are introduced to one aspect of the doctrine of the Lord—which is judgment. Elymas, the sorcerer, was full of demonic power, but Paul, on the other hand, was full of the Holy Spirit. What would have been the outcome if Paul had not been full of the Holy Spirit? What would have been the outcome if Paul had not allowed the gifts of the Holy Spirit to operate through him? Suppression of the Holy Spirit will always affect the harvest the church is called to bring in. The deputy witnessed God's power in manifestation—and it changed him.

19. MANY JEWS AND RELIGIOUS PROSELYTES

Acts 13:43

"Now when the congregation was broken up, many of the Jews and religious proselytes followed Paul and Barnabas: who, speaking to them, persuaded them to continue in the grace of God."

Note: It was Paul's preaching that was convincing many to follow Christ. Signs and wonders are tools to assist in the harvest of the nations, but there is nothing more vital than the preaching of the Word of God—which never returns void (Isaiah 55:11).

20. MANY

Acts 13:48

"And when the Gentiles heard this, they were glad, and glorified the word of the Lord: and as many as were ordained to eternal life believed."

Note: When the Gentiles heard Paul declare the Word of God concerning his calling to preach to them, they were filled with joy. This word from the Lord directed Paul's life and ministry and brought great joy into the hearts of those originally thought to be outside the boundaries of salvation.

21. A GREAT MULTITUDE OF JEWS AND GREEKS

Acts 14:1

"And it came to pass in Iconium, that they went both together into the synagogue of the Jews, and so spake, that a great multitude both of the Jews and also of the Greeks believed."

Note: This harvest in Iconium came to the Lord through Paul's preaching. No signs and wonders were documented as being needed to convince the listeners. The voice of the Lord is mighty upon the waters (Psalms 29:3).

22. INCREASED IN NUMBER DAILY

Acts 16:5

"And so were the churches established in the faith and increased in number daily."

Note: The spirit of faith (2 Corinthians 4:13) must be the dominating spirit in the local church. A church established in faith, which pleases God, has the potential to increase in number daily.

"But without faith it is impossible to please God."
Hebrews 11:6

23. LYDIA AND HER HOUSEHOLD

Acts 16:15

"And a certain woman named Lydia, a seller of purple, of the city of Thyatira, which worshipped God, heard us: whose heart the Lord opened, that she attended unto the things which were spoken of Paul. And when she was baptized, and her household, she besought us, saying, If ye have judged me to be faithful to the Lord, come into my house, and abide there. And she constrained us."

Note: Lydia was a worshipper of God that needed to be born again through faith in Christ. The work of God in Lydia's heart was so powerful that her house became the temporary base of Christian operation in that region. I would have to think that the discerning of spirits also came upon Lydia to know she could trust these men, that these were good men—men sent from God. It is also important to note that this harvest of Lydia, her household, and ultimately the region came because of Paul's vision of the man from Macedonia. The gifts of the Holy Spirit in operation definitely were responsible for this new door opening into that region.

24. KEEPER OF THE JAIL AND HIS HOUSEHOLD

Acts 16:30–34

"And brought them out, and said, Sirs, what must I do to be saved? And they said, Believe on the Lord Jesus Christ, and thou shalt be saved, and thy house. And they spake unto him the word of the Lord, and to all that were in his house. And he took them the same hour of the night, and washed their stripes; and was baptized, he and all his, straightway. And when he had brought them into his house, he set meat before them, and rejoiced, believing in God with all his house."

Note: As Paul and Silas prayed and sang praises, the operation of God's special faith, fully mature and full of power, shook that jail to its core. Those two missionaries simply received God's power delivering them. In this occurrence, though the shackles fell off and the doors opened, no one escaped. Most likely, the other prisoners sat paralyzed in their dark cells, too afraid to move.

This operation of God's special faith was a sign and wonder both to the jailor and to every prisoner. Through the word of knowledge, Paul cries out to the jailor, *"don't harm yourself."* This further astounded the jailor, who was kept from self-destruction. The operation of the gift of faith upon that prison positioned all therein to hear the preaching of the gospel. The result of this operation of power was household salvation for the jailor.

25. SOME JEWS

Acts 17:4

"And some of them believed and consorted with Paul and Silas; and of the devout Greeks a great multitude, and of the chief women not a few."

Note: Paul establishes the Thessalonian church through the preaching of the gospel. The Word of God will never return void, and in Thessalonica it accomplished much. In this passage the first part of this harvest only included some Jews.

26. GREAT MULTITUDE OF GREEKS

Acts 17:4

"And some of them believed and consorted with Paul and Silas; and of the devout Greeks a great multitude, and of the chief women not a few."

Note: The result of his preaching was a great multitude of Greeks believed, in contrast to *"some"* Jews.

27. CHIEF WOMEN

Acts 17:4

"And some of them believed and consorted with Paul and Silas; and of the devout Greeks a great multitude, and of the chief women not a few."

Note: The result of his preaching affected every level of society. Here we see the *"chief"* women of Thessalonica come to Christ. In this one verse, we see how different groups within society are touched by the power of the gospel.

"Having therefore obtained help of God, I continue unto this day, witnessing both to small and great."
Acts 26:22

28. MANY JEWS IN BEREA

Acts 17:12

"Therefore many of them believed (Jews in Berea); also of honourable women which were Greeks, and of men, not a few."

Note: Because of the persecution that arose in Thessalonica, the disciples sent Paul to Berea. The Bereans were noble and searched the scriptures to prove Paul's preaching. Paul preached from the Old Testament prophets, line upon line, and proved Jesus was the Christ—resulting in many Jews believing.

29. HONORABLE GREEK WOMEN AND MEN

Acts 17:12

"Therefore many of them believed; also of honourable women which were Greeks, and of men, not a few."

Note: Paul preached from the Old Testament prophets, line upon line, and proved Jesus was the Christ. Not only was there a harvest of his own countrymen, but honorable Greek women and men came to the Lord. The term "*honorable*" refers to those who were educated, wealthy, and of a higher social status. The gospel was reaching people in every culture and every level of societal order. Simply put, Jesus is building His church, which is comprised of people—all people. Later, in the book of James, the Holy Spirit confronts favoritism in the church based on wealth and societal order (James 2:1,2).

30. DIONYSIUS, DAMARIS, AND OTHERS

Acts 17:34

"Howbeit certain men clave unto him, and believed: among the which was Dionysius the Areopagite, and a woman named Damaris, and others with them."

Note: In Athens, Paul is given the opportunity to declare the resurrection of Jesus right in the heart of Greek humanism in a place called the Areopagus. It seems that Paul had not originally planned to go to Athens, but due to the persecution in Berea, the disciples sent him away, yet again, to save him. In Athens, while waiting for Timothy and Silas, Paul was troubled. It must have been very grieving for Paul to be living and walking in the light of Christ, while discerning such darkness in Athens—a darkness the world called light. Paul was moved in his spirit to preach to them. Though it may have seemed like preaching to a brick wall, the power of the Holy Spirit was still saving those appointed unto eternal life. Though not many came to Christ, a few did and that is why Paul's spirit was stirred. The Lord, the Great Shepherd, will leave the ninety-nine to find the one. That one, in turning to Christ, causes the angels in heaven to rejoice. Of course, in this passage it was more than one.

31. CRISPUS AND HIS HOUSEHOLD

Acts 18:8

"And Crispus, the chief ruler of the synagogue, believed on the Lord with all his house; and many of the Corinthians hearing believed, and were baptized."

Note: In Corinth, Paul reasoned with the Jews through scripture. The Jews blasphemed, causing Paul to shake his garments and declare, *"from now on, I will go to the Gentiles."* Though many of the Jews there rejected, there were those who received the Lord, such as Crispus and his household.

32. MANY CORINTHIANS

Acts 18:8

"And Crispus, the chief ruler of the synagogue, believed on the Lord with all his house; and many of the Corinthians hearing believed, and were baptized."

Note: Though most of the Jews rejected, many Corinthians accepted. This acceptance by the Gentiles provoked the Jews to greater envy against Paul. In Deuteronomy 32:21, the Lord declared that He would drive the Jewish nation to jealousy by a people that are not a nation. The religious Jews envied Jesus, and they also envied the fullness of the blessing (the double blessing) of Abraham upon the church—which now was comprised of both Jews and Gentiles.

33. ABOUT TWELVE OF JOHN'S DISCIPLES

Acts 19:5–7

"When they heard this, they were baptized in the name of the Lord Jesus. And when Paul had laid his hands upon them, the Holy Ghost came on them; and they spake with tongues, and prophesied and all the men were about twelve."

Note: Paul brings twelve disciples of John into a complete understanding of salvation. After baptizing the men in water, they then received the baptism of the Holy Spirit, speaking in tongues and prophesying. In this passage, the gifts of the Holy Spirit occur after Paul baptizes the men in the Holy Spirit. It is important to note that both salvation and the baptism of the Holy Spirit were being demonstrated together, having started in Jerusalem, Judea, Samaria, and now to the ends of the earth.

34. MANY

Acts 19:18

"And many that believed came, and confessed, and shewed their deeds."

Note: Paul had revelation that the healing power of God could saturate garments and cloths, as in the case with Jesus' garments. Perhaps while spending time with Peter, James, and John in Jerusalem, they told these unique stories of people being healed by touching Jesus' clothes. With faith operating on the same principle, Paul prayed over handkerchiefs. The tangible anointing of the Lord's healing ministry was so strong upon Paul's body that the handkerchiefs absorbed the healing power of God. Many, through this special operation, were healed and delivered from demonic influences. This demonstration of power so shook Ephesus that vagabond Jews decided to adopt similar methods of ministry. The sons of

Sceva, hearing of the power of God in Paul's ministry, attempted to cast out demons in the name of Jesus, whom Paul preached. This went terribly wrong for these *"want to be"* exorcists. When the demonic powers stripped and beat the sons of Sceva, it again shook Ephesus. Through Paul's preaching, heaven had descended upon that pagan city, and it was being turned upside down. The Bible says that the fear of the Lord fell upon all those that heard of these events. Because of the power of God that was being demonstrated, many turned away from witchcraft. They cleaned out of their houses everything that was unclean—it was a true revival. When the fear of the Lord is mixed together with miracles, it becomes a mighty catalyst for change in society. We must hunger for both.

35. SOME BELIEVED

Acts 28:24

"And <u>some believed</u> the things which were spoken, and some believed not."

Note: The book of Acts closes with Paul in Rome speaking to the Jews who came to hear him. He used the law of Moses and the prophets to convince them that Jesus is the Christ. The result was *"some"* believed. Others, by an act of their will, choose not to believe.

36. GENTILES

Acts 28:28

"Be it known therefore unto you, that the salvation of God is sent unto the Gentiles, and that <u>they will hear it</u>."

Note: This, by far, is my favorite recorded harvest in the book of Acts because it includes you and me. With Paul, a captive in Rome, we have experienced roughly thirty years of church history. From the outpouring of the Holy Spirit in Jerusalem to Paul before Caesar, the final harvest is spoken by a word of wisdom, *"the Gentiles will hear!"* After chapter 28, the road of church history has been set forth, a road that has encircled the globe. From tyrannical kings and governments that have sought to destroy Christianity to stories of great revivals that turned nations upside down, truly Christianity is built on a rock, and the gates of hell have not prevailed—nor will they ever (Matthew 16:18).

DOCUMENTED PERSECUTION

"BLESSED ARE YE,
WHEN MEN SHALL REVILE
YOU, AND PERSECUTE YOU,
AND SHALL SAY ALL
MANNER OF EVIL AGAINST
YOU FALSELY, FOR MY SAKE."
MATTHEW 5:11

DOCUMENTED PERSECUTION

A DEFINITIVE LOOK AT PERSECUTION IN THE BOOK OF ACTS

"If the world hates you, ye know that it hated me before it hated you."
John 15:18

"Remember the word that I said unto you, The servant is not greater than his lord. If they have persecuted me, they will also persecute you."
John 15:20

"We are troubled on every side, yet not distressed; we are perplexed, but not in despair; Persecuted, but not forsaken; cast down, but not destroyed; Always bearing about in the body the dying of the Lord Jesus, that the life also of Jesus might be made manifest in our body."
2 Corinthians 4:8–10

PREFACE

I am sure that there were times in Jesus' ministry when he remembered back to Bethlehem, to the vivid reality of Satan's hatred for His life. There in His birth town, thousands of little boys were slaughtered at the hands of Herod's government in hopes of destroying Him. Jesus was always aware of the hatred the world had for Him. In John 15:18, Jesus warned His disciples that it would be the same for them. Through His death and resurrection, Jesus has empowered His church to trample on the works of darkness. With such authority, Jesus never gave them power to trample on man. They were commanded to love the world as He did. Persecution comes when men yield or open doors in their thinking to demonic powers which seek to control humanity.

In the book of Acts, there are thirty-one examples of persecution. These persecutions range from religious leaders to government leaders and even from business leaders. As you read through these accounts, stop and think about each one. In doing so, you will discover a strength in Christianity that is more than able to handle the hatred of the devil and wicked men. As you study these references, I pray that the Lord will impart a new fervency into your spirit to strengthen your faith in Christ in these perilous days in which we live. If Christians 2000 years ago prevailed through such turbulent times, so shall we 2000 years later.

PERSECUTION
QUICK REFERENCE

Reference	Description of Persecution
(Jerusalem, Judea, Samaria)	
1. Acts 4:1,3	The first persecution
2. Acts 4:18,21	The first command and the first threat
3. Acts 5:18	Second account of assault and jail
4. Acts 5:40	Jewish religious leaders beat the apostles
5. Acts 6:11	The first perjury
6. Acts 7:58	First stoning (the first martyr)
7. Acts 8:1	Great persecution (jail, torture, death)
8. Acts 9:1	Great persecution continues
9. Acts 9:23	Jews in Damascus conspire to kill Paul
10. Acts 9:29	Jews in Jerusalem conspire to kill Paul
11. Acts 12:1–2	King Herod kills James
(To the Uttermost Parts of the Earth)	
12. Acts 13:8	First persecution by witchcraft
13. Acts 13:45	Jews contend verbally, speaking against
14. Acts 13:50	First city-wide persecution
15. Acts 14:2	First account of persecution from Gentiles
16. Acts 14:5	Jews and Gentiles assault Paul
17. Acts 14:19	Jews stone Paul
18. Acts 16:19–24	Gentiles in Philippi beat and imprison Paul
19. Acts 17:5	Non-believing Jews moved with envy
20. Acts 17:13	Persecution follows Paul
21. Acts 18:6	Jews in Corinth oppose and blaspheme
22. Acts 18:12	Jews in Corinth made insurrection against Paul
23. Acts 19:9	Ephesian Jews speak evil of *"The Way"*
24. Acts 19:23,29	Persecution from local business leaders
25. Acts 20:3	Jews in Greece lay in wait for Paul
26. Acts 21:27	In Jerusalem, Jews from Asia take Paul
27. Acts 21:30–32	The mob, beatings, and attempted murder
28. Acts 23:2	Paul is slapped
29. Acts 23:10	Roman captain rescues Paul
30. Acts 23:12–13	Forty Jews conspire to kill Paul
31. Acts 28:22	Christianity is spoken against everywhere

PERSECUTION
A DEFINITIVE LOOK

(Jerusalem, Judea, Samaria)

1. **THE FIRST PERSECUTION**
   Acts 4:1, 3
   "And as they spake unto the people, the priests, and the captain of the temple, and the Sadducees, came upon them,"
   "And they laid hands on them, and put them in jail unto the next day: for it was now eventide."

   Note: In this first account of persecution, the apostles felt the aggression of angry men approaching them and then of hands grabbing them. They had never experienced this while Jesus was with them. Now, Jesus was at the right hand of God, and these disciples were learning to depend on the Holy Spirit the same way He had. The words Jesus had spoken, *"I will never leave you or forsake you,"* must have been rising in their hearts as they were being thrown into a jail cell for the night. Peter and John had experienced such an outpouring of God on the day of Pentecost with signs and wonders along with thousands of men and women coming into the Kingdom of God, and now, sitting in a dirty cell, they are sobered by Jesus' words, *"They hated me, and they will hate you."*

2. **THE FIRST COMMAND AND FIRST THREAT**
   Acts 4:18
   "And they called them, and commanded them not to speak at all nor teach in the name of Jesus."

   Acts 4:21
   "So, when they had further threatened them, they let them go, finding nothing how they might punish them, because of the people: for all men glorified God for that which was done."

   Note: In this second account of persecution, the religious leaders employ a new tactic in hopes of silencing the church—namely, a command backed by threats. The apostles now have experienced the grip of angry hands squeezing their arms as well as being thrown into a jail cell for the night. Now, on top of it all, they receive a command which is baptized with intimidation. Words that threaten carry a spirit of fear with them. Those words were working in the spirit realm by Satan, who is the spirit of fear, in hopes of crippling the church's accuracy in fulfilling the great commission.

3. **SECOND ACCOUNT OF ASSAULT AND JAIL**
Acts 5:18
"And laid their hands on the apostles, and put them in the common prison."

Note: Once again, hands are laid upon the apostles, and they are thrown into jail for a second time. There is a clear frustration growing in the religious community in Jerusalem. Also, up until this time, the religious leaders have only persecuted the apostles, leaving the individual members of the congregation alone.

4. **JEWISH RELIGIOUS LEADERS BEAT THE APOSTLES**
Acts 5:40
"And to him they agreed: and when they had called the apostles, and beaten them, they commanded that they should not speak in the name of Jesus, and let them go."

Note: In this passage, we see the first beating. The apostles' bodies were physically bruised for their love of Christ. Peter and John, at this point, were growing into a deeper appreciation for Jesus and all that He did at the cross. The religious leaders, clearly frustrated, had ramped up their persecution because the apostles were not obeying their commands to stop preaching the name of Jesus, coupled with a call to repentance. The persistence of the apostles while ministering in such tangible power brought great hatred and envy into the ranks of Jerusalem's religious order.

5. **THE FIRST PERJURY**
Acts 6:11
"Then they bribed men, which said, "We have heard him speak blasphemous words against Moses and against God."

Note: Once again, the religious leaders realized they were not stopping the message of resurrection. In this passage, we see the first account of perjury (bribing with money) used. Their goal was simple—a quick trial followed by a community stoning.

6. **FIRST STONING (FIRST MARTYR)**
Acts 7:58,59
"And cast him out of the city, and stoned him: and the witnesses laid down their clothes at a young man's feet, whose name was Saul. And they stoned Stephen, calling upon God, and saying, Lord Jesus, receive my spirit."

Note: In this passage, we see the first murder of a Christian witness. The religious order realized they were not stopping the church, and the only thing they had left was the tool of murder. With this murder, they revealed which god they really served. The glory upon the church brought into the open how wicked Jerusalem's religious hierarchy had become. In Mark 11:14, Jesus cursed the fig tree as a prophetic act of what God was going to do with this dying *"fig tree"* of Jewish religion. In AD 70 this religious *"fig tree"* withered when Titus leveled Jerusalem and destroyed Herod's temple—scattering Jews outward to the ends of the earth.

7. **GREAT PERSECUTION (JAIL, TORTURE, DEATH)**
Acts 8:1
"And Saul was consenting unto his death. And at that time there was a great persecution against the church which was at Jerusalem; and they were all scattered abroad throughout the regions of Judea and Samaria, except the apostles."

Acts 8:3
"As for Saul, he made havock of the church, entering into every house, arresting men and women committed them to prison."

Acts 26:10–11
"Which thing I also did in Jerusalem: and many of the saints did I shut up in prison, having received authority from the chief priests; and when they were put to death, I gave my voice against them. And I punished them often in every synagogue, and compelled them to blaspheme; and being exceedingly mad against them, I persecuted them even unto strange cities."

Note: The key to this passage is the word *"great."* With the martyrdom of Stephen came a new wave of aggression against the newborn church. The religious leaders had found what they thought was the model that would ultimately stop the church. Saul, later known as Paul, was a key front man in this wave of unrest.

It is important to note that Stephen was not the only one murdered during this time of great trial. Many lost their lives—and there was Paul consenting to their deaths. Paul, filled with rage, had become a madman. Though tutored by a great man such as Gamaliel, Paul looked and acted nothing like his teacher (Acts 22:3). Gamaliel loved God and was slow to act—one who showed great wisdom. Most likely, Satan knew that there was something special about Paul and feared him. Therefore, he was trying to gain control over his calling. As you read through the life and writings of Paul, it doesn't take long to realize his deep love for the church. I imagine he never forgot the faces of those who died during this great persecution that he had helped lead.

8. GREAT PERSECUTION CONTINUES

Acts 9:1

"And Saul, yet breathing out threatenings and slaughter against the disciples of the Lord, went unto the high priest."

Note: In this passage, we have insight into the spread of Christianity. Christians went everywhere, even to foreign cities. Saul was so full of hatred that he went and requested letters of authority to arrest believers in Syria. It is also important to note that Saul's hatred fanned the flames of revival that scattered these evangelists everywhere. In one sense, Saul was responsible for bringing revival to Samaria through the preaching of Philip. Also, there is one truth that the religious leaders did not understand about Christianity and that being love. These believers knew Jesus loved them. These believers loved Jesus. And finally, these believers loved not their lives unto the death. A person who is not afraid to use his life as a weapon against his foe is greatly feared on the battlefields of life. These Christians laid down their lives, thus ensuring that the message of Christ was preached to the ends of the earth.

9. JEWS IN DAMASCUS CONSPIRE TO KILL PAUL

Acts 9:23

"And after that many days were fulfilled, the Jews took counsel to kill him."

Note: Saul was a Pharisee of Pharisees. He had grown up at the feet of Gamaliel in Jerusalem, which gave him status and prestige amongst his peers. He had always known favor within the Jewish religious circles, probably in part because his own father had been a Pharisee. Now, these Jews in Damascus were plotting his death. For the first time in His life, Paul feels what true hatred is, coupled with the fear of being murdered by those who once were deemed his colleagues and friends. Under this pressure, Paul most likely thought he needed to return to Jerusalem in hope of working out these misunderstandings.

10. JEWS IN JERUSALEM CONSPIRE TO KILL PAUL

Acts 9:29

"And he spake boldly in the name of the Lord Jesus, and disputed against the Grecians: but they went about to slay him."

Note: Upon arriving at the temple, Paul finds that Jerusalem is no longer a friendly place for him. Once again, he is forced to flee for his life.

11. KING HEROD KILLS JAMES

Acts 12:1–2

"Now about that time Herod the king stretched forth his hands to vex certain of the church. And he killed James the brother of John with the sword."

Note: In this account, we see the first persecution by government. Up until this time, the aggression had only been from religious leaders, but now a new chapter had opened in church history. Jesus had warned His followers to beware of the leaven of Herod and of the Pharisees. Both leavens are ultimately against the righteousness of God, and in this passage, we see that the ultimate manifestation of these leavens is persecution against Christ and His church.

> *"Why do the heathen rage, and the people imagine a vain thing? The kings of the earth set themselves, and the rulers take counsel together, against the LORD, and against his anointed, saying, Let us break their bands asunder, and cast away their cords from us. He that sitteth in the heavens shall laugh: the Lord shall have them in derision."*
>
> *Psalms 2:1–4*

(To the Uttermost Parts of the Earth)

12. FIRST PERSECUTION BY WITCHCRAFT

Acts 13:8

"But Elymas the sorcerer (for so is his name by interpretation) withstood them, seeking to turn away the deputy from the faith."

Note: Satan is always seeking influence and control in the realm of government. Governmental authority was ordained by God to protect the righteous. Paul warns all men not to give a place to the devil. All this means is to not provide a place for him to usurp and operate. In this passage, Satan, through the sorcerer Elymas, was seeking a place of influence in government. When witchcraft gains a foothold in governmental power, the devil can freely oppress the land. Paul's arrival with the gospel brought confrontation to Elymas' wicked plan. Here we see the first opposition coming from witchcraft.

13. JEWS CONTEND VERBALLY, SPEAKING AGAINST

Acts 13:45

"But when the Jews saw the multitudes, they were filled with envy, and spake against those things which were spoken by Paul, contradicting and blaspheming."

Note: Envy was at the root of Joseph's persecution from his brothers. Envy was at the root of why the religious leaders persecuted Jesus. Now, we see that envy is still an evil that hates everything that is good. These men didn't just hate Paul; they truly hated themselves, despising their own eternal salvation.

14. FIRST CITY-WIDE PERSECUTION
Acts 13:50
"But the Jews stirred up the devout and honourable women and the chief men of the city, and expelled them out of their coasts."

Note: Once again, envy is at the root of this persecution. The Jewish religious zealots stirred up the city leaders (the mayor and the city council) to persecute the apostles by expelling them from their coasts. This is the first example of city government rising up against the gospel.

15. FIRST ACCOUNT OF PERSECUTION FROM GENTILES
Acts 14:2
"But the unbelieving Jews stirred up the Gentiles, and made their minds evil affected against the brethren."

Note: Here, we see a battle for the minds of men. Paul wrote in 2 Corinthians 4:3–4 that Satan blinds the minds of those who believe not. The minds of the Gentiles in this passage had already chosen not to believe, thus allowing Satan to come in and keep them blind. Spiritual blindness is best described by Pharoah, who watched the Red Sea open, with water standing up on both sides. After the water parted, He then witnessed Moses and the Jewish nation walk through the sea on dry ground, and yet he still ordered his army to follow. That is the epitome of spiritual blindness. The Gentiles, in this example, were spiritually blinded through the hardness of their own hearts.

16. JEWS AND GENTILES ASSAULT PAUL
Acts 14:5
"And when there was an assault made both of the Gentiles, and also of the Jews with their rulers, to use them despitefully, and to stone them,"

Note: The persecution found in verse two moves from evil thinking to attempted murder.

17. JEWS STONE PAUL
Acts 14:19
"And there came thither certain Jews from Antioch and Iconium, who persuaded the people, and having stoned Paul, drew him out of the city, supposing he had been dead."

Note: What an emotional day Paul must have had. In fact, Lystra was probably a city he never really forgot. It was in Lystra that Paul while preaching, discerned faith in a crippled man's heart. The gifts of healings came into operation and a man, who had never walked, began walking. What joy it must have been to watch this miracle of healing unfold. But now, the pagan leaders in the city set out to worship Paul and Barnabas. It took much convincing to prove that they were not gods. This is where the devil got into the details. Those men never repented. Their hearts were hard and though they saw an undeniable miracle of healing, they did not desire Christ. It is in this darkness that they were convinced by zealot Jews to stone Paul. Miracles and manifestations of the Holy Spirit do not guarantee repentance. These miracles do guarantee either a hardening of the heart or a softening of the heart; there is no middle ground.

18. GENTILES IN PHILIPPI BEAT AND IMPRISON PAUL

Acts 16:19–24

"And when her masters saw that the hope of their gains was gone, they caught Paul and Silas, and drew them into the marketplace unto the rulers, And brought them to the magistrates, saying, These men, being Jews, do exceedingly trouble our city, And teach customs, which are not lawful for us to receive, neither to observe, being Romans. And the multitude rose up together against them: and the magistrates rent off their clothes and commanded to beat them. And when they had laid many stripes upon them, they cast them into prison, charging the jailor to keep them safely: Who, having received such a charge, thrust them into the inner prison, and made their feet fast in the stocks."

Note: Here, we have another first pertaining to persecution against the church. In this passage, the devil uses those in economic power to launch an assault against the church and its moral stance on human slavery. These economic leaders held influence over the city leaders, which, according to their bidding, beat Paul and Silas and threw them into jail. Until now, we have seen persecution through religion and government, and in this passage, we are introduced to the darkness in the world's economic system and its ability to persecute. Truly the love of money is a root of all evil (1 Timothy 6:10).

19. NON-BELIEVING JEWS MOVED WITH ENVY

Acts 17:5

"But the Jews which believed not, moved with envy, took unto them certain lewd fellows of the baser sort, and gathered a company, and set all the city on an uproar, and assaulted the house of Jason, and sought to bring them out to the people."

Note: Once again, envy is at the root of the persecution. It is also interesting to note that the city became involved. Satan hated Paul and the power of God that rested upon him; he was turning the world upside down, and no weaponized plan that had been formed against Paul had prospered (Isaiah 54:17).

20. PERSECUTION FOLLOWS PAUL

Acts 17:13

"But when the Jews of Thessalonica had knowledge that the word of God was preached of Paul at Berea, they came thither also, and stirred up the people."

Note: I really believe that Paul's thorn in the flesh was this demonic spirit assigned to harass him at every turn. These Jews followed him in order to stir up cities against him. The power of God's love enabled Paul to walk in miracles, establishing the church while sensing continual hatred and murder against himself. God's grace truly is sufficient.

"He said unto me, My grace is sufficient for thee: for my strength is made perfect in weakness. Most gladly, therefore will I rather glory in my infirmities, that the power of Christ may rest upon me."
2 Corinthians 12:9

21. JEWS IN CORINTH OPPOSE AND BLASPHEME

Acts 18:6

"And when they opposed themselves, and blasphemed, he shook his raiment, and said unto them, "Your blood be upon your own heads"; I am clean: from henceforth I will go unto the Gentiles."

Note: It is here that Paul fully turns to his high calling, which is to the Gentiles. It is important to note that as you read further, you will see that Paul continues to reach out to the Jews. But in his heart, he has turned completely to the Gentiles.

22. JEWS IN CORINTH MADE INSURRECTION AGAINST PAUL

Acts 18:12

"And when Gallio was the deputy of Achaia, the Jews made insurrection with one accord against Paul, and brought him to the judgment seat,"

Note: In this account, the Jews in Corinth banded together and brought Paul before the deputy. The Lord had already revealed to Paul that no harm would come to him in Corinth. As Paul began to open his mouth to speak, the deputy dismissed the crowd and rebuked the Jewish leaders for their religious strife.

23. EPHESIAN JEWS SPEAK EVIL OF *"THE WAY"*

Acts 19:9

"But when divers were hardened, and believed not, but spake evil of that way before the multitude, he departed from them, and separated the disciples, disputing daily in the school of one Tyrannus."

Note: Here, we see the effects of the gospel upon the human heart. These Jews heard the gospel and then chose not to believe. Their hearts were hardened by an act of their own will. Only people who are convinced of truth have the ability to harden their hearts against the truth.

24. PERSECUTION FROM LOCAL BUSINESS LEADERS

Acts 19:23

"And the same time there arose no small stir about that way."

Acts 19:29

"And the whole city was filled with confusion: and having caught Gaius and Aristarchus, men of Macedonia, Paul's companions in travel, they rushed with one accord into the theater."

Note: In this account of persecution, we see an attack come from the economic princes of the city. The craftsmen of Ephesus were rich and making idols was big business. Paul's gospel was interfering with the idol business, and this infuriated the devil and Demetrius. In 1 Samuel 5, we have the account where the Philistines captured the ark of the Lord and placed it into the house of their idol Dagon. In the morning, when they opened the door, they found Dagon on the floor with his head and his hands cut off. As it was with the Philistines, so it was in Ephesus. The gospel is the power of God unto salvation, and Paul's preaching was destroying the idol business in the region. In the confusion of the moment, when they could not find Paul, they grabbed (assaulted) two of Paul's fellow laborers. Things were definitely getting out of hand. Then Paul, when hearing of the commotion, attempted to go into the theater in hopes of shifting their hatred from Gaius and Aristarchus onto himself. Paul was a true leader. In this account, they were saved by a town clerk who stood on Roman authority and disbanded the crowd.

25. JEWS IN GREECE LAY IN WAIT FOR PAUL

Acts 20:3

"And there abode three months. And when the Jews laid wait for him, as he was about to sail into Syria, he purposed to return through Macedonia."

Note: As stated earlier, Paul's thorn must have been the continual sense of hatred and murder against him. In the midst of such persecution, the Lord continually delivered him.

26. IN JERUSALEM, JEWS FROM ASIA TAKE PAUL

Acts 21:27

"And when the seven days were almost ended, the Jews which were of Asia, when they saw him in the temple, stirred up all the people, and laid hands on him,"

Note: Paul knew that persecution awaited him in every city where he went. He also knew through the word of wisdom given by Agabus the prophet that he would be taken by the Jews and then by the Romans during his stay in Jerusalem.

On the seventh day of prayer in the temple, Paul's prophetic destiny to Rome began. From the temple of God in Jerusalem to Caesar in Rome, God was planting a seed for church expansion into Europe and from there to all nations.

27. THE MOB, BEATINGS, AND ATTEMPTED MURDER

Acts 21:30–32

"And all the city was moved, and the people ran together: and they took Paul and drew him out of the temple: and forthwith the doors were shut. And as they went about to kill him, tidings came unto the chief captain of the band, that all Jerusalem was in an uproar. Who immediately took soldiers and centurions, and ran down unto them: and when they saw the chief captain and the soldiers, they left beating of Paul."

Note: This persecution turns from physical aggression to attempted murder. The words *"all the city"* reveal the size of this persecution against Paul. In this account, Paul experiences the sheer weight of a crowd filled with such hatred for him. It is one thing to have one or two people come after you; it is another thing when it is thousands of people. Then, once again, Paul is beaten for his faith in Jesus. Therefore now, we have clarity *why* the Lord detoured Paul en route to Jerusalem to the house of Philip the evangelist. Philip's four daughters prophesied, and the Holy Spirit filled Paul's heart with strength and comfort. How we need New Testament (inspirational) prophecy (1 Corinthians 14:3)!

28. PAUL IS SLAPPED

Acts 23:2

"And the high priest Ananias commanded them that stood by him to smite him on the mouth."

Note: Paul, en route to Rome, must endure one more physical bruise at the hands of these religious leaders. They struck Jesus in the face, and now Paul was experiencing the same hatred for the gospel he preached. In AD 70, Jerusalem and its temple were destroyed, and these face-slapping religious leaders found themselves out of a job. They had missed their day of visitation.

29. ROMAN CAPTAIN RESCUES PAUL

Acts 23:10

"And when there arose a great dissension, the chief captain, fearing lest Paul should have been pulled in pieces of them, commanded the soldiers to go down, and to take him by force from among them, and to bring him into the castle."

Note: As tempers began to flare, the prophetic transition of Paul, originally taken by the Jews, now in the hands of Rome, had come to pass. With the change of hands from one cultural base (with its laws) to another cultural base (with its system of laws), Satan was temporarily hindered. Technically he could not use the same tactics on Paul that he had used on Stephen. This most likely enraged him. I believe that the devil did not know what to do. Satan was now hindered by Roman law as well as by the presence of the angel that stood by Paul—protecting him. This passage gives insight into the power of law and its effects upon societies that live apart from the light of the gospel.

30. FORTY JEWS CONSPIRE TO KILL PAUL

Acts 23:12–13

"And when it was day, certain of the Jews banded together, and bound themselves under a curse, saying that they would neither eat nor drink till they had killed Paul. And they were more than forty which had made this conspiracy."

Note: Paul, now firmly in the grip of Rome, was still considered a threat to Jewish religion. Jesus said that Satan, the god of religion, was a murderer from the beginning, and Paul really stirred up that side in Satan.

"Having a form of godliness (religion), but denying the power thereof: from such turn away."
2 Timothy 3:5

31. CHRISTIANITY IS SPOKEN AGAINST EVERYWHERE

Acts 28:22

"But we desire to hear of thee what thou thinkest: for as concerning this sect, we know that everywhere it is spoken against."

Note: Though the book of Acts deals primarily with the life of Peter and Paul, the fact is that all the apostles functioned in the power of God and had gone in different directions with the gospel. People all over the world knew about the message of Jesus Christ and the power of His resurrection. In this passage, we see that Christianity was spoken against everywhere, and yet it did not stop it! There is a saying, *"though the dog barks, the train keeps moving,"* and the concept of this saying holds true in describing the unstoppable power of Christ and His church.

DOCUMENTED ANGELS

"THERE APPEARED AN ANGEL
UNTO HIM FROM HEAVEN,
STRENGTHENING HIM."
LUKE 22:43

DOCUMENTED ANGELS

A DEFINITIVE LOOK AT ANGELS AND THEIR MINISTRY IN THE BOOK OF ACTS

"The angel of the Lord encamps round about them that fear him and delivers them."
Psalms 34:7

"For he shall give his angels charge over thee, to keep thee in all thy ways."
Psalms 91:11

PREFACE

There are over 313 mentions of angels in the Bible. The ministry of angels throughout the Bible is quite a study and rather exhaustive. In short, angels are used in a variety of ministry, such as giving messages to God's servants, they deliver, they fight battles, they perform judgments, and in certain situations they cook food, as was in the case with Elijah (1 Kings 19:5–8). In heaven there are armies that ride horses (Revelation 19:14) and even military divisions that ride in chariots (Psalms 68:17). Remember, it was a fiery chariot that picked up Elijah, taking him to heaven (2 Kings 2:11). In the book of Revelation, we see that angels differ in size and ability (Revelation 18:1,21). We also see that there are angels that can stand in the sun and not be affected by the natural power of its energy (Revelation 19:17).

In Abraham's life, the Lord and two angels walked into his camp and dined with him (Genesis 18:1–2). These two angels looked like men, ate like men, and were the size of normal men. But as the residents of Sodom found out, they were not normal men. They had been given authority to call down fire and brimstone upon the whole region (Genesis 19:22–24). These heavenly ministers obey the commands of the Lord, listening to the voice of His word, and doing what has been directed from His throne—whether for blessing or for judgment.

In short, the creation of angels and their ministry came forth from the heart of a loving God. Though out of the artistry of a loving Creator came forth these beings, the creation of man was different and brought forth a depth of God's love that creation had never seen. Man, who hasn't seen the face of God, was created in the image of God to be the sons of God, yes, His children! Without seeing the face of God, man was given a planet (earth) to develop and to harness the power of its wealth, and by faith to love the Lord, walking pleasing before Him. As we delve into this study, it is important to understand that angels marvel at the creation of man. The great psalmist penned the words, *"what is man that you are mindful of him?"* (Psalms 8:4). What did the angelic armies think as the Creator took on flesh and blood, became a man, and then died at the hands of those He created. They witnessed such love flowing from their Creator, who was willing to die to redeem the creation called man. Also, I think that angels marvel at the strength in a man or woman who believes and worships God, whom they have never seen with their natural eyes. Angels are real. When we get to heaven, we will see and know with perfection the reality of God's creation called angels. Without further ado, let us study angels in the book of Acts.

ANGELS
QUICK REFERENCE

Reference	Description
(Jerusalem, Judea, Samaria)	
1. Acts 1:10–11	Two angels standing with the Lord
2. Acts 5:19–20	An angel sent to deliver
3. Acts 8:26	Angels help in the harvest—Samaria
4. Acts 9:4	The angel of the Lord speaks
5. Acts 10:3	Angels help in the harvest—the Gentiles
6. Acts 12:7	Peter is delivered
7. Acts 12:15	Peter's angel
8. Acts 12:23	An angel removes a king
(To the Uttermost Parts of the Earth)	
9. Acts 27:23	An angel sent to protect

ANGELS
A DEFINITIVE LOOK

(Jerusalem, Judea, Samaria)

1. **TWO ANGELS STANDING WITH THE LORD**
   Acts 1:10–11
   "And while they looked steadfastly toward heaven as he went up, behold, <u>two men—stood by them in white apparel;</u>
   Which also said, Ye men of Galilee, why stand ye gazing up into heaven? this same Jesus, which is taken up from you into heaven, shall so come in like manner as ye have seen him go into heaven."

   Note: Jesus declared at the beginning of His ministry that angels would be ascending and descending upon the Son of man (John 1:51). It is interesting to note that Jesus did not say, *"upon the Son of God."* He came and ministered as a man and thus made it clear that the angels would come and go, bringing help from the throne of God to Him—as a man. Even so, it is with the body of Christ. Angels are sent to assist the Lord's body (comprising of men and women) throughout the earth.

In this first chapter of church history, two angels were standing with the Lord as He commissioned His disciples. Thus, we see that heaven was not trying to hide the ministry of angels and their role in assisting the church. As the Lord ascended, the disciples stood there with their mouths open in wonder and amazement. It was in this moment that the angels performed their first act of ministry to the newly formed church.

With the Lord taking His rightful place in heaven, the angels and the church were established on the earth to perform His will. The angels had been ministering with the Lord for three years of extremely exciting but intense battles against the powers of darkness. Now, the Lord was returning to heaven, and these battle-hardened angelic ministers delivered an extremely important message to those standing there (as well as to all who were to come), *"He is coming back as you watched Him go."* Jesus had conquered, and the Father's plan was in motion, and the angels of God were sent to help the church as they had helped Jesus during His earthly life and ministry.

2. AN ANGEL SENT TO DELIVER

Acts 5:19–20

"But the angel of the Lord by night opened the prison doors, and brought them forth, and said, Go, stand and speak in the temple to the people all the words of this life."

Note: Angels behold the face of the Father, and from the throne of His glory, they are sent. In this passage, the angel of the Lord, endued with God's faith and power, walked into the prison, and delivered the apostles out. The apostles did nothing for their deliverance; they simply received the power of God working on their behalf. After delivering the Lord's apostles, the angel then ministered a word of wisdom to them concerning the direction of God for their ministry, *"go, stand and speak."* The Holy Spirit also uses these ministers of the Lord in the *charisma* gifts of the Holy Spirit. Truly, the apostles were tasting of the powers of the world to come (Hebrews 2:5, Hebrews 6:5).

3. ANGELS HELP IN THE HARVEST—SAMARIA

Acts 8:26

"And the angel of the Lord spake unto Philip, saying, Arise, and go toward the south unto the way that goeth down from Jerusalem unto Gaza, which is desert."

Note: When Nicodemus came to Jesus at night, the Lord began to speak directly to his heart concerning his need (man's need) of being born again. In His sermon to the ancient scribe of Israel, Jesus likens the work of the

Holy Spirit in salvation to the moving of the wind. Going back to the beginning, when Adam and Eve sinned, God came looking for them in order to declare to them hope in the midst of their darkness. The Bible says that He came in the cool *wind* of the day. So it is here, in the life and times of Philip the Evangelist, where the wind of salvation was blowing towards Ethiopia, and God needed a man to move in the breath of His Spirit. It is in this operation of salvation that the Lord sent an angel to assist Philip. We often limit our understanding of the preaching of the gospel to the work of the evangelist only, forgetting that without the ministry of angels and the *charisma* gifts of the Holy Spirit, the harvest of the nations would not successfully come in. Therefore, angelic ministry is a critical part in the harvest of the nations.

"And of the angels he saith, Who maketh his angels spirits (winds), and his ministers a flame of fire."
Hebrews 1:7

4. **THE ANGEL OF THE LORD SPEAKS**
Acts 9:4
"And he fell to the earth, and heard a voice saying unto him, Saul, Saul, why persecutest thou me?"

Note: Throughout the Bible, we see that there are two angels that minister to the Lord; they are His personal angels. They walked with the Lord into Abraham's camp before destroying Sodom (Genesis 18:2). They were seen in the tomb after His resurrection (Luke 24:4), and they were present at His ascension (Acts 1:10). In this passage, the wording *"they heard a voice"* is important. To understand this more, we will need to look at an occurrence in the gospel of John where an angel spoke on behalf of the Father.

"Father, glorify thy name. Then—came there a voice from heaven, saying, I have both glorified it, and will glorify it again.
The people therefore, that stood by, and heard it, said that it thundered: others said, An angel spake to him."
John 12:28–29

Angels are often sent to speak on behalf of the Lord. In this passage, and all other corresponding accounts of Paul's conversion, the light shined upon all, and all heard the initial voice. Then, when Paul humbled himself and prayed, the Lord began to speak, manifesting Himself personally to Paul. The others in the group did not hear or see the Lord—only Paul did. In conclusion, it appears that the Lord's angel spoke first with heaven's authority, not only stopping this caravan of persecution but knocking them all to the ground. This account is very similar to Christ's resurrection when the angel descended and the glory light upon him knocked all the guards to the ground. As the guards lay on their faces, the Lord walked out of the tomb—completely clothed in victory (Mathew 28:3–4). So it is in this account, while everyone was stuck to the ground, the Lord stepped into their midst and revealed himself to Paul. Later, when Paul shares this account, he makes it clear that those with him did not hear the Lord's voice.

"And the men which journeyed with him stood speechless,
hearing a voice, but seeing no man."
Acts 9:7

"And they that were with me saw indeed the light, and were afraid;
but they heard not the voice of him (Jesus) that spake to me."
Acts 22:9

5. **ANGELS HELP IN THE HARVEST—THE GENTILES**
   Acts 10:3
   "He saw in a vision evidently about the ninth hour of the day an angel of God coming in to him, and saying unto him, Cornelius."

   Note: Though angels are active in the harvest of the nations, they do not preach the gospel directly to men. The role of preaching belongs to man. As mentioned above, the wind of God's Spirit was blowing for the Gentiles, and an angel was sent to assist in making sure that all the pieces and players were put into their proper position. In this passage, we see the ministry of angels and the ministry of men working together in the mighty outpouring of the Holy Spirit. It is proper to note that without the gifts of the Holy Spirit and the ministry of angels, this door to the Gentiles would never have opened. Thus, making it clear why the Lord commanded His body of believers to be baptized in the Holy Spirit, fire, and power. Everything about a move of God is supernatural. Whether it is the ministry of angels or the operations of the *charisma* gifts of the Holy Spirit, the Lord's body upon the earth must be clothed in His supernatural ability.

   "But ye shall receive power, after that the Holy Ghost is come upon you: and ye shall be witnesses unto me both in Jerusalem, and in all Judea, and in Samaria, and unto the uttermost part of the earth."
   Acts 1:8

6. **PETER IS DELIVERED**
   Acts 12:7
   "And, behold, the angel of the Lord came upon him, and a light shined in the prison: and he smote Peter on the side, and raised him up, saying, Arise up quickly. And his chains fell off from his hands."

Note: Standing before the throne of the Father and the exalted Jesus, this angel received an impartation of power for Peter's deliverance. Remember, the church was in constant, fervent prayer for his release. As the angel entered the prison, the light of his countenance lit the prison up, while the guards remained spiritually dumb and blinded to the whole event. The presence of the glory of God upon the angel caused the chains binding Peter to fall off. This story is a testimony of fervent corporate prayer and the privilege that belongs to the church—if she will rise up and engage in it.

7. **PETER'S ANGEL**
Acts 12:15
"And they said unto her, Thou art mad. But she constantly affirmed that it was even so. Then said they, It is his angel."

Note: The early church was not unfamiliar or ignorant of the ministry of angels in their midst. These believers were very familiar with Old Testament writings about the ministry of angels. In this passage, we are given insight into the heavenly helper that ministered to Peter and with Peter as he cared for the church and preached the gospel to the lost.

"For he shall give his angels charge over thee,
to keep thee in all thy ways."
Psalms 91:11

8. **AN ANGEL REMOVES A KING**
Acts 12:23
"And immediately the angel of the Lord smote him, because he gave not God the glory: and he was eaten of worms, and gave up the ghost."

Note: The Bible talks about angels with swords (1 Chronicles 21:16). What a thought! A flaming sword guarded the way to the tree of life in Genesis chapter three. An angel with a sword was sent to strike Balaam as he rode his donkey en route to curse the Israelites (Numbers 22:25). So it is here, except we see a man who was struck by the angel. It must have been an astounding sight to see a king fall off his throne with a slice through his body, causing his insides to fall out. There is a God in heaven, and He does rule!

"And he changeth the times and the seasons: he removeth kings, and setteth up kings: he giveth wisdom unto the wise, and knowledge to them that know understanding."
Daniel 2:21

"This matter is by the decree of the watchers, and the demand by the word of the holy ones: to the intent that the living may know that the most High

ruleth in the kingdom of men, and giveth it to whomsoever he will, and setteth up over it the basest of men."
Daniel 4:17

(To the Uttermost Parts of the Earth)

9. AN ANGEL SENT TO PROTECT
Acts 27:23
"For <u>there stood by me this night the angel of God</u>, whose I am, and whom I serve."

Note: This passage is the first mention of angelic ministry outside the boundaries of Israel. The Bible gives all believers spread across the nations the assurance of heaven's help through the ministry of God's celestial servants. Paul's love for the Lord and the assurance of his relationship with the Lord brings a wonderful nuance of understanding concerning the ministry of angels. The presence of the angel, emanating God's faith and power, brought such encouragement to Paul concerning his relationship with the Lord.

Though this is the last account of the ministry of angels in the book of Acts, it is by no way the last account of their labors on behalf of believers who would come after Paul. Even the writer of this study on Acts has experienced the faithfulness of the Lord's presence through the help and ministry of angels. Truly, the Lord has never left us as orphans (John 14:18). He is with us (Matthew 28:20).

DOCUMENTED JUDGMENT

"FOR IF WE WOULD JUDGE OURSELVES, WE SHOULD NOT BE JUDGED."
1 CORINTHIANS 11:31

DOCUMENTED JUDGMENT

A DEFINITIVE LOOK AT JUDGMENT IN THE BOOK OF ACTS

"For when thy judgments are in the earth, the inhabitants of the world will learn righteousness."
Isaiah 26:9

"I charge thee therefore before God, and the Lord Jesus Christ, who shall judge the quick (living) and the dead at his appearing and his kingdom."
2 Timothy 4:1

"Neither is there any creature that is not manifest in his sight: but all things are naked and opened unto the eyes of him with whom we have to give an account."
Hebrews 4:13

"For we must all appear before the judgment seat of Christ; that everyone may receive the things done in his body, according to that he hath done, whether it be good or bad."
2 Corinthians 5:10

PREFACE

When dealing with the topic of judgment, it would do us well to approach it cautiously and with great humility. Scripture has made it abundantly clear that the Lord will never change, being the same yesterday, today, and forever (Hebrews 13:8, Malachi 3:6). Therefore, man has a great Judge who not only presides over the far reaches of creation but over every action and word spoken upon the earth.

As we approach the topic of judgment in the book of Acts, we see that God is still sitting on His throne and actively involved with all men—both believers and unbelievers. The book of Acts gives six accounts of judgment, of which four of these were capital (life-ending) in nature, while the remaining two were temporal (for a season). Concerning these judgments, three of the six were against those who were followers of the Lord, two were against non-believers (one being a king and the other a sorcerer), and the third judgment, as in the case with Paul, was used as a tool in his conversion experience. It is appropriate to note that the three judgments that were against those who were followers of the Lord were life-ending. Of course, one of these was Judas Iscariot, whose judgment was written by the Holy Spirit a thousand years before as King David wrote in the Psalms.

God is a judge, and there is nothing in creation that is hidden from His sight. As we approach this topic, it is important that we maintain a healthy understanding of the Father's omniscience. Jesus, in building a DNA of trust and love into His disciples, assured them continually of His Father's ever-watchful care for them. It is from this foundation of the Father's love that we approach this study.

In closing, God is a judge, and the book of Acts gives clear examples of His role as man's ultimate overseer. There are many bad actors listed in the book of Acts, but only a few received a clear recorded judgment. God, who is man's judge, deals with some sin on the earth, as noted in this study—while all other deeds await judgment before His throne. Take each of the following examples slowly and let the Spirit of the Lord sow into your heart a healthy understanding of the fear of the Lord.

"Judge not, that ye be not judged."
Matthew 7:1

JUDGMENT
QUICK REFERENCE

References — Description of Judgments

(Jerusalem, Judea, Samaria)

1.	Acts 1:16–20	Judas Iscariot	Capital
2.	Acts 5:5	Ananias, a liar	Capital
3.	Acts 5:10	Saphira, agreement in sin	Capital
4.	Acts 9:8	Saul, a man forever changed	Temporal
5.	Acts 12:23	Herod and worms	Capital

(To the Uttermost Parts of the Earth)

6.	Acts 13:9–12	Elymas the sorcerer	Temporal

JUDGMENT
A DEFINITIVE LOOK

(Jerusalem, Judea, Samaria)

1. **JUDAS ISCARIOT** **(Capital)**
   Acts 1:16–20
   "Men and brethren, this Scripture must needs have been fulfilled, which the Holy Ghost by the mouth of David spake before concerning Judas, which was guide to them that took Jesus. For he was numbered with us, and had obtained part of this ministry. Now this man—purchased a field with the reward of iniquity; and falling headlong, he burst asunder in

the midst, and all his bowels gushed out. And it was known unto all the dwellers at Jerusalem; insomuch as that field is called in their proper tongue, Aceldama, that is to say, The field of blood. For it is written in the book of Psalms, Let his habitation be desolate, and let no man dwell therein: and his bishopric let another take."

Note: Just because you are a minister in the service of the Lord doesn't mean you have a ticket to heaven. Judas went to hell. The love of money was and still is a root of all evil (1 Timothy 6:10). It is also important to note in the first chapter of Acts that God, as a judge, has not changed. Every one of the Lord's apostles who knew and ministered with Judas during the Lord's three years of ministry witnessed this judgment, and it shook them to their spiritual core. Judas had been one of them. He proclaimed the kingdom of God, cast devils out of people, and healed the sick, yet he went to hell.

I believe that this judgment was placed in the first chapter of Acts in order to warn all ministers to come that heaven is not assured through ministry position but rather as a gift of grace through faith in the merciful Blood of Jesus Christ. With this gift of grace, we are admonished to judge ourselves lest we be judged, knowing that it is a fearful thing to fall into the hands of the living God—to whom we will all give an account (Hebrews 10:31).

"The Son of man indeed goeth, as it is written of him: but woe to that man by whom the Son of man is betrayed! good were it for that man if he had never been born."
Mark 14:21

2. ANANIAS, A LIAR **(Capital)**
Acts 5:5
"And Ananias hearing these words fell down, and gave up the ghost: and great fear came on all them that heard these things."

Note: God gave man the ability to think and generate thoughts. With this, man also has ability to receive thoughts—good or bad. In this case, Ananias' heart had been counseled by Satan—the father of all lies. Ananias agreed to the lie and then decided to operate in it—in the midst of the congregation. Who would ever know? There was one problem, as man draws near to God, God draws near to man—searching every inward thought and motive. While standing before the apostles, who were standing in the manifested grace of God's weighty glory, Ananias lied. Perhaps Ananias was vying for a position of leadership and respectability before the eyes of the congregation. When judgment fell upon Ananias, cleansing came upon the congregation. It is also proper to note that just as the altar Moses built was holy, so is the altar of blessing in the New Testament church.

The book of Hebrews (chapter 7) reveals that it is Jesus, our high priest, established after the order of Melchizedek, who receives offerings. In this case, the New Testament altar is not holy because of the gift, but rather because of the One present, receiving offerings and administrating blessing. Ananias walked right into the presence of Jesus that fateful day. God had to show the church that He had never changed. As He had manifested Himself in the Old Testament, He was, and is, and always would be the same holy God to them. I imagine that many of those present that day walked away, remembering the sons of Aaron who were consumed with fire before the presence of the Lord (Leviticus 10:1–2).

The last point is that everywhere this story was told, the fear of the Lord came upon those listening. This one act of judgment brought forth a revival, a turning to the Lord in the hearts of people across the region. As we pray for revival in our nations, perhaps a notable judgment could be one possible way that it comes.

3. **SAPPHIRA, AGREEMENT IN SIN** **(Capital)**
Acts 5:10
"Then fell she down straightway at his feet, and yielded up the ghost: and the young men came in, and found her dead, and, carrying her forth, buried her by her husband."

Note: Ananias and his wife Sapphira agreed to lie, and in their agreement, they were buried. The Lord allowed them to enter eternity united in their cause. It is important to note that Sapphira was given the opportunity to change course, thus being spared her place in Ananias' judgment. She chose unwisely. The love of money is a root of all evil, and the Lord, through judgment, cleansed the act so that it would not take root in the newly formed church. In the Old Testament, as mentioned above, God judged Aaron's sons for burning strange fire before the altar. Even so, in the New Testament, God was showing the church that He had not changed, and that the altar was equally as holy.

4. **SAUL, A MAN FOREVER CHANGED** **(Temporal)**
Acts 9:8
"Saul arose from the earth; and when his eyes were opened, he saw no man: but they led him by the hand, and brought him into Damascus."

Note: Paul was worthy of death. He had persecuted and tortured many Christians, but like us all, he was a candidate for God's bountiful mercy. Though Paul had never known Jesus in the flesh like the other apostles, he was granted a one-on-one visitation from Jesus. It is important to note that this very Jesus who met Paul on the road to Damascus had been restored to the glory He had with the Father before creation.

"And now, O Father, glorify thou me with thine own self with the glory which I had with thee before the world was."
John 17:5

Paul received a small taste of the absolute glory and light coming from the face of Christ Himself. Jesus literally lit up Paul's world that day. Though blinded, no doubt the image of Christ had been eternally burned into the heart and mind of Paul. Though Paul was physically blind, he finally could see. After several days, the power of God came upon Paul, and the season of his judgment was over. The blinding scales over his eyes simply fell off. I often wonder what effect all of this had on Paul's companions—the ones who were traveling to Damascus to arrest Christians. Though there is no record, one thing is for sure—they were never the same.

"For God, who commanded the light to shine out of darkness, hath shined in our hearts, to give the light of the knowledge of the glory of God in the face of Jesus Christ."
2 Corinthians 4:6

5. **HEROD AND WORMS (a tale of two angels) (Capital)**
Acts 12:23
"And immediately the angel of the Lord smote him, because he gave not God the glory: and he was eaten of worms and gave up the ghost."

Note: King Herod learned that day that all positions of authority (kings and priests) belong to the Lord. He also was without excuse, for he had knowledge of the story of Belshazzar, Nebuchadnezzar's foolish grandson, who also crossed sacred lines in his day and watched the hand of God write his personal judgment upon the wall—in front of his friends, relatives, and rulers (Daniel 5:5).

The writer of Acts, Luke, was granted a word of knowledge to reveal that an angel was sent from the throne of God to strike the proud king. Those standing before Herod most likely did not see the angel but witnessed the king fall from his throne, being opened in a way that only a sword can produce. These stories are given as a warning to men, especially to all those in positions of authority.

The final thought includes Peter, who, only a few verses before, was released from prison by an angel. When Herod killed James and had Peter arrested, the church went into fervent continual prayer—most likely praying in the Holy Spirit prayer language. Under such a burden of potential loss, they yielded to the Holy Spirit in prayer, and when they did, heaven orchestrated Peter's release and Herod's demise. As a result, two angels were sent from the throne of God, producing two different outcomes. One outcome being escape for Peter, while the other being judgment upon an evil king. What mighty deeds we would see in the earth if only the church would rise up in prayer—accessing the power and authority that has been provided to us.

(To the Uttermost Parts of the Earth)

6. **ELYMAS THE SORCERER** **(Temporal)**
Acts 13:9–12
"Then Saul, (who also is called Paul,) filled with the Holy Ghost, set his eyes on him, And said, O full of all subtlety and all mischief, thou child of the devil, thou enemy of all righteousness, wilt thou not cease to pervert the right ways of the Lord? And now, <u>behold, the hand of the Lord is upon thee, and thou shalt be blind, not seeing the sun for a season. And immediately there fell on him a mist and a darkness</u>; and he went about seeking some to lead him by the hand.
Then the deputy, when he saw what was done, believed, being astonished at the doctrine of the Lord."

Note: As Paul began preaching to the governor, a demonic power became unsettled and began to move Elymas against Paul *(just as fire awakened a sleeping serpent in a brush pile in Acts 28:3)*. Satan did not want to lose his place of influence in that region. Though the Bible gives no detail of how long this spiritual battle took place, we do know that it must have been intense in that John Mark quit the mission over it, leaving Paul and Barnabas to continue without him. Though I do not believe that this was a quick incident between Paul and the sorcerer, I do know that Paul didn't back away. He and his team continued to bind the strongman in prayer until heaven moved, breaking the power of the witch's influence (Matthew 12:29).

Does the church today forfeit such heavenly grace by lack of targeted prayer? If the government is upon the Lord's shoulders, then the church has influence through its ministry of prayer and authority. As the church takes her place before the throne of God, even civil leaders will change or be changed, causing peace and prosperity to come upon the land. Though the effects may not come overnight, they surely will come if the church refuses to grow weary. Though this is the last recorded judgment in the book of Acts, history reveals that the Lord's judgments are still in the earth. In closing, the book of Revelation is a book that settles this major truth—there is a God in heaven that rules over creation. He is man's Judge.

OTHER TITLES BY ERIC CASTO

"God's plan for our lives requires His leadership. As we yield to the Master Designer, He is able to impart into us that which unfolds and becomes a beautiful tapestry that carries the mark of the artistry of God. It is in this beautiful tapestry that we are able to look back and see the footsteps of God in the earth traveled through the frailness of our own feet."

In *Bearing Precious Seed*, author Eric Casto brings to life the operation of the Kingdom of God and how we can activate the power of God's kingdom through the principle of seed-time and harvest. Eric's journeys to over 40 nations have one single thread that carries the miraculous power of God in every adventure and through every adversity. The Kingdom of God is released in the earth when a man takes seed and plants it. This book will encourage the reader to do the same.

For More Information About Eric Casto
www.foursmiles.com

CPSIA information can be obtained
at www.ICGtesting.com
Printed in the USA
BVHW012104041122
651162BV00012B/403

9 781685 568054